AMERICAN EDUCATION

Its Men,

Ideas,

and

Institutions

Advisory Editor

Lawrence A. Cremin
Frederick A. P. Barnard Professor of Education
Teachers College, Columbia University

A MERICAN EDUCATION: *Its Men, Ideas, and Institutions*
presents selected works of thought and scholarship that have
long been out of print or otherwise unavailable. Inevitably, such
works will include particular ideas and doctrines that have been
outmoded or superseded by more recent research. Nevertheless,
all retain their place in the literature, having influenced educational thought and practice in their own time and having provided
the basis for subsequent scholarship.

THE CURRICULUM

BY

FRANKLIN BOBBITT

ARNO PRESS & THE NEW YORK TIMES

New York * *1971*

Reprint Edition 1971 by Arno Press Inc.

Reprinted from a copy in
  The University of Illinois Library

American Education:
  Its Men, Ideas, and Institutions - Series II
  ISBN for complete set: 0-405-03600-0
  See last pages of this volume for titles.

Manufactured in the United States of America

Library of Congress Cataloging in Publication Data

Bobbitt, John Franklin, 1876-
    The curriculum.
    (American education: its men, ideas, and
institutions. Series II)
    1. Education--Curricula. I. Title.
II. Series.
LB1570.B6 1971   372.1'9   78-165706
ISBN 0-405-03695-7

THE CURRICULUM

BY

FRANKLIN BOBBITT

Professor of Educational Administration
The University of Chicago

HOUGHTON MIFFLIN COMPANY

BOSTON   NEW YORK   CHICAGO

The Riverside Press Cambridge

The Riverside Press
CAMBRIDGE . MASSACHUSETTS
U . S . A

PREFACE

SINCE the opening of the twentieth century, the evolution of our social order has been proceeding with great and ever-accelerating rapidity. Simple conditions have been growing complex. Small institutions have been growing large. Increased specialization has been multiplying human interdependencies and the consequent need of coördinating effort. Democracy is increasing within the Nation; and growing throughout the world. All classes are aspiring to a full human opportunity. Never before have civilization and humanization advanced so swiftly.

As the world presses eagerly forward toward the accomplishment of new things, education also must advance no less swiftly. It must provide the intelligence and the aspirations necessary for the advance; and for stability and consistency in holding the gains. Education must take a pace set, not by itself, but by social progress.

The present program of public education was mainly formulated during the simpler conditions of the nineteenth century. In details it has been improved. In fundamentals it is not greatly different. A program never designed for the present day has been inherited.

Any inherited system, good for its time, when held to after its day, hampers social progress. It is not enough that the system, fundamentally unchanged in plan and purpose, be improved in details. In education this has been done in conspicuous degree. Our schools to-day are better than ever before. Teachers are better trained. Supervision is more adequate. Buildings and equipment are enormously improved. Effective methods are being introduced, and time is being economized. Improvements are visible on every hand. And yet to do the nineteenth-century task better than it was then done is not necessarily to do the twentieth-century task. New duties lie before us. And these require new methods, new materials, new vision. The old education, except as it conferred the tools of knowledge, was mainly devoted to filling the memory with facts. The new age is more in need of facts than the old; and of more facts; and it must find more effective methods of teaching them. But there are now other functions. Education is now to develop a type of wisdom that can grow only out of participation in the living experiences of men, and never out of mere memorization of verbal statements of facts. It must, therefore, train thought and judgment in connection with actual life-situations, a task distinctly different from the cloistral activities of the past. It is also to develop the good-will, the spirit of service, the social valuations, sympathies, and attitudes of mind necessary for effective group-action where specialization has created endless interdependency. It has the function of training every citizen, man or woman, not for knowledge about citizenship, but for proficiency in citizenship; not for knowledge about hygiene, but for proficiency in maintaining robust health; not for a mere knowledge of abstract science, but for proficiency in the use of ideas in the control of practical situations. Most of these are new tasks. In connection with each, much is now being done in all progressive school systems; but most of them yet are but partially developed. We have been developing knowledge, not function; the power to reproduce facts, rather than the powers to think and feel and will and act in vital relation to the world's life. Now we must look to these latter things as well.

Our task in this volume is to point out some of the new duties. We are to show why education must now undertake tasks that until recently were not considered needful; why new methods, new materials, and new types of experience must be employed. We here try to develop a point of view that seems to be needed by practical school men and women as they make the educational adjustments now demanded by social conditions; and needed also by scientific workers who are seeking to define with accuracy the objectives of education. It is the feeling of the writer that in the social reconstructions of the post-war years that lie just ahead of us, education is to be called upon to bear a hitherto undreamed-of burden of responsibility; and to undertake unaccustomed labors. To present some of the theory needed for the curriculum labors of this new age has been the task herein attempted.

This is a first book in a field that until recently has been too little cultivated. For a long time, we have been developing the theory of educational method, both general and special; and we have required teachers and supervisors to be thoroughly cognizant of it. Recently, however, we have discerned that there is a theory of curriculum-formulation that is no less extensive and involved than that of method; and that it is just as much needed by teachers and supervisors. To know what to do is as important as to know how to do it. This volume, therefore, is designed for teacher-training institutions as an introductory textbook in the theory of the curriculum; and for reading circles in the training of teachers in service. It is hoped also that it may assist the general reader who is interested in noting recent educational tendencies.

CONTENTS

PART I. ENDS AND PROCESSES

PART II. TRAINING FOR OCCUPATIONAL EFFICIENCY

PART III. EDUCATION FOR CITIZENSHIP

PART IV. EDUCATION FOR PHYSICAL EFFICIENCY

THE CURRICULUM

PART I
ENDS AND PROCESSES

THE CURRICULUM

CHAPTER I

TWO LEVELS OF EDUCATIONAL EXPERIENCE

CURRENT discussion of education reveals the presence in the field of two antagonistic schools of educational thought. On the one hand are those who look primarily to the subjective results: the enriched mind, quickened appreciations, refined sensibilities, discipline, culture. To them the end of education is the *ability to live* rather than the practical *ability to produce*. For them most of education is to be motivated by interest in the educational experiences themselves, without particular solicitude at the moment as to the practical use or uselessness of those experiences. If they expand and unfold the potential nature of the individual, therein lies their justification. The full unfoldment of one's powers is the primordial preparation for practical life.

On the other hand there are those who hold that education is to look primarily and consciously to efficient practical action in a practical world. The individual is educated who can perform efficiently the labors of his calling; who can effectively coöperate with his fellows in social and civic affairs; who can keep his bodily powers at a high level of efficiency; who is prepared to participate in proper range of desirable leisure occupations; who can effectively bring his children to full-orbed manhood and womanhood; and who can carry on all his social relations with his fellows in an agreeable and effective manner. Education is consciously to prepare for these things.

The controversy involves practically every field of training. For example, the advocates of culture would have science studied because it is a rich and vitalizing field of human thought. They would have the student live abundantly within the wide fields of his chemistry or biology or physics without at the time any great regard for the practical use or uselessness of the particular facts met with. If the experience is vivifying, if it satisfies intellectual cravings, therein is to be found its sufficient excuse. They assume that enough of the scientific facts, principles, and habits of mind acquired will be of use afterwards to justify the teaching from a purely utilitarian point of view. In fact, they assert that these things can be better mastered when studied as "science for science' sake" than when narrowed down to practical science for the work's sake.

The utilitarians, on the other hand, would have science studied in order that the facts may be put to work by farmers in their farming, by mechanics in their shops, and variously in the fields of manufacturing, mining, cooking, sanitation, etc. They would have an accurate survey made of the science-needs of each social class; and to each they would teach only the facts needed; only those that are to be put to work. In an age of efficiency and economy they would seek definitely to eliminate the useless and the wasteful. To cover the broad fields of the sciences without regard to the functioning value of the particular facts is a blunderbuss method in an age that demands the accuracy of the rifle. It is to waste time and energy and money that are needed elsewhere. It is to force upon unwilling students things that can be justified upon no practical grounds.

A social study like history or literature the culture-advocates conceive to be chiefly a means of lifting the curtain upon human experience in all lands and ages. It gives the pupil an opportunity to view and to mingle vicariously in the age-long varied pageant of world-wide human life. The pupil's business is simply to look upon this pageant as he would view a play at the theater. The experience is in itself a satisfying mode of living, enriching his consciousness, expanding the fields of his imagination, refining his appreciations. When in his reading he beholds the "glory that was Greece and the splendour that was Rome," the epics of Homer or the dramas of Shakespeare, he need not concern himself with the application of that experience in the performance of his practical duties. On the other hand, the utilitarians tell us that we would better eliminate ancient history and the older literatures. These deal with a world that is dead, a civilization that is mouldered, with governments that are now obsolete, with manners and customs and languages that are altogether impracticable in this modern age. In their judgment, in so far as we need history at all, it should be modern history drawn for the purpose of throwing light upon current practical problems of industry, commerce, and citizenship. The facts should be gathered in definite relation to the problems and not be mere blunderbuss history that aims at nothing in particular. And as for literature, they say, it would best be that which reveals the world of to-day: the present natures of men and women; present-day social problems and human reactions; current modes of thought; existing conditions in the fields of commerce, industry, sanitation, civic relationships, and recreational life; not classics, but current literature.

The controversy is particularly marked in the matter of foreign languages. Ancient languages do not function in the lives of men, say the utilitarians: therefore they should be cast out. For the vast majority, even the modern languages do not function. What does not appear in the lives of the people has no reason to appear in the education of the people. The argument is plausible, convincing; and yet the foreign-language advocate is not convinced. He asserts that important matters are lost sight of; that there are more things in human life than practical action, however efficient; that living itself is worth while; that it is the end of education; and that the various utilities are but to provide the means. He looks to a self-realization, to a humanism, to a world of satisfactions that lie above and beyond the mere means to be used in attaining those high ends. He accuses our practical age of aiming at a life for man that is too narrow, barren, mechanical, materialistic.

Now, which side is right? Doubtless both are right. It is like asking the question, "Which shall the tree produce, the flower or the fruit?" It must produce both or it will not perform its full function. We have here simply to do with two levels of functioning, two levels of educational experiences, both of which are essential to fullness of growth, efficiency of action, and completeness of character. Both are good, both are necessary; one precedes the other. One is experience upon the play-level: the other experience upon the work-level. One is action driven by spontaneous interest: the other, by derived interest. One is the luxuriation of the subjective life which has a value for objective experience even though one be not conscious of the values at the time. The other looks to the conscious shaping and control of the objective world; but requires for maximum effectiveness the background of subjective life provided by the other.

The culture-people are not wrong in demanding an education that looks to the widening of vision, the deepening of the general understanding, the actualizing of one's potential powers, the full-orbed expansion and maintenance of the personality, the harnessing-up of native interests, the development of enthusiasms and ideals; or briefly, the full humanization of the individual. They cannot too much insist.

The practical-minded people are not wrong in affirming that man's life consists, and must consist, largely in the performance of responsible duties; that these are to be capably performed; that responsibilities are to be efficiently absolved; that there is need of technical accuracy, dependableness, industry, persistence, right habits, skill, practical knowledge, physical and moral fiber, and adherence to duty whether it be pleasant or painful; and that these results are not to be sufficiently achieved without education of the practical work-type. Upon these things they cannot too much insist.

CHAPTER II

EDUCATIONAL EXPERIENCE UPON THE PLAY-LEVEL

RECENT psychology tells us that man has a long period of childhood and youth in order that he may play. He plays, not because he is young, but he is long young in order that he may play; and thus through active experience secure his education. Play is Nature's active mode of education. Shall a boy unfold his physical powers so that he can run with speed and endurance, or throw accurately or fight with strength and skill, or exert himself long hours without undue fatigue? Nature provides that in his play he shall run and throw and fight and otherwise exert himself; and thus make actual his potential powers. Physical play is Nature's physical education. Shall the boy develop the social abilities necessary for full coöperation with the members of his social group? Nature provides instinctive tendency to participate in group-plays, social games, conversation, etc., which develop his social nature, fix his social habits, and cement social solidarity. Social play is Nature's active method of social education. Shall the boy possess an unspecialized mechanical ability of a type that is even more needful to-day than in the age when man's nature was shaped? Fortunately, here again we find the strong constructive and operative play-instincts which drive boys to make and operate things. Give a normal-minded boy a rich opportunity to make things and to "make them go," — and one has then only to leave him alone with his opportunity. Nature's method of education will do the rest. Shall he be observant of men and affairs about him? Shall he fill his mind concerning the things with which he is to be concerned throughout life? Shall he acquire and maintain masses of knowledge through the possession of an inquiring disposition? Again Nature has provided the deep-lying and powerful mental-play instinct of curiosity, the intellectual appetite, the desire to know. The boy is made watchful of everything that goes on about him, especially the actions of men. Thus he learns and thus he continues to learn throughout life. Mental play is Nature's active method of filling the mind with information.

Since education is so largely a matter of learning things, let us first take up this topic of mental play as the basis of intellectual education. One observes men and their affairs, the things of one's environment, and the natural phenomena by which one is surrounded, simply as a mode of living. Through such observation he is continuously gathering facts through all of his waking hours; and without question as to the use or uselessness of the information. He makes no attempt to observe merely the things that can be of practical service in his personal affairs. He lives most fully who keeps himself awake to everything before him and who sees all in due relation and proportion even though most of it has no visible relation to his practical affairs.

Not only does he observe directly, but he listens with consuming interest to the stories of things which he has not seen. Most of the gossip of the daily papers relates to things with which he has no immediate concern. And yet he reads and learns, and feels that if he does not do so he does not fully live. The avidity with which he absorbs the news or the eager curiosity with which gossips delve into the affairs of the neighborhood show the universality and the intensity of this hunger after knowledge, even of useless type. One drinks endlessly at this fountain without ever so much as raising the question whether the knowledge so obtained is or can ever be of any use. Like breathing, one feels it to be a natural portion of living which requires no justification.

Learning things because of curiosity without reference to the use of that knowledge is really one of the largest normal activities of man. Knowledge-getting because of curiosity is analogous to food-getting because of hunger. One wants the food when hungry whether he knows anything about its functional value or not. The hunger is Nature's way of ascribing value to things that the man needs. Equally, the healthy mind wants to know the things that appeal to the mental appetite without care at the time as to their practical application. This knowledge-hunger is Nature's method of ascribing value to the things that the man needs — when he is too immature or too stupid to know what he needs. Such strong and continuing instincts impel only to things that are on the whole useful and necessary.

It is play; but it has its values. Although most things observed have no visible relation to his immediate affairs, yet everything in the community is related to everything else in subtle, intangible, and usually unknown ways. Each individual is the center of a vortex of influences. He needs an understanding of the total life of the community in order that he may adjust his actions to the factors of the situation as a whole. His current information concerning apparently useless things really gives him fullness of vision of the total pageant of community life of which he forms a part. This fullness of vision is necessary for understanding; for valuations; and right social attitudes.

While traveling to my work in the Orient, some years ago, I had occasion to observe a portion of the educational experiences of two boys about twelve years of age. The ship on which we were traveling stopped for a day or two at each of a number of ports: Hongkong, Shanghai, Nagasaki, Kobe, Yokohama, etc. Scarcely had the ship come to anchor when

the boys were off and away on an exploring expedition. For
them it was a region strange and new. There was no assign-
ment of anything for them to learn; they were not sent;
they were not going ashore to get information so that they
might recite upon it at night; it was not a thing upon which
they were later to be examined. Simply a rich field of experience opened before them and they eagerly embraced their
opportunities and went forth to partake to the full. It was
simply play-experience resulting from their intellectual
hungers. During the day they visited as many different
portions of the city as their time and their means of loco-
motion would permit. They looked into the residences of
rich and poor, into the shops, amusement places, religious
temples, soldiers' barracks, streets and alleys, the conditions of life among the well-to-do and among the poor, etc.
They came back to the ship at night with rich stores of
experience and full to overflowing with information. It
required no effort on the part of the adult members of their
party to secure extended and enthusiastic verbal reports.
The boys were living. They were not simply memorizing
facts. It was all upon the play-level; and yet they were securing the best possible type of education. Had it been made
a work-task for them with definite program and time allot-
ments, with reports that had to be put up in specified form
and with examinations to see that nothing had been overlooked,—would they have left the ship? And in what mood?

This experience of the two boys seems to indicate the kind
of intellectual play-experience needed throughout the fields
of education. In the same way, impelled only by curiosity
and the play-motive, following the leadings of interest,
children and youth should, it appears, wander through
every important field of human knowledge and human
experience. Without any particular consciousness of the serious values or purposes of the learning, they should thus

lay a wide and secure foundation of understanding of all important aspects of reality. So far as possible, this should be by observation. But one's horizon is narrow, and most of this world lies beyond, and stretches backward through history. Most is to be explored vicariously in imagination on the basis of the reports of others. For this, pupils need books that vividly reconstruct the experiences of others.

There is a great wealth of geographical readings, especially travels, which present a vivid reconstruction of life in other lands. As children travel, for example, in their readings with Peary to the North Pole, or with Amundsen and Scott to the South Pole, their experiences will bring them to appreciate the nature of the polar regions almost as clearly as if they had been there in the flesh. Let them travel in spirit with Livingstone and Stanley and Roosevelt into the heart of Africa aħd they will have an appreciation of the nature of Central Africa that they can obtain in no other way. Let them travel with Captain Cook and Darwin and Stevenson through the South Seas, with Dana in his voyage around the "Horn," with Tyndall and Jordan in the Alps, with John Muir and Enos Mills in the Rockies, with George Kennan in Siberia, etc., — let them thus travel vicariously through the various lands and regions of the earth, and they will come to have a full appreciation of the nature of the world. In the reading of literature with geographical background like *Captains Courageous, Heidi, Kim, The Iron Trail, The Lumberman,* etc., children are permitted further to relive the lives of peoples in various lands and under various conditions; and thus through living acquire understanding. These geographical readings should aim, not at information, but at experience. Like the two boys roaming through the cities merely as a mode of living, the children in our schools should roam through the wide earth in the pages of their reading merely as a satisfying mode of living.

The more unsophisticated, the less they are conscious of the serious values, the more they simply follow interest, probably the better will be the experience for education.

History presents another rich and endless field for exploration upon the play-level. This children should read for the sake of their interest in the human story, in the anecdotes, the biographies, the struggles, the adventures, and all of the other things that appeal to childhood and youth. Thus they should become acquainted with all the family of nations. They should participate in the historical experiences of all important countries for the same type of delight that actuated the boys in exploring the foreign cities. They need not know at the time the values of this experience in developing large-group consciousness, national and planetary sympathies and understandings, the bases of civic judgment, or the solid foundations of any "Federation of the World" which we may ever produce.

The teacher must see the serious ends in order to adjust conditions, to control motives, and to guide. But children should not be greatly conscious of the growth-ends of play-experience. The play-spirit is a skittish thing that tends to take flight when it sees itself harnessed up and set to prosaic productive labors. On this level it is enough for the children that the historical reconstructions be true, vivid, interesting, voluminous, and rapidly read; that the experience be a satisfying mode of living, like going to a play, or reading an exciting story. On this level it should not be conscious learning of facts, — for the reason that we want more learning than can be accomplished that way; and other things equally valuable that cannot be accomplished that way at all.

One has a natural interest, not only in the affairs of men, but also in the things and forces with which men are surrounded and with which they must deal: the phenomena of nature, the fields of science. Give healthy-minded children

a full opportunity to indulge in the playful manipulation of
toys, tools, machines, appliances, and materials that involve
mechanical principles; the making and operation of electrical
devices; the manipulation of sound-producing apparatus and
instruments; of lenses; projection apparatus; photographic
apparatus; experimentation with the chemical elements;
exploring geological formations; keeping pets; visiting the
Zoo, the Aviary, the Aquarium, or the plant conserva-
tory; observing plants and animals in their native haunts
and habitats; — give the unspoiled child proper opportunities at these things and he asks no better fun. He
brings to them the same eager intellectual desires to know
that inspire the trained scientist who delights in scientific
"knowledge for its own sake." Let the child, therefore,
explore the world of reality as widely and deeply as he can
be enabled to get at it; and when he has reached the limitations imposed by conditions, let him read the stories of
insect life, of flowers, birds, bees, rocks, stars, animals wild
and tame, electricity and its applications, chemistry and its
wonders, mechanics and inventions, light and sound and
heat, and all the rest. Naturally he will explore according
to his maturity. Much of this can be accomplished in the
elementary schools — more than school people have usually
thought possible. Still more of it should come in the high
school. Probably the scientific interest is no stronger in the
high school than in the elementary; simply pupils are capable
of seeing wider and deeper relations. It is probable that the
science experience of the elementary level should cover a
wide range. Then upon the high-school level they will
simply go into greater detail and attain the higher levels of
generality. After one is familiar with the concrete details,
the tracing-out of general relationships and discovering the
natural organization of the field are among the normal
intellectual delights.

Neither the laboratory nor reading experiences upon this level need be functional in the consciousness of the children any more than the daily newspaper or one's observations out of a car window. The experience is not to be so systematized that the spontaneous play-spirit is destroyed. There is not to be too much *teaching*. What the children crave and need is *experience*. The school's main task is to supply opportunities that are so varied and attractive that, like the two boys when they arrived at a port, pupils will want to plunge in and to enjoy the opportunities that are placed before them.

All of these preliminary studies or experiences, whether geographical, historical, literary, or scientific, like children's play in general need to be rich in details, full of human color, infinitely varied, touched lightly and then left behind, taken up as prompted by interest not by logic, superficial, repetitious, and loosely organized. There is need of movement, irregularity, caprice, variety, and incessant interplay of all the factors that compose the human spirit. For such are the ways of childhood; and even of youth and adulthood in the hours of their freedom.

Enough has been said to illustrate the nature of educational experience upon the play-level in fields that involve a large intellectual element: but there are other kinds of play. The usual manual training shop is a play-shop, and the kitchen a play-kitchen. The experiences in the main are but a liberation of the constructive and operative play-instincts. And upon the early or preliminary levels of one's education this is as it should be. For where the equipment is such as to permit diversity of experience with tools, machines, materials, and processes, there is nothing so good as play-experience for laying the solid foundations for the later industrial studies.

It is generally conceded nowadays that the best type of

physical training is the liberation of the physical play-impulses of children. Systematic gymnastics and calisthenics are being discarded and in their stead we are introducing a great variety of indoor and outdoor games, sports, rhythmic dances, folk-dances, hiking expeditions, etc., of the types in which well-trained children and youth indulge in the hours of their freedom. We are making this change, not because it is easier to manage or less expensive or more economical of time, for it is none of these things; but rather because physical experience upon the play-level is a more effective kind of physical education than spiritless mechanized physical exercises at word of command from which the play-spirit is absent.

The social training likewise that we are introducing into our schools is mainly upon the play-level. It is accomplished in connection with the plays and games, the social clubs, the dancing, the civic leagues, the Boy Scouts and the Camp-Fire Girls movements, and the general social life of the school. The greater the spontaneity, other things equal, the greater the values.

To say that portions of serious education are to be on the order of play no longer shocks a practical-minded people as it once did. Our biology, psychology, and sociology have recently shown us the serious values of play and the vital function it has always performed and must perform in human life. For whatever the field of man's activity, it is this that lays the foundation for the serious, specialized matters that are to come later. It is man's basic training, and in the present world of infinite complexity, demanding world-wide vision and sympathies, it needs to be full, rich, and extensive.

We are also coming to recognize the value of harnessing up the play-motive when we wish strenuous exertion. It does not mean lack of effort; rather intensification of effort. A boy will play till he drops from fatigue, and do it all voluntarily for the love of the cause. He will not voluntarily do that in his *work*, where the play-spirit is omitted. It is the boys or girls who enter with the greatest zest into the actions of men as reconstructed in their histories, who take sides in the struggles, and who are warmed by their sympathetic and vicarious participation in the historical actions, who have most historical experience and get the greatest good from their history. It is the boy who wants to win in the spelling match who will manfully master the entire spelling book as a part of the game. The pupil who sees his mathematics as a series of interesting puzzles and games, is the one who will come nearest to conquering every difficulty that shows its head. The thing that one enjoys is the thing at which one will strain every nerve. Given a healthy play-motive and the right opportunity, it is like a high-power engine and a straight track ahead.

We find here a partial answer to the contention that education on the basis of interest results in softness and flabbiness. Really it is the one who finds his educational prescriptions pieces of drudgery who most tries to evade them, consciously or unconsciously; and who consequently suffers from softness and flabbiness. The boys on the athletic fields who most enjoy their opportunities are the ones who most often over-develop physically; and later suffer therefrom. Interest-driven exercise is not only efficacious for developing fiber, but it must even be guarded against because of its over-efficacy where conditions are specially favorable. It is no less true in the intellectual realm. Find the student in mathematics or physics or Latin who has the best general command over the subject, who sees relations in clearest perspective, who has least intellectual flabbiness, — it is always one who delights in his studies in that field; one who loves the subject "for its own sake." It is never the one for whom the experience is drudgery.

CHAPTER III

EDUCATIONAL EXPERIENCE UPON THE WORK-LEVEL

ALTHOUGH play has its place in the process, education aims at preparation for the serious duties of life: one's calling, the care of one's health, civic coöperations and regulation, bringing up one's children, keeping one's language in good form, etc. Educational experience upon the work-level is intended to prepare consciously for the efficient performance of these and all other serious duties. By *work* in this chapter we refer not merely to one's calling, but to all of one's responsible activities.

Even one's play has ends that are as serious as those of one's work, for they are the same ends; but the relations are different. Although one may be unconscious at the time of the serious values of his play, Nature is thereby aiming definitely at his physical upbuilding, his mental expansion, and his social development. Neither the play-instincts nor the pleasures thereby occasioned are given as purposeless luxuries. The pleasure is not an end; it is a lure. It is a primitive method of impelling serious developmental activities where the intellect cannot be depended upon to direct the work. It is serious activity impelled by instinct; whereas work is serious activity impelled by ideas. The play is short-sighted; even blind in the face of modern conditions. Work when fully developed is far-sighted, clear-sighted, fully conscious of ends and means. The accompanying diagram may assist in showing the identity of play and work ends, and also the differences in relationships.

The figure shows four things, A, B, C, and D, all obviously involved in the preparation for, and performance of, responsible activities. Play is conscious of only the first; but this really looks to the second; the second is involved in the third; and the third then produces the fourth. As indicated

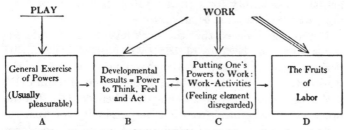

FIG. 1. To represent the relations of play-activities and work-activities to education and to each other.

by following the arrows, the play, without the individual's knowing it, is leading him toward the fruits of serious labors. But since he does not see the ends, there is no feeling of responsibility.

Work-activity differs in that it looks consciously to all of the factors. It is conscious primarily of the fruits of the labors. Here is where the fundamental interest lies. This casts a derived interest back over the other factors since they are prerequisites. The worker, while in training, has a double interest in the work-activities: the primary one is due to the fact that they produce the fruits that he is after; the secondary, that they further develop his powers to act, lifting them to higher levels of efficiency. He is then interested in the general exercise of the play-level, not because of the pleasures thereby derived, but because of its value in developing the powers to think and act.

The diagram shows the place in the total scheme of the two levels of educational experience. A represents experiences of the play-level; C those of the work-level. Both are factors in developing the individual's work-powers. A comes

earlier and lays the foundations; and may continue throughout life alongside or mingled with the work for maintaining
the foundations. C comes only after one has come to feel
actual responsibility for serious results. *It is not to be something like work; it must be actual work.*

It must be observed that the work-level actually differen-
tiates into two, because of the two types of fruits to be
derived from the work-experiences. One may perform the
work-activities (C) for the sake of the ultimate results (D)
without consciousness of the educational effects (B). On the
other hand, one may, from felt responsibility for final results and consciousness of inferiority of his powers, perform
the work-activities for the sake of the developmental results (B) alone. These are as genuinely the fruits of the
labors as the ultimate objective results. There cannot be
felt responsibility, however, for these developmental work-
results except as it is derived from a feeling of responsibility
for securing the ultimate results.

*Whether the work-experiences, therefore, look toward sub-
jective or objective fruits, both interests and responsibilities
relate primarily to the objective; and only in derived form to the
subjective. The strength of the derived interests and responsibilities is determined by the strength of the primary ones. Even
when the developmental results are the things primarily sought
by teachers in directing education, the students must be aiming
primarily at the objective results, and only secondarily at the
prerequisite developmental ones.*

An awakening education is everywhere coming to realize
the need of work-activities as the only possible normal method
of preparing for the work of the world. In the occupational
field, we are developing schools and courses for trades,
commerce, household occupations, agriculture, mining, etc.,
in special schools, continuation schools, and in general high
schools. In the more progressive of these, there is every-

where attempt to perform a real portion of the world's work as the means of training. This may be accomplished by transferring a portion of the community's occupational activities to the schools and having the work done there; or by distributing the students throughout the community where they can find their work-experiences in those situations provided by the work-activities of the adult world.

Both plans are used. On the one hand, vocational activities are being transferred to the schools, and the work done there under regular shop conditions involving genuine responsibility. Thus the boys in the shops, instead of the old-type manual training exercises, are engaged in manufacturing school equipment, furniture, farming implements, playground apparatus, articles needed for Red Cross work and for community poor-relief, laboratory apparatus, electrical appliances for home use, etc. They are also in places doing actual community printing, milk-testing, seed-testing, repair-work on furniture, tools, machines and automobiles, cement construction, building portable houses, garages, gymnasiums, playground pavilions, etc. The girls, instead of formal cooking exercises, are nowadays more and more put to preparation of the daily school luncheon, home canning and preserving, sometimes doing baking for home use, or even for the general market. And their sewing is the making of actual garments.

Since it is often difficult to transfer actual work-activities to the schools, another method is for the students to go out into the community where the work is being carried on by the adult world and there to share in the labors for training purposes. Although difficult enough to arrange and manage, this is often the easier method of the two because of the frequent practical impossibility of transferring the actual responsibility to the schools. As a result of this recognition we are substituting home gardening for training purposes for the old ineffective school gardening; the home-project type of agriculture for the school farm; and part-time work in shops, stores, offices, etc., for mere drill exercises in school shops and commercial rooms.

In training for citizenship, also, practical activities are being introduced. Pupils are helping to make the city clean, sanitary, and beautiful; to care for the city's trees and shrubbery; to prevent flies and mosquitoes; to protect the birds and to destroy noxious insects. They are engaged in making things for school or community use. Boy Scouts at times patrol dangerous street-crossings morning and afternoon to protect the little children going to and from school. School civic organizations are making local surveys of community conditions for responsible report to the authorities or to adult civic organizations.

For practical hygienic training, pupils are often made responsible for some portion of the school ventilation, building cleanliness and sanitation, the regulation of temperature, humidity, and sunlight. Through the school medical department and through giving credit for home work, children are stimulated to outside practical hygienic activities: home ventilation and sanitation, cleansing the teeth, rational choice of foods, regulation of sleeping conditions and hours, adjustment of exercise to needs, care of the eyes, etc.

In the pupil's language, also, we are introducing the work-motive of felt responsibility. Pupils are brought to aim at social results that for attainment require a correct and effective type of language. This compels them to see their language as a work-activity employed for getting results. Responsibility for ends then impels them to watchfulness and effort in organizing their thought, in paragraph and sentence construction, in choice of words, pronunciation, spelling, handwriting, etc. They are given the opportunities in problem-solving, oral reports, written reports, letters, news

items, communications to civic organizations, applications
for position, debates, social-club activities, etc.

But after enumerating all of these things we must confess that professional vision is far in advance of professional
practice. For really, except for the language field, taking
schools the country over, there is not much training experience of genuine work-type, the criterion being felt responsibility for serious results. Even trade-school experiences are
most often exercises in isolation from the world's actual work.
Far more is this the case with courses bearing vocational
names in the general schools; and with training for citizenship, hygiene, and sanitation. The list of things being done
somewhere in the country is very long; but it is a rare school
system that has found a way so to share in community work-
responsibility as to secure a sufficient portion of actual work-
experience for training purposes.

There is insufficient realization of the need or the legitimacy for public education of actual work-experiences.
Even yet our schools appear to be well-named from the old
Greek word *schole*, meaning *leisure*. In the main, education
in grammar grades, high school, and college of liberal arts
— we except the mastery of the school arts in the elementary
school and the training in professional and technical schools
— is yet a life of leisure. Teachers are often able to prevent
students' enjoying it; but that does not make the activity
an organic portion of the world's work, which is set aside for
training youth in the processes of that work.

In technological and professional schools we have long
recognized the need of work-activities. Young physicians
in training are helpers in hospitals; engineering students have
field and shop work; agricultural students, work on the
school farm; but even in these schools the amount of work-
experience is usually felt to be inadequate. This is revealed
by such a movement as that in the University of Cincinnati,

where the students in mechanical engineering have been given opportunity to work half-time in manufacturing establishments of the city, bearing actual responsibilities and receiving wages for their work. This is to provide work-experience that is genuine in character and adequate in quantity.

The need of work for training has long been understood by the skilled trades. The apprenticeship system trained through experiences of the work-type. The recent agitation for vocational training in public schools is due, not to a new need, but to new conditions. The apprenticeship system, never very efficient, has broken down in the face of complicated conditions. Public education is coming to the rescue. But even though we organize schools for the purpose, we must no less than in the old days include actual work-experience. Indeed, we must now have a greater quantity of responsible work than was provided by the old apprenticeship system, because of the greater present complexity of work and of the higher levels of efficiency to be reached. And it must be not less real than the old.

Finding work-experience for training presented no difficulty to the apprenticeship system. It had little else to provide. But that is just the thing that has been most absent from public education. Schools have been places of leisure occupations; not places where the world's work is being performed. They can provide any amount of experience on the play-level. But they are not in command of the world's work-activities, whether production, distribution, civic regulation, community sanitation, or other. In their traditional form they are therefore not in a position to provide much training on the work-level. Hence, education requires a profound transformation before it is able to take adequate care of work-experience as training for work. Schools must become sharers in the world's work of every kind by way of finding the only possible training opportunities.

Experiences of the work-type may well begin in a small way even in kindergarten and primary grades. The expansion of the pupils' understanding of ends and means will be gradual up through the grades. It ought to be fairly full by the later years of the high school — in spite of present usual practices to the contrary. It is not unreasonable to suppose that it should be dominant on the college level — again in spite of current contrary practices. The academic tendency has been to delay educational activities of the work-type. They have been withheld from college students until the professional schools have been reached; and from most high-school students until they reach technical schools, or the school of the world's work. This is the way of ease and economy; but the world is rapidly coming to think it a mistake.

CHAPTER IV

THE PLACE OF IDEAS IN WORK-EXPERIENCE

EVEN the crude activities of the past were directed by ideas. The farmer in his fields, the machinist at his lathe, the housewife at her cooking, the citizen in arriving at judgments of public affairs, or in staving off disease, — all considered the conditions before them, and applied the means and processes that appeared to them the most rational. But they lacked accurate scientific knowledge of the factors involved. The ideas that they put to work were crude; and that is why their labors were crude and inefficient. The thought or subjective part of the work *is the work* essentially. One indispensable thing for making work efficient is a full supply of accurate scientific information concerning all the factors. The second thing is a correct performance of the ideational portion of the practical work. Let us begin with the latter and call it

The antecedent performance

The practical performance of any task divides itself naturally into two parts. First, there is the planning of the work: making decisions as to exact objectives and as to the specific materials and processes to be employed. This task involves performance in imagination of the entire labor from incipiency to finished product. It involves marshaling all of one's science relative to both objectives and processes; and drawing plans as dictated by the science. One must also test out in imagination each step in the series to see that everything fits into everything else, and that there is no contradiction, interference, or other obstacle.

Any complete task will serve to illustrate. Let us take

the case of the boy in the machine-shop who sets out to construct a gas-engine. He first constructs it in his imagination. This antecedent construction involves all of the parts, sizes, designs, and relations. In this way, without any risk or waste of materials, he may construct it over and over again, to see that there are no mistakes, no interference of parts, and no insurmountable difficulties. He may construct it in many ways, using different designs, sizes of parts, or proportions; and he may test out each design in order to determine the working plan that seems best. For these antecedent labors, he must mobilize all of his science and put it to work both in the planning and the testing. His thought may be concentrated into a few hours or distributed over months. But when this antecedent construction and testing are satisfactorily accomplished and decision made, the more fundamental portion of the work is done. There remains the objectification of his plans. This is not mere mechanical registration of his decisions. Back of his hands, his thought is still busy directing, guiding, and supervising. His hands are the tools of his intellect. Such manual labors, before being mechanized into habit, — a later process, — are essentially intellectual labors.

This must be emphasized because of the frequent tendency in the training to commit 'one or the other of two fundamental errors. One is to leave out a large portion of the ideational element, by giving ready-made plans to the students which they are simply to follow: shop-manuals, books of recipes, blue-print plans, ready-made patterns, detailed directions. In such case pupils may get practically no vision of the controlling science, and are not even putting second-hand ideas to work. They may get nothing more than ideas of mechanical manipulation without any insight into the reasons for the processes. As training experience, it is barren and ineffective.

The opposite error is the attempt to teach the science without any relation to the work-situations. This no more than the other is putting ideas to work; it is therefore not intellectual work-experience. It may accomplish much as intellectual play. Practical experience proves that it lays a good foundation for later actual work-training, — as where the man trained in "pure" science goes into practical industry, and rapidly gets his next level of training. We do not deny that the play-level provides an excellent foundation for training of the work-type; we have everywhere affirmed it. But it is not training on the work-level. And in the degree in which the latter is necessary, the experience is incomplete, inefficient, unfocused, fails to provide work-valuations, work-habits, attitudes, and sense of responsibility. As a method of training for serious duties, it too is ineffective.

We must point out an important difference between the antecedent or subjective performance of the act and the later objective performance. In the former, one draws on all his ideas that are in any way related to the task in hand. If he has abundant ideas and a fertile imagination, he may be brought into contact with about every important thing in the field. He comes to know the science and properly to value it, as he thus chooses the things that can serve his purposes and rejects those that are of no service. The planning, the antecedent performance of the task, is, therefore, from an educational point of view, the most important part of it. But it cannot have vitality for education unless it is really antecedent to intended action; unless it is an organic portion of a total act of which the outward performance is but the culminating portion.

On the other hand, after decisions are made, plans drawn, and only execution remaining, then one's mental life is much narrowed. It is concerned intensively with the one design that has been decided upon, the one set of materials and methods. This culminating activity has many educational values: it gives motive and substantiality to the whole process; it gives depth to one's understanding and appreciations; it confers operative skill. But it cannot be compared with the antecedent labors for giving width of intellectual vision.

The pupil must, therefore, not be robbed of the antecedent performance by having the finished plans prescribed by the teacher or by a class manual.

The antecedent performance possesses another important value. Novices will not acquire a sense of responsibility unless they are forced to take the initiative, to make plans and decisions for themselves, and to bear the responsibility of making the plans successful. But with novices, this involves mistakes, waste of materials, and losses. Since penalty alone can enforce responsibility, and since loss is the normal penalty of mistakes, serious waste appears to be the price of initiative and responsibility, — if they are to be real, and not merely make-believe.

We have a way out of the difficulty as we distinguish between antecedent and culminating performance; and as we develop educational technique appropriate to the two. *Full and complete initiative can be given students for the antecedent performance of the action.* Then, before the steps planned are actually taken, they can be reviewed, step by step, as frequently as necessary by the student by way of seeing that no mistake is involved. Plans can be taken up in class discussion, and tried out in the critical testing imagination of teacher and pupils. Serious defects will thus be discovered. Mistakes can be seen before they are made actual. Losses can be realized, and the penalty enforced in imagination sufficiently to restrain wrong action. As a matter of fact, this is the way Nature enforces her penalties

most of the time in the case of the successful man. He is
successful because he anticipates mistakes and corrects
them before they are made. The unsuccessful man is the
one of narrower vision and duller imagination who does
not see his mistakes until he is injured or crushed beneath
them. "Experience is the best teacher." But experience in
anticipating mistakes and correcting them before they are
made is a better teacher than loss and injury. The plan
demands full development of the technique of antecedent
performance.

The technical information

On the work-level, the task to be performed is central;
and the science is organized about it. A boy, for example,
in the school shop wishes to construct and operate a tele-
graphic apparatus. This ambition will serve as the center
of the science training. He will be motivated to gather
information concerning batteries, wiring, electro-magnets,
making and breaking of circuits, etc. He will learn just the
things that he needs for the task in hand; and nothing more
at the time. Through using his ideas in the planning and in
the actual construction he comes to realize the full significance of the various facts. The derived interest aroused is
for most individuals more potent than the native interest
in the abstract science facts and principles. For this reason
the knowledge is more effectively driven home and remembered.

There is a strong drift in public education toward this
project-method of organization. The school corn clubs, for
example, assemble all possible information relative to the
growth of corn and use it for the control of practical procedure. Children engaged in an anti-mosquito campaign
assemble just the entomological, bacteriological, and other
information needed in their labors, rejecting for the moment

all irrelevant scientific information. The tree-protecting league gathers all possible facts concerning the species of trees attacked by insects, fungi, etc., together with the scientific information needed for combating the destructive influences. They reject for the time all botanical or entomological information that has no bearing on the problem in hand. In weeding out the grammatical mistakes made by children in their speech, the grammatical information is assembled that relates to the specific mistakes found; all other grammatical facts are passed by as irrelevant. In brief, one learns the things needed for directing action in connection with the situations in which the action is to take place, and just previous to the drawing-up of the plans. Only under such circumstances can knowledge properly reveal its significance, be rightly focused upon human affairs, or be normally assimilated. Knowing and doing should grow up together.

In spite of these virtues, the project-method as a mode of teaching science is not always in good repute. This is not due to any inherent defect in the method — when it is complete. It is by far the most complicated method; and differs most from familiar traditional ones. It is not, therefore, surprising that teachers often develop an incomplete and ineffective form of the method. Whenever a training task involves practical performance, this is so visible, tangible, and solid to sense that it often comes to be conceived as being the whole thing. The teacher attempts to get the pupils in the most economical and expeditious way to perform the practical actions by way of securing the results. The teachers, therefore, often do the thinking, draw up the plans, and prescribe procedure for the students. This is exceedingly common in sewing-rooms, kitchens, and shops. So far as the pupils' experience is concerned, the intellectual element is largely dropped out. In such case the pupils do not themselves perform the most vital portion of the work. The part given over to them does not require that they master the science involved for the sake of planning and self-guidance.

The technique of the project-method requires that in the teaching the major attention be given to what we have called the antecedent performance rather than to the objective or culminating performance. It also requires that the antecedent activities be performed by the students.

In the use of this method the necessary ideas are to be got from at least three places. To make the matters clear let us resume our illustration of the gas-engine: —

1. In the first place, the boy, motivated by intention to make the engine, will observe such engines in as great variety as available. For fullness of understanding, he should operate them, and see the workings of the parts. He should take them to pieces, and reassemble them. This experience brings him into direct contact with all the science realities involved — the first vital step in learning science. After he has thus experienced the realities, he is prepared to isolate them, verbalize them, and appreciate quantitative relations. The situation does not contain all that he needs for these latter purposes, and certainly not enough for full scientific generalizations; but the things it contains he needs as part of the total process.

2. In the second place, he will read descriptions, pictures, drawings, and diagrams of engines that he has not seen, by way of extending his vision of possibility. If he can have direct access to two or three types of actual engines, he will have an apperception-alphabet that will enable him easily and quickly through reading to examine another ten or twenty types. It would be well in such case to begin with the historically earliest and simplest types, noting both the structures and the science involved; then to trace the

changes that have been made by way of improvement and of adaptation to special needs, and reasons for these changes. When this experience is added, he is provided with a better basis for generalizations. But probably even this is not enough.

3. For illustrating the third step, let us isolate the single feature of the ignition system. Instead of further widening his understanding of the electrical science involved by looking to still more engines, — there is a limit beyond which little or nothing new appears, — he might look off and view the wide field of electricity in general and its applications in general. He is still motivated, let us say, by his project of developing an improved type of ignition system. He reads a full treatise on electricity and its applications. Where his apperception is defective, he tries things out in the laboratory. But, though taking a full survey of the "pure" science, he is only sorting over the possibilities of the field, locating suggestions, trying to find the ideas that he can put to work. This pure-science overview is the ultimate level of project-science experience.

While in a sense this is "pure" science, it is very different from the usual non-functional type. Here the primary thing in the student's consciousness is the project, the piece of work to be done; not the satisfaction of intellectual interests. He examines every fact and principle in relation to his practical problem, and not merely as a field of intellectual sight-seeing. The two types of experience differ as play differs from work.

CHAPTER V

WHERE EDUCATION CAN BE ACCOMPLISHED

EDUCATIONAL experiences must take place where they can be normal. Frequently this is not at the schools. The nature of the problem can be made clear by illustrations of varying character. Let us take first the case of the training of girls in sewing. The practical activities will transfer to the schools with ease. The continuing need of garments and other household necessities involving needlework gives rise to the normal responsibilities. While the activities may take place in the individual homes, the teacher going about from home to home to supervise it, the plan is not administratively economical. The schools can easily provide the simple appliances needed. The materials can be carried to the schools as easily as books, and the practical labors performed there as normally as at home. When tasks can be so transferred without loss of normal responsibility, this is administratively desirable.

The training in home cooking will not transfer with any such ease. Food materials are bulky, and not easily carried to the school for the work, nor easily returned to the homes. They are perishable, easily subject to contamination in transit, and often should be served as soon as preparation is complete. Most of the practical activities therefore must take place in the home kitchen, not in the school kitchen. For supervising it, teachers need to be in intimate contact with the homes. A few such cooking tasks can be transferred to the schools at times, as for example, certain special baking, a portion of the canning, preserving, jelly-making, etc. These can occasionally be performed at the school and the product then returned to the homes of the girls.

Owing to the difficulty of providing normal responsibilities, and therefore normal training conditions, many schools at present are using a substitute. The preparation of the school luncheon is used to provide responsible training conditions. The girls in relays provide daily one or two dishes for the luncheon. In other cases they prepare luncheons for the teachers, regularly or occasionally. In a few schools they even go so far as to provide an entire noonday meal each day including a dozen or more dishes, served cafeteria-fashion for several hundred students. When a needed activity will not transfer, it is thus possible occasionally to find a sufficient substitute that is not mere make-believe.

Recognition of the necessity of normal responsibility as a factor of educational situations is a relatively recent development. Not many years ago it was felt, for example, that training in gardening could be given in our little school gardens. Recently it has been discovered that in so far as the school garden omits normal responsibility for securing actual results that are to be used in serious ways, it is but a play-garden. As such it is of value for preliminary training of the play-type. It can introduce the subject and give some beginning ideas as to gardening; and it can serve for demonstration and experimental procedure; but it is insufficient for serious training. It is being discovered that gardening responsibility transfers to the school only with great difficulty, and that therefore the training should take place in the home gardens with the teacher going about from home to home to supervise the work. *The training needs to be taken care of where the work can be normal, not where it may be most convenient for teachers.*

Formerly we thought we could train machinists and carpenters in our high-school manual-training shops. Now we see that our shops of the usual type provide play-situations, not work-situations. The constructive instinct is strong in boys, and whether in school or not their play inclines them to constructive activities. The usual school shop offers these instincts a favorable outlet. This is of large value. Constructive play, distributed from kindergarten to high school, is a highly profitable training of the preliminary type. It introduces novices to the field of serious mechanical occupations. It can carry them but a portion of the way, however. After such introduction the thing needed is responsible work, where the boy can participate in serious mechanical activities, under actual working conditions. The practical responsible aspects of shop training will transfer to the schools under present conditions only with great difficulty. It is scarcely possible to organize in any sufficient way at our schools actual machine-shop production or the actual building of houses. At the school only preliminary, laboratory, and demonstration portions can be taken care of. The culminating portions of the educative process are to be found out in the world of responsible industry. To that must the students be sent for the later levels of their mechanical training.

Our schools have tried to train for health by imparting textbook and lecture information concerning matters of anatomy, physiology, and hygiene. If the children got the facts in mind well enough to recite and pass the examinations, they were considered educated. Application of the information has been looked upon as a thing to be done by the pupils only *after* the examination has attested the completeness of their education. The application has been looked upon as being in no sense a part of the training process; certainly not a part of the school's responsibility. Recently we are becoming better informed. We are discovering that the application of the information is the culminating process of education; that without the processes in which the knowl-

edge is put to work, education is only half done. We are
coming to see that education in hygiene is accomplished,
not in the moments of acquiring the preliminary technical
information at the school, but *in the moments of using that
information in the control of conduct; and in the recurring
moments of such actual use of knowledge while health habits are
being fixed.* The training is accomplished as one puts his
ideas to work in the ventilation of his sleeping-room; in his
choice of food; in caring for his teeth; in keeping up his muscular strength and tone, in work and play; in evading
bacterial infection; and in the countless other matters in
which he is called upon *to act.*

Most of these hygienic training activities will not transfer
to the school. The training has to be accomplished where
the activity can take place normally. The school can give
necessary antecedent information; it can aid students in
forming judgments as to what to do; it can through teachers
and school nurses coöperate with parents in stimulating
and supervising the activities of the students; but in most
cases the self-directed activities that round out and fix the
training cannot be transferred to the schools. The home-
visiting health-nurse in continual contact with the home
situations in which the pupils live is the one ideally situated
for supervising the culminating aspects of the training.

When in later chapters we look at the responsible activities involved in training for citizenship, for leisure occupations, for parenthood, for religion, for social intercommunication, etc., we shall discover that in most fields of training
there are some of the culminating activities that transfer
to the schools with entire ease; that there are others which
transfer with difficulty; and that there are still others which
will not transfer at all. It will be found, too, that the relative value of any aspect of training is in no wise related to
the place where it has to be carried on. Very many activi-

ties most urgently needed can be transferred to the schools only with great difficulty, or not at all. Education is no less imperative, however, simply because of this difficulty or impossibility of transfer. Our profession must find ways of going out to the activities that cannot be brought to the schools. This is now being done in part-time work, in giving credit for home activities, and in school-club work of various kinds.

A good example comes from Iowa. The bulletin of the Iowa Home-Work School-Credit Club enumerates three hundred and thirty home activities of wide diversity for which credit is given. It is unfortunate that space precludes the presentation of the entire list; but the following table shows the number of activities of each class for which credit is given: —

	Number of activities
Agricultural activities: —	
Plants	45
Animals	18
Agricultural construction and farm economics	21
Home economics: —	
Sewing	23
Cooking	29
Laundry	17
Housekeeping	18
General construction, repairs, and other work with tools	59
Home duties of boys and girls	9
Health activities	20
Self-culture (home reading, music, etc.)	16
Helping the aged, the weak, the ill, etc.	11
Business practice	6
Thrift activities	4
Civic activities	10
Club projects	24
Total	330

Naturally such non-transferable activities require direction and supervision. Much of this is to be taken care of at the school building in the antecedent planning for the activities. This involves the previous mastery of the necessary information. So far as possible the children will do their own planning and thus know what they are about. If the antecedent portions of the activity are fully taken care of, the need of personal supervision is greatly diminished. But pupils need leadership and encouragement. While parents here have a part to perform, the major responsibility rests upon the teachers. It demands that they mingle in the community life and come into contact with their pupils while the latter are securing their educative experiences. As teachers educate for efficient performance of life's affairs, they must be a portion of the active world of affairs. In the degree in which the experience itself cannot be transferred to the classroom, in this degree the teacher himself cannot be placed within a classroom for directing the work.

The part-time school or course is another practical recognition of the fact that, where normal experience cannot be transferred to the school, the children must be sent to the places where such normal experience can be had. In such well-known examples as those of Cincinnati or Fitchburg, the boys in the shop courses spend one half of the school year in the classes, laboratories, and shops of the high schools and the other half of the school year in the shops of the city, doing real work for wages under shop foremen. The plan is worked out by having two boys assigned to one job in the shop. Each boy works a week in the shop and a week in the school alternately. When one is in the shop the other is in the school; both are in the shop on Saturdays.

This part-time activity can be indefinitely extended; and the extension is at present being actually and rapidly made. The young men in the shops of high schools and industrial schools are being used by the educational authorities of certain cities in taking care of the repairs upon school buildings and school equipment, under the direction of responsible repair foremen. In a technical high school recently visited, the boys in the agricultural class had contracted with the fruit-growers of the region roundabout to care for the orchards for a certain price per year. They went out Saturdays, holidays, vacations, and did the spraying, pruning, cultivation, harvesting, etc., under the conditions of normal responsibility. Arrangements are being made in many places whereby students in typewriting, bookkeeping, salesmanship, advertising, window-dressing, etc., work for a few hours per week or certain weeks during the year on part-time work within commercial establishments.

We discover here a further administrative reason for making clear distinction between the antecedent portion and the objective portion of practical action. The planning and all the preparation incident thereto can in practically all cases be most economically and effectively taken care of at the schools. The actual putting of ideas to work under responsible conditions must be accomplished in the diverse and scattered situations where those conditions obtain. Administratively this actual accomplishment often presents difficult problems. In the degree, however, in which the antecedent portion has been adequately performed, these difficulties are minimized. The novices when they go out find themselves prepared to put the right ideas to work; to do the things with confidence; to do them correctly; and with little supervision. The world knows how to use that kind of ability.

CHAPTER VI

SCIENTIFIC METHOD IN CURRICULUM-MAKING

THE technique of curriculum-making along scientific lines has been but little developed. The controlling purposes of education have not been sufficiently particularized. We have aimed at a vague culture, an ill-defined discipline, a nebulous harmonious development of the individual, an indefinite moral character-building, an unparticularized social efficiency, or, often enough nothing more than escape from a life of work. Often there are no controlling purposes; the momentum of the educational machine keeps it running. So long as objectives are but vague guesses, or not even that, there can be no demand for anything but vague guesses as to means and procedure. But the era of contentment with large, undefined purposes is rapidly passing. An age of science is demanding exactness and particularity.

The technique of scientific method is at present being developed for every important aspect of education. Experimental laboratories and schools are discovering accurate methods of measuring and evaluating different types of educational processes. Bureaus of educational measurement are discovering scientific methods of analyzing results, of diagnosing specific situations, and of prescribing remedies. Scientific method is being applied to the fields of budget-making, child-accounting, systems of grading and promotion, etc.

The curriculum, however, is a primordial factor. If it is wrongly drawn up on the basis merely of guess and personal opinion, all of the science in the world applied to the factors above enumerated will not make the work efficient. The scientific task preceding all others is the determination of the curriculum. For this we need a scientific technique. At present this is being rapidly developed in connection with various fields of training.

The central theory is simple. Human life, however varied, consists in the performance of specific activities. Education that prepares for life is one that prepares definitely and adequately for these specific activities. However numerous and diverse they may be for any social class, they can be discovered. This requires only that one go out into the world of affairs and discover the particulars of which these affairs consist. These will show the abilities, attitudes, habits, appreciations, and forms of knowledge that men need. These will be the objectives of the curriculum. They will be numerous, definite, and particularized. The curriculum will then be that series of experiences which children and youth must have by way of attaining those objectives.

The word *curriculum* is Latin for a *race-course*, or the *race* itself, — a place of deeds, or a series of deeds. As applied to education, it is that *series of things which children and youth must do and experience* by way of developing abilities to do the things well that make up the affairs of adult life; and to be in all respects what adults should be.

The developmental experiences exist upon two levels. On the one hand, there is the general experience of living the community life, without thought of the training values. In this way, through participation, one gets much of his education for participation in community life. In many things this provides most of the training; and in all essential things, much of it. But in all fields, this incidental or undirected developmental experience leaves the training imperfect. It is necessary, therefore, to supplement it with the conscious directed training of systematized education. The first level we shall call undirected training; and the second, directed training.

The curriculum may, therefore, be defined in two ways: (1) it is the entire range of experiences, both undirected and directed, concerned in unfolding the abilities of the individual; or (2) it is the series of consciously directed training experiences that the schools use for completing and perfecting the unfoldment. Our profession uses the term usually in the latter sense. But as education is coming more and more to be seen as a thing of experiences, and as the work- and play-experiences of the general community life are being more and more utilized, the line of demarcation between directed and undirected training experience is rapidly disappearing. Education must be concerned with both, even though it does not direct both.

When the curriculum is defined as including both directed and undirected experiences, then its objectives are the total range of human abilities, habits, systems of knowledge, etc., that one should possess. These will be discovered by analytic survey. The curriculum-discoverer will first be an analyst of human nature and of human affairs. His task at this point is not at all concerned with "the studies," — later he will draw up appropriate studies as *means*, but he will not analyze the tools to be used in a piece of work as a mode of discovering the objectives of that work. His first task rather, in ascertaining the education appropriate for any special class, is to discover the total range of habits, skills, abilities, forms of thought, valuations, ambitions, etc., that its members need for the effective performance of their vocational labors; likewise, the total range needed for their civic activities; their health activities; their recreations; their language; their parental, religious, and general social activities. The program of analysis will be no narrow one. It will be wide as life itself. As it thus finds all the things that make up the mosaic of full-formed human life, it discovers the full range of educational objectives.

Notwithstanding the fact that many of these objectives are attained without conscious effort, the curriculum-discoverer must have all of them before him for his labors. Even though the scholastic curriculum will not find it necessary to aim at all of them, it is the function of education to see that all of them are attained. Only as he looks to the entire series can he discover the ones that require conscious effort. He will be content to let as much as possible be taken care of through undirected experiences. Indeed he will strive for such conditions that a maximum amount of the training can be so taken care of.

The curriculum of the schools will aim at those objectives that are not sufficiently attained as a result of the general undirected experience. This is to recognize that the total range of specific educational objectives breaks up into two sets: one, those arrived at through one's general experiences without his taking thought as to the training; the other, those that are imperfectly or not at all attained through such general experience. The latter are revealed, and distinguished from the former, by the presence of imperfections, errors, short-comings. Like the symptoms of disease, these point unerringly to those objectives that require the systematized labors of directed training. Deficiencies point to the ends of conscious education. As the specific objectives upon which education is to be focused are thus pointed out, we are shown where the curriculum of the directed training is to be developed.

Let us illustrate. One of the most important things in which one is to be trained is the effective use of the mother-tongue. It is possible to analyze one's language activities and find all of the things one must do in effectively and correctly using it. Each of these things then becomes an objective of the training. But it is not necessary consciously to train for each of them. Let an individual grow up in a cultivated language-atmosphere, and he will learn to do, and be sufficiently practiced in doing, most of them, without any directed training. Here and there he will make mistakes. *Each mistake is a call for directed training.*

The curriculum of the directed training is to be discovered in the shortcomings of individuals after they have had all that can be given by the undirected training.

This principle is recognized in the recent work of many investigators as to the curriculum of grammar. One of the earliest studies was that of Professor Charters.[1] Under his direction, the teachers of Kansas City undertook to discover the errors made by pupils in their oral and written language. For the oral errors the teachers carried notebooks for five days of one week and jotted down every grammatical error which they heard made by any pupil at any time during the day. For the errors in writing they examined the written work of the pupils for a period of three weeks. They discovered twenty-one types of errors in the oral speech and twenty-seven types in the written. The oral errors in the order of their frequency were as follows: —

	Per cent
1. Confusion of past tense and past participle.....	24
2. Failure of verb to agree with its subject in number and person.............................	14
3. Wrong verb................................	12
4. Double negative...........................	11
5. Syntactical redundance......................	10
6. Wrong sentence form.......................	5
7. Confusion of adjectives and adverbs...........	4
8. Subject of verb not in nominative case........	4
9. Confusion of demonstrative adjective with personal pronoun...........................	3
10. Predicate nominative not in nominative case....	2
11. First personal pronoun standing first in a series.	2

[1] Charters, W. W., and Miller, Edith. *A Course of Study in Grammar based upon the Grammatical Errors of School Children in Kansas City, Missouri.* University of Missouri, Education Bulletin, no. 9.

12. Wrong form of noun or pronoun.................. 2
13. Confusion of past and present tenses........... 2
14. Object of verb or preposition not in the objective case...................................... 1
15. Wrong part of speech due to a similarity of sound 1
16. Incorrect comparison of adjectives............. 1
17. Failure of the pronoun to agree with its antecedent 0.3
18. Incorrect use of mood........................ 0.3
19. Misplaced modifier........................... 0.3
20. Confusion of preposition and conjunction....... 0.2
21. Confusion of comparatives and superlatives..... 0.1

Each error discovered is a symptom of grammatical ignorance, wrong habit, imperfect valuation, or careless attitude toward one's language. The nature of the deficiency points to the abilities and dispositions that are to be developed in the child by way of bringing about the use of the correct forms. Each grammatical shortcoming discovered, therefore, points to a needed objective of education. It points to a development of knowledge or attitude which the general undirected language experience has not sufficiently accomplished; and which must therefore be consciously undertaken by the schools.

Scientific method must consider both levels of the grammar curriculum. One task is to provide at the school as much as possible of a cultivated language-atmosphere in which the children can live and receive unconscious training. This is really the task of major importance, and provides the type of experience that should accomplish an ever-increasing proportion of the training. The other task is to make children conscious of their errors, to teach the grammar needed for correction or prevention, and to bring the children to put their grammatical knowledge to work in eliminating the errors. In proportion as the other type of experience is increased, this conscious training will play a diminishing rôle.

In the spelling field, Ayres, Jones, Cook and O'Shea, and others have been tabulating the words that children and adults use in writing letters, reports, compositions, etc. In this way they have been discovering the particularized objectives of training in spelling. But words are of unequal difficulty. Most are learned in the course of the reading and writing experience of the children without much conscious attention to the spelling. But here and there are words that are not so learned. Investigations, therefore, lay special emphasis upon the words that are misspelled. Each misspelled word reveals a directed-curriculum task. Here, as in the grammar, error is the symptom of training need; and the complete error-list points unerringly to the curriculum of conscious training.

In the vocational field, and on the technical side only, Indianapolis has provided an excellent example of method of discovering the objectives of training. Investigators, without pre-suppositions as to content of vocational curriculum, set out to discover the major occupations of the city, the processes to be performed in each, and the knowledge, habits and skills needed for effective work. They talked with expert workmen; and observed the work-processes. In their report, for each occupation, they present: (1) a list of tools and machines with which a workman must be skillful; (2) a list of the materials used in the work with which workers need to be familiar; (3) a list of items of general knowledge needed concerning jobs and processes; (4) the kinds of mathematical operations actually employed in the work; (5) the items or portions of science needed for control of processes; (6) the elements of drawing and design actually used in the work; (7) the characteristics of the English needed where language is vitally involved in one's work, as in commercial occupations; (8) elements of hygiene needed for keeping one's self up to the physical standards demanded by the work; and (9) the needed facts of economics.

Many of the things listed in such a survey are learned through incidental experience. Others cannot be sufficiently learned in this way. It is by putting the workers to work, whether adolescent or adult, and by noting the kinds of shortcomings and mistakes that show themselves when training is absent or deficient, that we can discover the curriculum tasks for directed vocational education.

The objectives of education are not to be discovered within just any kind or quality of human affairs. Occupational, civic, sanitary, or other activity may be poorly performed and productive of only meager results. At the other end of the scale are types of activity that are as well performed as it is in human nature to perform them, and which are abundantly fruitful in good results. Education is established upon the presumption that human activities exist upon different levels of quality or efficiency; that performance of low character is not good; that it can be eliminated through training; and that only the best or at least the best attainable is good enough. Whether in agriculture, building-trades, housekeeping, commerce, civic regulation, sanitation, or any other, education presumes that the best that is practicable is what ought to be. Education is to keep its feet squarely upon the earth; but this does not require that it aim lower than the highest that is practicable.

Let us take a concrete illustration. The curriculum-discoverer wishes, for example, to draw up a course of training in agriculture. He will go out into the practical world of agriculture as the only place that can reveal the objectives of agricultural education. He will start out without pre-judgment as to the specific objectives. All that he needs for the work is pencil, notebook, and a discerning intelligence. He will observe the work of farmers; he will talk with them about all aspects of their work; and he will read reliable accounts which give insight into their activities. From these sources he will discover the particular things that the farmers do in carrying on each piece of work; the specific knowledge which the farmers employ in planning and performing each specific task; the kinds of judgments at which they must arrive; the types of problems they must solve; the habits and skills demanded by the tasks; the attitudes of mind, appreciations, valuations, ambitions, and desires, which motivate and exercise general control.

Facts upon all of these matters can be obtained from a survey of any agricultural region, however primitive or backward. But primitive agriculture is the thing which exists without any education. It is the thing education is to eliminate. The curriculum-discoverer, therefore, will not investigate just any agricultural situation. He will go to the farms that are most productive and most successful from every legitimate point of view. These will often be experimental or demonstration farms which represent what is practicable for the community, but which may not be typical of actual practices in that community. Where such general practices are inferior, agricultural education is to aim not at what is but at what ought to be.

When the farming practices are already upon a high plane, education has but a single function: it is to hand over these practices unchanged to the members of the new generation.

Where the practices of a region are primitive or backward, education has a double function to perform. It is not only to hand over to the new generation a proficiency that is equal to that of their fathers, but it is also to lift the proficiency of the sons to a height much beyond that of their fathers. Within such a region, therefore, agricultural education has the additional function of serving as the fundamental social agency of agricultural progress.

What we have said concerning agriculture is generally applicable throughout the occupational world. For discov-

ering the objectives for a training course in bricklaying one
will analyze not the activities of bricklayers in general, but
those where bricklaying has been carried to its highest
practicable level of efficiency, — as this efficiency is judged
on the basis of all legitimate standards. Education will aim,
not at average bricklayers, but at the best types of bricklayers.

When stated in broad outline, the general principle is
obvious. In practical application, it presents difficulties.
Men do not agree as to the characteristics of the most desirable types of work. The employers of the bricklayers will
be inclined to use maximum productiveness as the criterion
of superior work; and unquestioning obedience to orders
and contentment with any kind of hours, wages, and working conditions as proper mental attitudes. The employees
will judge otherwise as to some of the factors. The employers will invite the curriculum-discoverer to investigate situations where productiveness in proportion to costs is greatest;
the employees, where the total welfare of the worker is considered alongside of the factor of productiveness. Both sides
will agree that education should aim at the best and that
scientific investigations as to objectives should seek to
discover the characteristics of only the best. They disagree
as to what is the best, and therefore where the investigations
are to be made.

The general principle of finding the scholastic curriculum
in the shortcomings of children and men is quite obvious
and entirely familiar to teachers in its application to the
curriculum of spelling, grammar, and other subjects that
result in objective performance, such as pronunciation,
drawing, music, computation, etc. It is not so clear in connection with the highly complex subjects of history, literature, geography, etc. What are the social shortcomings
that are to be eliminated through a study of these social

subjects? Our ideas are yet so vague, in most cases, that we can scarcely be said to have objectives. The first task of the scientific curriculum-maker is the discovery of those social deficiencies that result from a lack of historical, literary, and geographical experiences. Each deficiency found is a call for directed training; it points to an objective that is to be set up for the conscious training. The nature of the objectives will point to the curriculum materials to be selected for these subjects. A major obstacle is lack of agreement as to what constitutes social deficiency. There is however no justification for scholastic training of any kind except as a gap exists between the training of general experience and the training that ought to be accomplished.

Society agrees sufficiently well as to many social shortcomings. Education needs to assemble them in as accurate and particularized a form as possible. They can then be used as the social symptoms which point to the objectives of history, literature, geography, economics, and other social studies. Society will disagree as to many suggested deficiencies. A program can be scientific, however, without being complete. The thousand spelling words presented by Mr. Ayres is a good list notwithstanding the fact that it presents not more than a quarter of the words needed. It is a secure beginning that can be completed by further studies. In the same way in our social training, we shall do very well if we can set up a quarter of the desirable objectives. That would be a great advance over none at all, as at present; and would provide the nucleus, the technique, and the vision of possibilities, necessary for gradually rounding out the list.

The principle involves us in similar difficulties in its application to civic, moral, vocational, sanitational, recreational, and parental education. It is equally valid, however, in connection with each of these. Only as we agree upon *what ought to be* in each of these difficult fields, can we know at what the training should aim. Only as we list the errors and shortcomings of human performance in each of the fields can we know what to include and to emphasize in the directed curriculum of the schools.

PART II
TRAINING FOR OCCUPATIONAL EFFICIENCY

CHAPTER VII

PURPOSES OF VOCATIONAL TRAINING

WITH only occasional exceptions, each of the twenty million children now in the public schools of America will in time be obliged to earn his living. The schools should, therefore, deal with every normal child and youth on the theory that, when adulthood is reached, he must earn his living. Each is to be a producer to the extent that he consumes.

In any survey of civilized conditions the most obvious thing is that men and women must work; that to their callings they must devote a major portion of their time and energy. They find Nature very parsimonious with her supplies of food, clothing, fuel, shelter; more illiberal still in supplying books, pianos, theaters, railroad and steamship tickets, church pews, and college courses. Nature supplies only the crudest raw materials. The rest must be created by human labor.

Were man content with what Nature supplies, he would not be man, but only an exceptionally intelligent animal species. But he has not been content. He has manfully taken raw Nature in hand and through heavy labor controlled it and shaped it to his high human purposes. Thus he has laid the foundations of his civilization; won his measure of freedom from stern biological necessity; and thus alone can he hold his gains. Through productive toil he has won his leisure, his surplus energies, and the means for his art, his literature, sports, travel, science, religion.

Occupational labors clearly represent the basic service to humanity, the most fundamental social service. In a day when the watchword of the world's humanitarian religion is "social service," it is well to note that the most solid and never-relaxing portions of this service are the labors of farmer and merchant, plumber and carpenter, housewife and seamstress, miner and engineer, physician, teacher, and journalist, and the rest of the valiant army of men and women who labor.

Those who object to vocational education in public schools because manual labor is sordid and unclean, should note that its frequent unloveliness is due, not to the fact that men work, but to the conditions of their labor. Insanitary shops, factories, and mines sap the physical vitality of the workers. Their inertia, ignorance, and inefficiency result in too long a work-day and a too-extended deadly mechanical monotony. They live usually within a narrow mental and social horizon. There is a great dearth of humanizing influences, companionships, and associations; and owing to this absence of uplifting influences and opportunities, they all too often tend to vicious and destructive animal pleasures. Too often they are compelled to live in crowded, unwholesome houses; are too often ill-fed, ill-clad, and uncleanly of habit; and have wages that permit little better even if they should desire and attempt a higher standard of living. The frequent ugliness of labor conditions is sufficiently evident.

The undesirable conditions are debasing, even destructive. Their malign influence year after year does degrade or even destroy the laborer. After long exposure to them, his character cannot usually be of socially desirable type. Men should, however, clear the scales from their eyes, and see that while the maleficent influences may be the usual concomitants of labor, they are not necessary concomitants. Each is really a foe to right labor; a demonstrable obstacle to efficiency.

The purpose of occupational education is the removal through general enlightenment of the injurious or destructive labor conditions. To admit that much of labor is debased and debasing is not an excuse for faltering before the task of vocational training. It is the very reason for manfully undertaking it. It is the presence of imperfections in the labor field that justify the ameliorative labors of education. As in the field of language, where there are no imperfections, there is no reason for training in grammar. The more mistakes there are, the more the reasons for education. In the same way in the labor field, the greater the number of imperfections, the greater is the need of vigorous occupational education.

In objection to the social-service doctrine of labor, it may be urged that vocations are and ought to be individualistic. It must be admitted, however, that there are some vocational classes upon whom does rest the moral obligations of social service. The physician, for example, supported by a given community is expected to serve that community to the best of his ability. He will respond to calls for service at any hour and under all conditions. Not his convenience, but theirs, is to be served. He must respond to the call of the poor who cannot pay with the same promptness and good-will that he extends to the call of the well-to-do. He must keep inviolate all information professionally confided to his care. In these matters the ethics of the medical vocation is clearly social. The work is recognized as social service. The physician's measure of honor is the greater because it is so.

Most professional service is of analogous type. And it is these social-service vocations that we regard as the highest. Men of the largest intelligence and ambitions regard them as the ones most desirable. To develop an ethics of social service about a calling does not deprive it of honor or desirability. On the contrary, it is thereby exalted.

These professional labors are not the only ones about

which public opinion is weaving systems of social ethics. We hear much nowadays of "public-service" corporations. The phrase is one of recent coinage. Until within a few years corporations were expected to serve the stockholders and directors. Now we have faced them the other way. They are to serve the public. A railroad company, for example, can no longer fix the qualities, rates, or conditions of service in ways dictated solely by self-interest. These are fixed in the interests of efficient public service. Manufacturers of foodstuffs and of clothing are no longer wholly free to follow the dictates of individual self-interest in the choice of the raw materials, the labeling of the product, the labor conditions under which produced, or, in extreme cases, even prices, when self-interest runs counter to community welfare. Where the two interests conflict, the public interest is coming to be dominant. The old plan was to "charge all that the traffic would bear." In other words, there was to be a maximum of social extortion for a minimum of social service. The new situation reverses the terms. Its aim is a maximum of social service for a minimum of social expenditure.

This weaving of a social ethics about vocational groups proceeds with almost disconcerting rapidity. Many are finding it difficult to readjust their systems of ideas fast enough to keep pace with social changes. But the movement appears to be the irresistible movement of civilization. Many vocations, hitherto self-centered and materialistic, are being humanized, socialized, and lifted into a purer atmosphere. Bankers, manufacturers, and railroad officials, for example, in recognizing and absolving their recently discerned social responsibilities, are taking places in social esteem formerly reserved only for the few so-called "learned" professions.

Far less clear is this movement of the public consciousness as regards the work of the farmer, the small merchant, the housekeeper, the artisan, the factory-worker, and the unskilled laborer. It is easy to see that these classes serve the general welfare as fully and as fundamentally as the other classes mentioned above; but their labors are not yet so fully recognized as community service. Their labors are looked upon as simply self-seeking modes of making a living. The difference in the social-service situation is not a difference of reality, but only one of social understanding and recognition. The farmer, for example, performs an indispensable community service in supplying the original elements of food and clothing. His service is not less high than that of the physician simply because he ministers to the bodily side of man. The physician also ministers to the bodily welfare; and in a less fundamental way. We can do without the labors of the physician most of the time; but the services of the farmer extend to every day of our lives. His labors are fully as strenuous, involve as long hours, and require as great disregard of physical discomforts.

Recognition of the social-service position of the farmer, although inadequate as yet, is developing visibly and rapidly. The general public is coming to see that many of its ills are due to inadequate service received at the hands of the men on the farms. The public is coming to scrutinize the service of the farmer, and to point out, through public opinion and legislation, ways in which he may better serve the general welfare; as in the handling of milk, the tuberculin test of cattle, etc. Only a few regulations of this type have yet been extended to the farmer's work. In general his social responsibilities are yet unrecognized. Whether the soil socially entrusted to his care shall bring forth twenty or one hundred bushels to the acre is altogether an affair of his own, and in no wise an affair of the rest of the men and women whom that land must feed. He is in the position of the street-car company that runs cars or not just as the company pleases without regard to the general welfare; or of the physician who responds or not to a call for help according to his own personal desires. The countless suggestions made nowadays by bankers, merchants, packing-house directors, grain-dealers, ultimate consumers, etc., to "educate" the farmer so as to bring about better and bigger crops of all kinds, to keep him and his family healthy, happy, and efficient, and to keep the sons upon the farm, are indications of a growing recognition of the indispensable social-service aspect of the farmer's work. In spite of any desires on his part, a social ethics is being woven about the farmer's work in the public consciousness.

Responsibility is not all on one side, however. In serving all other groups efficiently, the farmer puts upon all of them the responsibility of serving his interests equally in return. He must have opportunities for himself and family for self-realization as full as those accorded to the groups which he serves. Current discussions of rural education, churches, social opportunities, rural surveys, etc., indicate a rapidly growing realization of these return social responsibilities. In developing this recognition of mutual obligation, the farmer loses nothing: he gains much. It means improved material conditions, a widened mental and social horizon, more numerous social contacts and opportunities, and heightened social esteem. His measure of honor and of reward must be in proportion to the general consciousness of his measure of service.

It should be mentioned here that the development of a social ethics about any vocation is perhaps always done *by those who receive the service, not by those who perform it.* Food manufacturers are not the ones who pointed out the community-service aspect of their labors, and the resulting obligations of purity, honesty of label, and full weight.

Recognition of their obligations had to be forced upon them by those to whom they owed their responsibilities. This is equally true of railroads and municipal-service corporations, of journalists and Congressmen, of teachers and clergymen, judges and physicians. An occupational class does not of itself develop its own social ethics. This must be done by the general public, and perhaps always in the face of opposition from the class that is being socially assimilated. The superintendent of schools in a large city recently stated that after fifty years of service within the city as teacher, principal, and superintendent, he had never known a progressive educational movement to be proposed that was not opposed in the beginning by the majority of the teachers. If such is the case with an occupational group already so enlightened as teachers, and already so imbued with the spirit and traditions of service, much more may initial oppositions be expected of social groups which are in less close contact with enlightenment, and which have not yet the social momentum of tradition.

Social service does not mean self-renunciation. Self-interest cannot be eliminated. It is the steam that runs the whole machine. It has always been and must always be the mainspring of human action. It must be noted, however, that, on the one hand, there is a narrow, ignorant, materialistic self-interest; and on the other, an enlightened, humanistic self-interest characterized by wide social vision, which recognizes that individual welfare at its highest comes only through general community welfare at its highest.

The growing zeal for the vocational education of all classes, shown by clear-sighted men and women whose primary interest is general human welfare, is closely related to this changed and still rapidly changing attitude toward all useful vocations. They see that every useful calling is not only in itself social service, but that it is coming to be so recognized; and that it is being more and more given its proper measure of social reward and honor.

This is solving a problem hitherto insoluble, although our schools pretended to solve it by an impossible method. A certain few occupations, the professional and the managerial, have been looked upon as possessing an ethical superiority to commercial, mechanical, agricultural, or household occupations. It has been felt that in the professions men can live honorable, worthy social lives, while in the other callings men are of necessity sordid-minded, self-seeking, and generally more or less debased. It has been felt that education must close the gates of full opportunity to no child. The only gates of full opportunity are those that open toward the professions. These are the ones, therefore, that are to be held open to every child — these and no others. To start him toward anything else is to deprive him irrevocably and forever of the opportunity of full-statured, socially-honored manhood. The result has been that we have offered pre-professional training to all pupils. And we have refrained from recommending to students that they prepare for the so-called "lower" occupations. In this attitude teachers have been honest and high-minded. They have felt that only the best was good enough for their pupils. Their highest service, they have felt, has been to help their pupils to the highest.

While honest and well-intentioned, the plan is incredibly shortsighted. The doors of opportunity are not opened to our twenty million children and youth in any such easy way. If all of them should take advantage of the opportunities and fit themselves to enter upon professional or managerial labors, they would find, when they reached the world of affairs, that there are positions of this type for less than ten per cent of them. More than ninety per cent would after fruitless preparation be compelled to enter the ranks of tradesmen, merchants, miners, farmers, factory operatives, etc. Nearly all would be turned back into the so-called "lower" vocations. Our people must be given credit for seeing the fallacy of the plan. The withdrawal of pupils of adolescent grades, of which we hear so much lament, appears to be indicative of a certain amount of common sense. Men see that the plan only pretends to offer high opportunity to all; it does not really do so. If every man and woman were a college graduate, the useful labors of the world would still have to be performed. Productive labor is not to be escaped by shunting everybody into the professions.

So long as equally useful vocations have been so unequally honored and rewarded, and so long as labor conditions have offered such unequal opportunities for self-realization, this educational problem has been insoluble. The solution is coming, not through the impossible plan of lifting all people into the professions, but through lifting all vocations to the social level of the professions. The process is making the door to *any* useful vocation a door of opportunity.

The objectives of occupational training

In the imperfections of the occupational world, one finds the call for directed vocational training.

If all occupational affairs were efficiently and harmoniously conducted by the present adult generation, education would have but a simple task to perform. It would be nothing more than to hand over to the members of the rising generation the fully developed occupational heritage of the present generation. Educators would make a survey of actual occupational conditions by way of finding the particular objectives for which the young people are to be trained. It would be easy to discover demonstrable objectives accepted by everybody, because they would be already actual in the world of affairs.

Unfortunately, the present world of occupation is not of the type described. Affairs in general are managed neither efficiently nor harmoniously. As a matter of fact, the advocates of most vocational training are often chiefly interested in raising the labors of agriculture, mechanical trades, commerce, etc., to higher levels of efficiency. They are interested not so much in the education of youth as in the improvement of the work in the world of practical affairs. The improved education of the worker is simply a means of bringing about this result.

Education under the circumstances has, therefore, a double task to perform: (1) to act as a primary agency of social progress, lifting the occupational world to a higher and more desirable level; (2) to do this by educating the rising generation so that they will perform their occupational functions in a manner greatly superior to that of their fathers. The task is to develop in the rising generation, not merely the degree of proficiency found in the world about them, but to carry them much beyond; to look, not merely to the actual practices, but rather to those that ought to be. It is so to train them that the occupational mistakes, weaknesses, imperfections, maladjustments, etc., that now appear so numerously in the occupational situations of their fathers shall be as fully as practicable eliminated in that more harmonious and more efficient occupational regime that they are to establish and maintain.

Since the training is for the purpose of eliminating the various undesirable weaknesses, obviously one of the first tasks of education is to discover what these are. This at present is a baffling and in part an impossible task because of the vagueness of our knowledge as to *what ought to be.* Large portions of the occupational realm have not yet been sufficiently explored by scientific investigators. These unexplored regions constitute fields of great disagreement on the part of differently situated interested parties. A list of occupational weaknesses drawn up by an employers' association will differ in essential particulars from one drawn up by a labor organization. A group of social or civic workers will prepare a list that will differ in important respects from either.

Educators meet here with a grave difficulty. The correction of grammatical or spelling errors, for example, has no important economic results. Property distributions are not affected. Men do not, therefore, greatly care what the list of grammatical or spelling weaknesses may be that are to be corrected by the training in our schools. They give little heed to our lists, however complete they may be. But in the occupational field, property is affected. An undesirable occupational condition very frequently gives increased profits to one group and does harm to a second. It is, therefore, considered good and desirable by one and evil by the other. Each side develops a special economic theory. One justifies, the other condemns. Public education, however, must train the individuals of both groups for the occupational and economic things that ought to be. We cannot employ two systems of thought in the drawing-up of the training; and each side forbids our using that of the other. And in the face of such a blocked situation, each side demands of the schools that something adequate be done.

Apparently the only practicable thing for the present is to assemble that quite considerable list of occupational deficiencies upon which all sides can now agree sufficiently for getting a program under way. This can be only a partial program; but it can provide a common ground of understanding which can be gradually extended until in time it embraces the whole field.

A long list of occupational deficiencies can be obtained from the Report of the United States Commission on Industrial Relations. This commission visited all portions of the country and secured testimony from representatives of eighty-two labor organizations; thirty-six employers' associations; one hundred and thirteen firms and corporations; thirty-eight civil organizations; and fifty public institutions. Naturally witnesses of different types did not agree as to occupational maladjustments, or remedial measures. But education cannot wait till the world has settled all its differences. We must secure a list of deficiencies that can be agreed upon by at least a majority of citizens. In the following brief list we present a mingled sample of occupational deficiencies and maladjustments as reported to the commission by employers, employees, and social workers; or as implied in their testimony.[1]

Occupational deficiencies

1. Inefficiency of workers.
2. Inefficiency of managerial officials in organization, administration, and direction of work.
3. Dearth of high ideals and standards of workmanship.
4. The misunderstanding and misvaluation on the part of each other of both labor and capital; the lack of mutual confidence; the class prejudices.
5. The failure of workmen to appreciate the superior power of intelligence over force in the correction of social and economic difficulties.
6. Inaccessibility of facts concerning the various occupational fields to many or most interested parties.
7. Violence in labor troubles: lockouts, strikes, black lists, boycotts, use of provokers, spies, and gunmen, sabotage, "soldiering," etc.
8. A lack of industrial democracy; the presence of industrial feudalism.
9. The presence of opposing special interests which make neces-

---

[1] Mainly taken from a summary of the Report of the Commission, published in *The Survey*, December 12, 1914.

sary opposing organizations and the resulting inevitable class warfare.

10. Employers and employees both largely lacking in the social-service point of view, and in social conscience.

11. The deadening effect of long mechanical monotony in highly specialized industry.

12. Insanitary and dangerous conditions in many industries. The prevalence of occupational diseases.

13. The insecurity which the wage-earner feels at all times. Unemployment.

14. The lack of a voice on the part of workers in the regulation of the conditions under which they labor.

15. The loss of the feeling of individual responsibility, as men are swallowed up in large factories or other corporate organizations.

16. The lack of the scientific attitude of mind, in the consideration of the conditions of workmen, wages, relations of employers and employees, relation of the vocational group to the general public, etc.

17. Lack of principles or accepted standards of judgment for fixing wages or just income for the various social classes.

18. A general ignorance on the part of occupational groups as to the social relationships of their labors: their rights, and their responsibilities.

19. A highly fragmentary and inadequate knowledge of the occupational situation on the part of the general public.

20. Public indifference to the welfare and general success of occupational groups.

21. The unawareness on the part of the general public of the ways in which facts can be used in the settlement of occupational difficulties.

22. The different ethical levels to which equally useful occupations are assigned in the public consciousness.

23. The decay of old ideas of honesty and thrift.

24. The lack of standards of judgment as to where one's individual economic rights end; laxity in the search for any such limiting standards.

25. Square pegs in round holes, and *vice versa*.

26. Low standards of living; and the undesirable living conditions that are made necessary by low wages.

27. Inertia, indolence, laziness, — usually symptoms.

28. Inability to meet new labor conditions effectively.
29. The mechanization of men through years of automatic labor, who are then thrown upon the scrap-heap because of the general atrophy of their powers, and their inability to turn to new types of labor.

When we examine reports of vocational surveys to see to what extent they have discovered the serious occupational difficulties that are to be met by better occupational education, we are disappointed in finding that many of them have discovered little beyond the technical inefficiency of the worker. The program of training which they recommend, therefore, is too often but training for technical efficiency. This cannot be too much emphasized. But technical inefficiency is but one of many shortcomings; and from an educational point of view, it presents the simpler problems. Some of those on the wider social level are educationally more baffling and will require more extended and elaborate educational treatment.

In such a list of occupational weaknesses we can discover the objectives of occupational education. The purpose is so to train men and women that the weaknesses will not appear. Occupational education will seek to develop those abilities, dispositions, bodies of knowledge, types of skill, social attitudes and valuations, etc., the possession of which negative or prevent these and other technical and social deficiencies.

More and more schools are recognized as the agencies of social progress. Where deficiencies are discovered in any aspect of social life, schools are being called upon to overcome and prevent. For example, let agricultural production fall short of needs and of what experiment stations show to be easily possible, and business men, Congressmen, and all others interested set up a great clamor for agricultural education. Millions of dollars are then voted and agricultural courses introduced into land-grant colleges, high schools, continuation schools, extension systems, etc. There is provision for long courses, short courses, and brief institute opportunities. County agents are appointed to lead and supervise. The practical men are very much convinced that education is the way to bring social progress. Let factory production be inefficient, and business men call in no uncertain tones for industrial education. Where commercial and clerical work is not well done, the call is for commercial and clerical education. When figures show the extent of physical defects, illness, and premature deaths, there is a demand for efficient health training in our schools. When our young men in large numbers are found to be physically unfit for military duty, there is widespread demand for military training in our high schools that will prevent our being caught unprepared. When traffic accidents grow common on our crowded streets, the cry goes up for "Safety-First" training in our schools. When a generation appears that seems insufficiently to value money and tends to squander it, the call is for teaching "Thrift" in our schools. And so it goes. Practical business men are the first to call on the aid of the schools, and thus to recognize their fundamental position as agencies of social progress.

As agencies of social progress, schools should give efficient service. And efficient service, we are nowadays coming to know, is service directed, not by guess or whim or special self-interest, but by science. To be efficient, schools are not to wait till somebody guesses that a certain type of social progress is desirable, or until it is prompted by desires of larger personal profits, or of avoidance of paying damages. Scientific management demands *prevision — accurate prevision*. It demands understanding that sees all factors in true and balanced relation without any distortion due to claims or oppositions of special interests. This means that scientific survey and analysis of human needs must be the method of discovering the objectives of the training that is demanded, not by individuals, but by the conditions of society. Such surveys will demand only what is practicable. But they will look to human conditions from no partial angle. In a democracy they will look impartially to all things that promote the total human welfare. They will be disproportionately interested in no special class, whether high or low, rich or poor, cultured or uncultured; but without prejudice or partiality will look equally to all.

CHAPTER VIII

SPECIALIZED TECHNICAL TRAINING

SPECIALIZED technical training aims at a productiveness far beyond that of a pre-scientific generation. The efficient farmer, for example, in terms of proved standards, is one that raises, not one hundred bushels of potatoes to the acre, which is about the average, but rather two hundred to five hundred bushels. The efficient cotton-planter raises, not the average three eighths of a bale to the acre, but one full bale. The efficient bricklayer lays three hundred and fifty bricks per hour, instead of the usual one hundred and fifty. The efficient machinist in cutting steel turns out, not, as in the recent past, his ten units of product per day, but rather his forty, sixty, or one hundred units.

This setting forward the standards of accomplishment is not chimerical. Scientific industry has proved its entire feasibility. It is to be done through the application of science to labor. It is the next step in the increase of productiveness. Labor-saving machinery has been able to double, quadruple, or even at times to multiply the product a hundred-fold without increasing human labor. We are now being told that through the application of science to industry an equal further gain may be made.

Each occupation is to be analyzed into the tasks that make it up; each task into the factors that require control. The science needed for the regulation of each factor is then to be assembled, and placed in secure control of every work-situation. The science is in control when it dominates the consciousness of the worker. He must think each factor in terms of the science of that factor. His planning consists of putting his science-ideas to work. Thus he predetermines and foresees maximum results before a stroke of the work is done.

Along with the primary matter of technical intelligence there is the secondary matter of operative skill. In some occupations, as, for example, stenography or telegraphy, the amount of practice needed for skill is large; and requires more time and effort than the technical information. But in general the large educational tasks relate to developing understanding rather than operative skill.

The work of the farmer affords a good illustration. Raising a crop of corn, for example, presents the problem of controlling a large number of independently variable factors: soil ingredients, lime, nitrates, phosphates, sand, clay, moisture, soil oxygen, weeds, quality of seeds, temperature, light, plant parasites, and a number of others. For each factor in a given situation there is one optimum degree of strength; if its influence is either too weak or too strong, the crop is lessened. He must see each factor in its separate working in order to control it. Most of them are invisible or indistinguishable to the eye of sense; they are to be seen only by the inner eye of technical agricultural science. The trained farmer has this inner light and this inner vision. He can see and control the factors so as to secure his sixty or one hundred bushels per acre, while his unseeing rule-of-thumb neighbor secures only his twenty-five or forty bushels. The difference is not mainly due to a greater amount of manual labor or of operative skill; but to the ability to see the conditions requiring control and a knowledge of the adjustments that are best under the conditions.

After the trained farmer has examined all the factors that enter into a given situation, and has drawn up his plans, naturally he must have the operative skill for performing the processes: the ploughing, harrowing, cultivation, harvesting, storing, etc. Some practice is required; but this presents no large problem.

We have not been sufficiently accustomed to think of science as the source of maximum occupational productiveness. We have, for example, ordinarily thought of efficiency on the part of a machinist or a plumber as mainly a matter of general intelligence and manual dexterity. There must be skill of eye and hand, as we have phrased it. There must be operative skill. We have given insufficient thought to the intellectual elements.

Technical efficiency in a surgeon is very differently conceived. He, too, must possess great operative skill. Hand and eye must be as thoroughly trained as in the case of the mechanic — even more so. But back of the hand and guiding it, and back of the eye giving it vision, there must be fullness of technical knowledge. With the surgeon, skill of hand and eye is mainly a matter of intellectual discernment.

The case of the surgeon exhibits the two factors of technical efficiency in proper balance and relation. The mechanic, as popularly conceived, represents an incomplete stage in the development of technical efficiency. Trained to strength and dexterity on the operative side, and this alone, he has had but one side of the training he needs, and the less fundamental side. He lacks the thought-materials in terms of which to think the factors of his work-situations. Without this he lacks power to see his work on anything but a rule-of-thumb level, or to know that there can be any other level. His great need also is a knowledge of technical science back of the hand for guiding it, and back of the eye for giving it vision. For the tradesman as well as the surgeon, effective operative performance must in the long run be mainly a matter of scientific discernment.

In all parts of the occupational world to-day, rapid change is the rule. Workmen everywhere are being confronted with new tasks and new conditions. In the presence of a new and strange work-situation, the technically untrained workman does one of three things: (1) he blindly applies his rule-of-thumb procedure, trusting that it will work well enough. Generally it is inefficient, and sometimes wholly unworkable. (2) He guesses at an adaptation that will meet the new conditions. Scientific studies have proved that there are incalculably more ways of going wrong than right. He therefore usually guesses wrong; and the work is inefficient, or a failure. (3) He is nonplussed by the situation. He cannot make even a plausible guess.

Not one of the three things that he can do is usually the right thing. And for him in his intellectual blindness there is no fourth possibility. He finds himself caught hopelessly unprepared. He can act only as directed by others; and usually only inefficiently. The condition of feudal servitude in which he works is the necessary result of his ignorance. And in his rewards he can reap only the fruits of ignorance and inefficiency. In his work he can never have any proper human opportunity; never possess the full-grown man's independent outlook and ability. And what is more, outside of his work, because of his inefficiency, he never can have any full human opportunity. In general, — and the conception is becoming more accurately defined each year, — one can have only in proportion as one earns. Unfitted to produce the means required for life upon a proper humanistic level, he never can attain it. His ignorance largely shuts him out both from work and from life.

On the other hand, the technically trained individual is not perplexed by new occupational situations. He does not have to guess. He does not mechanically apply blind habit. And the reason is simple. The new situations that he meets are not new in the elements that compose them. He sees within them the same familiar factors, only differently balanced and arranged, with which he has been dealing all the time. He simply takes the measure of the factors in their new forms and goes on applying the same science. In his work he can feel himself a full-grown man; and with the fruits of his efficient labors, he can provide for himself and his family a full human opportunity.

There is another closely related matter. The education which comes in youth must consider the technical intelligence needed for a lifetime. But a large proportion of the science needed in most fields is yet undiscovered. And naturally this portion of it cannot be now taught. But many of the things needed by those now entering upon their work will be discovered within a few years. If they are not to be left behind and cast upon the scrap-heap at an untimely age, they must keep abreast of discoveries and inventions relative to their specialty. For the technically untrained individual such progress is impossible. Lacking the main body of science, he has no apperceptive basis for apprehending new developments, nor any vital interest in them. Inferior position or the scrap-heap is his inevitable portion. The technically trained individual is prepared to make the additions, the emendations, and otherwise to keep abreast of his science. He alone can value it. He will keep up with it as it appears in his technical journals; assimilate it without effort; and put it to practical use. While the schools cannot teach the undiscovered, yet they can provide the conditions that later will automatically take care of the matter.

The technical training is here treated briefly because many of its aspects were presented in chapters iii-v.

CHAPTER IX

THE SPECIALIZED TRAINING OF GROUP-WORKERS

THE day of independent tradesmen and of other disassociated workers is past or rapidly passing. In their places we have great factories, department stores, public-service corporations, railroad systems, school systems, hospitals, ecclesiastical organizations, building-construction companies, mining companies, etc. The productive capacity of specialized individuals in a coöperative labor-group is much greater than that of the same individuals working independently. They turn out a larger product, a better product, and at a reduced cost. Because of the greater efficiency it is probable that the movement will continue until it embraces most occupational fields. Education's larger problem of technical training relates, therefore, not to the training of the independent specialist, but rather to the specialized training of associated workers.

We can make the educational problem clear with an illustration or two. In the old days a shoemaker was master of his entire craft. He took the original order, prepared the leather, designed the shoe and each of its parts, cut each piece, did the sewing, the finishing, and finally the selling. For efficiency he had to have a command over all of the technical factors. At the present time, however, one man cuts out the sole; a second cuts the parts for the upper; a third, the lining; a fourth man sews the top to the vamp; a fifth sews on the toe-cap; a sixth gashes the insole preparatory to sewing it to the vamp; and so the process continues, the shoe passing down the line of several dozen workmen before it reaches the last one who places the finished shoes in the box ready for shipment.

In this factory situation it is the manager who controls everything. Like the old-time shoemaker he has command of the technical information, makes all the necessary judgments, and operates his man-and-steel machine in such a way as to perform all the processes. The one difference is that he uses a more elaborate set of tools and has devised a complicated machine that uses all of them at once. The men along the line are but fingers and wheels and levers in one large shoemaking machine. So far as their function is concerned, they are scarcely men at all. Had the manager all the inventions that he would like, he would have a machine into which he could feed the leather at one end, and out of which he could receive the finished product, ready boxed for shipment at the other, — about such an arrangement as we already have in the production of our large newspapers. As a matter of fact, he has just that kind of a machine, though not yet perfected. The men scattered along the line are there temporarily to supply flexible fingers of flesh until cheaper and more skillful fingers of steel can be invented to fill the gaps, and the machine thereby completed.

Lest it be thought that all tendency to mechanization of the workers is to be found only in the field of material production, let us note a case upon the professional level: that of teachers. One finds in a large city building a line of highly specialized teachers, each performing, as in the factory, a small portion of the total task. The first teacher in line receives the original raw material in the kindergarten and performs the first process. It is then taken by the I–B primary teacher for a half-year. She passes it on to the I–A primary teacher, who gives to it her half-year of effort. And so the product in more and more finished form is passed down the long line of specialists. In the later years of departmental teaching, the tasks are more minutely specialized and the material passes through many hands.

Now, here, as in the shoe factory, the things aimed at are the finished products, and the labors from beginning to end must all aim at the same products. But since each teacher performs but a fragment of the total process, the results of which usually do not greatly resemble the ultimate objectives, it follows that somebody whose vision is single for the final product and who sees all the steps to be taken must think for the whole organization and direct the steps. Superintendent and principal, therefore, lay out the courses of study, choose the books, supplies, and equipment, and direct the methods. The supervisory brain, so to speak, does the thinking for the whole organization; the teachers are but hands and voices to this brain.

This feudal theory tends at present to be strong wherever organization develops — whether in factory or school, railroad or hospital, department store or ecclesiastical organization. It appears to demand specialized technical training for the five or ten per cent who lead and think and plan; but for the vast majority only such little training as they need for skill in routine labor. The less they trouble their superiors by thinking and insisting upon being heard, the better for all.

This feudal theory is being supplanted rather rapidly by a democratic theory. Let us resume our two illustrations by way of explaining its basic conceptions. Instead of its being the manager of the shoe factory who takes the place of the original independent tradesmen, it is the *total group* who takes his place. In the school field, it is not the superintendent or principal who takes the place of the general teacher of a century ago, but it is the *total group*. It is not the manager, the superintendent, or other head of an organization who is to do the thinking that goes into the work; it is rather the entire associated group. Managers and superintendents are those who have specialized in leadership. They are generalists; while the individual workers are specialists. Where all are made intelligent as to the group-labors, the sum of the knowledge of the specialists added to that of the generalists is greater than that of the generalists alone; and this aggregate is a more effective directive agency. And as workers are changed from industrial serfs to freemen with minds and rights to think and with responsibility resting upon them for thought and suggestions, they are filled with a new spirit. Recognized as men, they become men; act like men; and the curve of their operative efficiency mounts rapidly upward.

The accompanying diagram will show the relations within the school organization; and is typical of right relations in

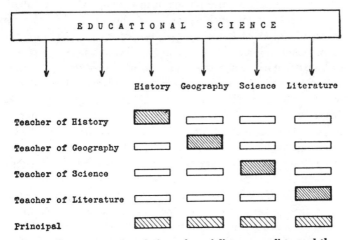

Fig. 2. To represent the relations of specialists, generalists, and the controlling science in the management of group-labors.

all organizations. Over all the group, specialists as well as generalists, is the science that should control in taking every step. Both must read it. But it is not to be read in books of abstractions; however valuable they may be as helps. It is to be read within the practical situations where they work; and by those in contact with the actualities in their details. Some things can be seen most clearly by the generalist; other things most clearly by the specialist. As indicated by the width of the bars, the generalist will see everything equally in balanced relation, his function being interpreter and coördinator for the whole. But every part of the work is vitally related to every other part. The specialist cannot see his duties if he looks to them alone without regarding the labors of the whole organization. He can rightly see any task only as he sees it as a part of the whole organization-task. As shown by the width of the bars, he will have a fuller understanding than the principal in his special field; but he must also have an understanding of the whole field that is much like that of the principal, except as to its completeness. Each teacher is, so far as possible, to be his own co-ordinator. Otherwise there can be no efficiency in organization labors. The principal cannot be always at the elbow of every teacher dictating every coördinating adjustment. It is educational science that must preside at every teacher's desk and do the dictating. The teacher is, therefore, to be a specialist in one thing and a generalist in all. Having operative skill in one thing, he needs nothing more than the generalist's skill in the others. He needs *to think* all, but *not to do* all. *For his thinking he needs to be trained in the work of the entire organization; for operative skill, he needs to be drilled and practiced only in the special tasks required of him.*

An orchestra provides us with a perfect illustration. The conductor is a generalist; but every individual player must also be a generalist, or *he cannot be a perfect specialist.* He must think the whole piece, his consciousness must move as the full current of the total music, in order rightly to place his special part. The kettle-drummer, for example, must strike at exactly the right instant, with the right degree of loudness, and with his instrument properly attuned. Conductor and music-score are necessary helps to his thinking; but they alone cannot determine any one of the three enumerated elements with exactness. He needs to be trained *on the conscious side* to the whole of the music rightly to play his part. But *on the operative side* he may be skillful with but the one instrument.

The two illustrations are taken from fields where it is admitted that the specialized workers must be generalists in thought in order efficiently to coördinate their specialties. Not so obvious is the need in the case of factory, railroad, or large department store. Recently, however, in all these types of organization, schools are being voluntarily established in which specialists are not only trained for their specialties, but also to an understanding of the whole in order rightly to understand each specialty. This movement shows promise of abundant growth. Industrial and commercial organizations are becoming conscious of the interdependencies of all the parts, and of the subtle and infinitely numerous ways in which inefficiency or maladaptation in one portion affects all the rest. They are realizing the consequent need on the part of each to see and continually to think the whole in order rightly to think one's own part. As the science is developed in terms of which to do all the necessary thinking, what is now obvious in the case of the school or the orchestra will become equally obvious in the case of all group-labors.

Enough has been said to indicate the curriculum solution. On the thought side, workers are to be taught as though they were to work in all parts of the organization. This will mean not only full intellectual studies relating to all aspects of the work, and systematic observation of all; but also some opportunity to *work* in all portions of the field.

To work means to bear participative responsibility of some kind, which will differ according to the nature of the work. Sometimes he will work at a thing quickly learned on the operative side, or one requiring no special operative skill; in such case he may well bear full responsibility. In other cases, involving specialized skill which requires long preparation, he may serve as a helper to the skilled operative so as to bear enough responsibility for acquiring the generalist's necessary insight and appreciation.

So far as public education takes care of this training, it may leave the individual on the semi-specialized level, — a generalist within some broad occupational field. Carried thus far his training is practically complete. Usually the final specialization will be left until the individual is employed in the occupation itself. Understanding the whole, he will quickly master his specialty. But it cannot usually take place in any school. It usually must take place in the occupational situation where he is to work, as directed by technical specialists employed for the purpose.

Occupational education must concern itself largely with the preparation of workmen and managers for *right mental attitudes* toward the work. The general technical intelligence referred to must constitute much of the basis for these right mental attitudes. The manager as a generalist among trained specialists actually *does* but a small portion of the total group-task. But seeing the whole and thinking the whole, as he does his small part, he *feels* himself doing the whole. Just so it is with the fully enlightened specialized worker. Let him as he works at his minute task have a clear intellectual vision of the total group-task. With his discernment of interdependencies, and of the way his labor is concerned in and supports all the rest, he too feels his power and his responsibility to extend outwards to the farthest limits of the group-labors. In his consciousness, the specialist may feel himself a *master* about as fully as the generalist. The main difference between the laggard specialist as a slave and the vigorous specialist as a master is in having or not having the intellectual vision of the work as a whole. The one feels his personality and his responsibility to be as small as his petty task. To the other, both are greatly magnified since his vision of the group-labors becomes his vision of his own labors.

At Beverly, Massachusetts, in their part-time shop school, where they are training machinists for the United Shoe Machinery Company, they have equipped a small shop with all the kinds of machines used in the large factory. As the boys are trained, they pass from machine to machine so as to become proficient in the entire range of labor to be found within the large factory. In both school and factory, they are bringing each of the workmen to a full understanding of all of the labors performed in the shop. This same width of industrial training is attempted in all well-developed industrial schools. Apprenticeship contracts usually specify that the boy shall be moved about from one kind of work to another so as to have an opportunity to master all of the processes.

Under the so-called "Taylor System" of scientific management, all the thinking is done by specialized officials in the "planning-room." Decisions are there made as to what is to be done every hour during the day by every man in the shop. Instructions are typewritten, and sent out to the workmen. The latter are not expected to do any thinking or judging or deciding; this is all done for them; they are only to obey orders.

This system is looked upon by many factory managers as the most perfect that has yet been devised. It puts science in the saddle. Yet the system is not popular. Where it is tried, it is frequently abandoned. It usually breaks down, we are told, because most labors are so complicated that the planning-room cannot foresee all contingencies; and therefore cannot make provision for all necessary coördinations. It takes responsibility for thought and initiative off the men. When instructions are deficient or obscure, work has to stop until further orders are received. Where instructions to different workmen are contradictory, the plan gives them no power to adjust matters. The relative failure of the Taylor System seems to result from insufficient attempt to enlist the intelligence and initiative of the men. The system claims that both managers and men are working under the control of science; yet, as a matter of fact, this science is mostly visible only to the management; and is little or not at all visible to the men. They see only the orders. The system represents a halfway step, however, toward actual and inevitable scientific management. Science rules in the planning-room; it must also rule in the consciousnesses of the workmen.

The human element

Recently there has been an awakening on the part of leaders of organized industry as to the far-reaching significance of *the human element*. The independent tradesman did not have to manage men; he had no such problem. It has arisen with organization, where men work in groups, and where the generalist must be in part the director — at least the leader — of the specialists; where he must play upon them and through them as does the conductor of an orchestra.

Of large occupational organizations, it is education that has most fully recognized the need of taking into account the human element. In a school system, for example, the pupils are the ultimate workers. Using the terminology of the factory, the teachers rank as foremen. It is their business not to do the work that educates, but to get it done by the pupils. In doing this, *they must know the pupils:* know their varying mental capacities, their interests, their aptitudes and abilities, their states of health, and their social *milieu.* They must know how to arouse interest; how to motivate them from within; how to adjust the conditions of the work to child-nature; how to keep up an abundant physical vitality in the children; and how to employ community influences for vital stimulation of the pupils.

Now come the leaders of scientific management in industry and commerce and proclaim their recognition of the human factor as a great and revolutionizing discovery. Superintendents and foremen in factories must know their men, their psychology, aptitudes, interests, motivating influences, etc., so as to be able to stimulate them to the greatest desirable degree of productivity. It has been found that arbitrary driving will not work with men any more than with pupils. *The driving force must lie within the will of the worker.* The foreman must adjust conditions of work, wages, factory sanitation and comforts, opportunities of promotion, of social recognition, etc., so that this inner driving force will awaken naturally and of itself within the worker. The foreman must be able to read the nature and needs of his men as fully as the teacher reads his pupils. He needs to be proficient in practical psychology, practical sociology, industrial hygiene and sanitation, and other *human* studies that are at the same time technical studies for him.

In the relations of foremen, managers, etc., to their men, the greatest single source of coördination is a large ground of common understanding, community of thought, and mutual confidence in the motives actuating both sides. Where all are informed as to the controlling science, where all have access to all the facts relative to the economic and other vital affairs of the group, in ways otherwhere specified, these grounds of mutual confidence and understanding are securely laid. In the bitter antagonisms of labor and capital, the need is being voiced by both sides. One of our well-known captains of industry is reported recently to have said:

> If capital and labor do not get together in the right spirit, the future of America is doomed. If they do not come to see that the interests of each are inseparably bound up with the interests of the other, and that each must be mutually recognized and respected, then capital's resources are doomed, just as the workers' prosperity is doomed.
>
> One cannot exist without the coöperation of the other. To drive this stupendous fact home to each of these two forces, to make each know that it is but the complementary force of the other, and not an antagonistic force, is the most vital problem before the United States to-day.
>
> Let the officers of this company understand that there is never to be another strike in our company, that every man is to be treated as a partner and not as an enemy or an underling. . . .

Now, to be partners, to coöperate intelligently and effectively, to be able mutually to recognize and respect the interdependent interests of the other, etc., — these things imply that all must have access to the same body of facts; and that all have the trained powers of mind necessary for rightly interpreting and judging of those facts. As yet, taking the industrial world in general, neither of these things has been provided for. And so long as this is the case, industrial antagonisms, occasionally flaring forth into actual warfare, will and must continue. But just as the industrial leaders are now calling on the schools for remedying technical weaknesses on the side of labor processes, so they must likewise depend upon the schools to provide much of the training needed for those other weaknesses on the side of the human factor. *Neither side is now consciously trained for mutual understanding. Both sides are equally in need of extended training, that has community of thought, and outlook, and valuations, as its conscious purpose.*

CHAPTER X

SOCIAL ASPECTS OF OCCUPATIONAL TRAINING

ONE hears much nowadays concerning "occupational efficiency." But the term may refer to either of two widely different conceptions. One may take the short and narrow view, and conceive the term as meaning only "high material productiveness." The degree of efficiency in such case is to be measured by the amount of economic product. Beyond this, it does not go. It leaves the product in the hands of the producer without further inquiry.

On the other hand, the term may refer to "high efficiency in the promotion of the general human welfare." The degree of efficiency is to be measured by the quantity of human service. Whereas the narrow view looks at the material product as the finished product, this humanistic view sees the finished product only within those human results that arise from the use of the economic product. The latter is a means; not an end. Not unnaturally this is the view that is coming to be preferred by the world at large. Even though labor because of great technical knowledge and skill may turn out a large product, if that product falls into only a few hands where it is selfishly misused so as to produce or to permit continuing human ill-fare instead of welfare, then the occupation cannot be looked upon as efficient in any desirable way. In terms of human service, it is inefficient.

Efficient management of the *social factors* is as vital as technical efficiency. The economic mechanism is to be operated by society in general for the sake of maximum human service. This task is immeasurably more complicated than operating a lathe or a locomotive or raising a crop of corn. If technical training is needed for the latter, certainly then technical training of all people for the effective operation of our vast economic mechanism is much more needed.

Division of labor has created the problem. To see this, let one first think of our country civilized as at present and producing as much as possible of the things used to-day — but without any division of labor. Within such a situation vocational education would be highly desirable. But it would be only for technical information and skill. There would be no need for training in the social aspects of occupation because there would be no social aspects. Production would be wholly individualistic; and distribution nonexistent. Each worker would receive in proportion as he produced — neither more nor less. Each would have in proportion as he earned. There would be no economic mechanism to be operated by society; and consequently no need of community training in the technique of operation.

But specialization of labor has introduced social interdependency. Each produces one thing; and this not for himself alone, but for all the group. In return each receives from the others that portion of their product which they have produced for him. The obverse side of division of labor is the organic interdependence of the group. The individualistic situation disappears in proportion as specialization appears. In the degree in which the group is divided for the performance of specialized labors, it must be united for any effective coöperative distribution of the fruits of those labors. Without the latter, the purpose of the divided labor is defeated.

This coöperation of specialists demands general understanding on the part of all as to the common ends; of the means of attaining them; and a disposition to obey the social dictates. It seems that each member of society needs to be informed as to the total occupational situation: the working conditions that are supplied to all classes of specialized workers; the relation of these to right standards; the productivity of the various occupations; the distribution of the products; the nature and mode of operation of the economic mechanism necessary for accomplishing all of the social purposes. And along with information, he also needs social attitudes and valuations. The social studies of our schools, the history, geography, literature, economics, etc., have the large and inadequately recognized task of developing both information and attitudes. The ends demand a program of large proportions that has been mostly unrecognized and unattempted.

The conception that the labors of an industry are to be supervised by those who are served is really as old as industry itself. It was formerly done by the consumer's acceptance or rejection of the product. If it did not suit him, he went elsewhere. This plan is operative still. But industries have grown large and complex. Competition is eliminated through price agreements, or division of the field. Often one cannot now go elsewhere for supplying his needs. Processes and products have grown so complicated that he can no longer judge of quality of commodities or justice of prices. He cannot know whether he ought to go elsewhere or not. Should he do so, being unable to distinguish the better from the worse, he still cannot know whether he is improving matters. Men are coming to see that a kind of intelligence and a mode of supervision of the services of others that worked well in a simpler economic age can no longer serve our purposes. New conditions demand new methods.

Public-service labors are coming to be supervised by the public through public-service commissioners, committees of city councils, the United States Interstate Commerce

Commission, etc. These representatives of the public keep a continuous oversight over quality, quantity, costs of service, etc. Year by year this community supervision is augmented and strengthened; and freedom to serve or not as dictated by self-interest is diminished. Each year sees the extension of this supervision to hitherto unsupervised occupational fields. For some time it has been accepted as a matter of course, in the case of railroads, express companies, telegraph and telephone companies, city traction, gas, and electrical supply companies, the work of plumbers as regards sanitation, of carpenters and electricians as regards fire protection, etc. More recently the supervision is being extended to food and drug manufacture and distribution, the milk-supply, packing-house industries, the handling of perishable foods, etc.

But all useful specialized labors are public-service labors. It becomes ever more difficult to draw any line of division between industries that are to be socially supervised and those that are to be left only to the control of individual self-interest. The logical end of the process is the extension of social supervision to all that serve and the suppression of all that do not serve. And all social movements set strongly in' that direction. Where done wisely and justly, its influence is salutary both to industry and general community.

Whether the supervision does good or harm to the occupations, and thus to the community itself, depends upon the quantity of sympathetic occupational enlightenment employed by the public in the supervision. Where present in sufficient degree, a community can maintain a high character of service while keeping costs on a level that is just to all concerned. On the other hand, ignorant or mercenary supervision can diminish or destroy the power of an industry for service, and thus do harm both to industry and community.

To require of a railroad, for example, a high character of service, but at the same time to keep the rates so low that necessary expenses cannot be met, may injure or destroy the service that the supervision is intended to improve.

The supervision at bottom must be performed by the men and women of the general community. They may delegate legislative and executive action so far as these are required. But they must first know what they want their representatives to accomplish before they can delegate the responsibilities; or check up the work to see that the right things are done. There must be informed public opinion and right community attitudes and valuations. While this community mind may partly control through governmental mechanism, in the main it doubtless must act directly in influencing the acts of its specialized members. When all members of an industry know what is expected of it, and when they know that the public knows, and that the public will be instantly aware of any missteps that they may make, — this is the situation that crystallizes into "social conscience." It is this that will supervise and exercise social control. One can appreciate the relations by noting the analogous "grammar conscience." It is not necessary to employ legal machinery for enforcing the laws of grammar. To know what is right usage, and to know that one's associates will instantly detect and silently condemn any deviations therefrom, is enough to hold the well-informed individual pretty close to the straight and narrow paths of grammar. In the same way it is public knowledge of an occupation that through public opinion must directly and indirectly supervise that occupation. And education must confer the necessary enlightenment, social attitudes, and occupational conscience.

The acceptance-rejection method of supervision of early days was of a democratic type. Everybody knew products, processes, and social relationships sufficiently to supervise;

and on the basis of this knowledge, through accepting or rejecting the products everybody was continually engaged in the task of supervision. Each did it for himself, however. Special training was not needed. Coöperative and systematic methods of diffusing the necessary intelligence were not needed. In one fundamental aspect that was a day of industrial democracy. Except as labor was purely individual, each served all, and all supervised each. The present is asking nothing more. It is asking only for new methods that can be as effective for present-day conditions as the older methods were for the old days. One of the major differences must be in the mode of diffusing the necessary enlightenment. As much as in the old days, all need now to understand products, processes, and occupational relationships. But the knowledge cannot be picked up incidentally. What could formerly be well enough done without the help of the schools can no longer be accomplished in any such unsystematic and incidental way. A school task always arises when the incidental method breaks down in the face of complicated conditions. The economic revolution of the past few decades has in this manner created an educational task of gigantic proportions.

One has but to examine the newer courses of study and textbooks to note the growing realization of this task. *Industrial Studies of the United States, Commercial Geography, Industrial History, Makers of Many Things, Wheat-Growing in Canada, United States, and the Argentine, How the World is Fed, Clothed, and Housed, Diggers in the Earth, The Farmer and his Friends, The Book of Wheat, Book of Cotton, Book of Corn, The Story of Sugar, Story of Oil, Leather Manufacture,* — such occupational books are rapidly finding place in schools everywhere. The movement indicates a realization of the need of enlightenment as the basis of occupational adjustment in a democracy.

One finds a complete list of occupations in the reports of the Census. They are classified into nine major fields as shown in the accompanying table: —

	Men	Women
1. Agriculture, forestry and animal husbandry.......	10,851,702	1,807,501
2. Manufacturing and mechanical industries.......	8,837,901	1,820,980
3. Trade.................	3,146,582	468,088
4. Transportation..........	2,531,075	106,596
5. Domestic and personal service................	1,241,328	(25,000,000)
6. Clerical occupations.....	1,143,829	593,224
7. Extraction of minerals...	963,730	1,094
8. Professional service......	929,684	735,885
9. Public service (not elsewhere classified)..........	445,733	13,558

Geography divides the world up into a few grand divisions; these grand divisions into several score countries and states; and then presents the situation in each country one after the other. In the same way, in acquiring an understanding of the world of occupations, we may well divide it into nine grand divisions; divide the latter into several score occupational fields; and then present studies of the important ones. As in the geography, it is possible to group related divisions, and study many cognate occupations at one time. Much can be done on the basis of type-studies, where a single occupation studied intensively can be used to reveal the situation in several similar fields. It is also possible to view and study the whole occupational realm at once by considering single aspects one after the other; as for example, wages, hours of labor, seasonal fluctuations, profits, desirability of different vocations from a hygienic point of view, social desirability of different occupations, etc. When these methods of attacking the problem are considered, it is not so formidable as may at first sight appear.

What are the things that people need to know for supervision of occupational groups? Let us here mention seven things: —

1. They need definite knowledge of the human needs that are to be ministered to by the different occupations.

2. They must know definitely the character of occupational service required for meeting the needs fully and without waste.

3. They must know the extent to which any occupational group is actually delivering the required character of service.

4. They must know what material and other facilities are needed by each occupation for performing service of the kind required.

5. They need to know the extent to which the community is actually providing the needed facilities.

6. They need a knowledge of technical processes only sufficient for understanding the findings of inspectorial experts concerning the efficiency, economy, and general social effectiveness of occupational services.

7. They need full appreciation and understanding of the dependence of group upon group. It is this vision of interdependence, of common membership within a common group, which creates those sympathetic attitudes necessary for considerateness in the supervision.

Naturally it is not meant that memories shall be stored with great masses of recallable facts relative to all of these things; or that the educational task is any such memorization. Man has no such memory-capacity. And more serious educational malpractice can scarcely be imagined.

The things which the public needs to know about each

occupation has a counterpart in the things that the specialized workers need to know for willing and intelligent acquiescence in the supervision. This represents a vital portion of specialized vocational training, treatment of which was deferred because of its intimate relation to the supervisory problem.

The specialized workers need a more detailed knowledge than society in general concerning their own occupation along the seven following lines: —

1. Full knowledge of the human needs which their occupation is to serve.
2. Specialized knowledge of the character of service which they are to render.
3. The extent to which they are actually rendering such service.
4. Accurate knowledge of what they must demand from the general public in order that they may have the facilities needed for effective service.
5. Accurate knowledge of the extent to which they are being supplied with the needed facilities.
6. Such full knowledge of technical processes and of results secured by their group that they can adjudge the justice of the findings of community inspectorial experts; and accept them when just, and correct them when unjust.
7. Full and specialized understanding of the dependence of their group upon the social whole; and of the total community upon their group. This consciousness of sharing a common lot, and of requiring reciprocal support, lies at the root of willing submission to the general mandates and of willing service on the part of those supervised. It is this which shows the specialized workers that the road of self-interest and the road of service are one and the same.

When both general public and occupational specialists have these types of information, the intelligence-basis will be laid for effective social control in this difficult field. Each side has rights; and each has duties. The knowledge referred to permits a clear definition of both rights and duties by all interested parties. It also lays a broad foundation of common understanding upon which all can meet in the current adjustment of conflicting claims. For it must be kept in mind, as we shall hereafter discuss, that the push and pull of specialized groups, in which each tends to exaggerate its services and its rights, are inevitable. Social tensions and strains, requiring constant and ever-renewed adjustment, are inherent in the nature of the life-process, whether physiological, biological, or social. Intelligence cannot obliterate them but it can control. The stronger they are, the greater is the indication of life and of power. But also the greater is the need of social education.

Enlightenment alone can bring genuine industrial democracy. An examination of the factors shows the futility of much of the controversy as to the best type of economic mechanism. We have public ownership and coöperative management in some of our occupational fields, such as public education, letter and parcel transportation, fire protection, street and road construction and maintenance, etc. We leave to private ownership and volunteer management most of our industries, believing that on the whole this is best. But as a matter of fact whether the labors are of one type or of the other, the thing needed and wanted is *service*. The kinds of enlightenment needed for social supervision of both types are exactly the same. Where society is introducing and developing effective supervision, the methods are scarcely affected by the question whether the industry is publicly or privately owned, — i.e., whether by a few stockholders, or by the many stockholders of a total community. Either plan is good or bad according to the way it is managed. With enlightened social supervision, effective service can be secured under either plan. But without enlightened supervision, effective service can result from neither. *Not the mechanism, but the intelligence, is the principal thing.*

Before education can proceed, it must have the facts concerning the various occupations. At present many of the necessary facts are inaccessible. Secrecy in the interest of individual ends rather than publicity in the interest of the public weal is the rule, not the exception. As a nation we have not yet come to value enlightenment as the basis of democracy. But the light is nowadays being turned into all sorts of places. Occupational surveys are being made. Official public-service bodies are accumulating facts for their purposes, to many of which publicity is being permitted. In proportion as an industry is performing actual public service, it is always glad to have it known; and since the quantity increases year by year, the quantity of voluntary publicity increases also. When an industrial group is particularly anxious to prevent publicity, more and more the public is coming to suspect that there is exactly where publicity is needed.

Enlightened business men are coming to understand the publicity implications of social interdependence. The salutary attitude of the business world was recently well expressed by Mr. E. H. Gary, chairman of the United States Steel Corporation, in an address before a business convention, for which he took as a theme the Biblical quotation: "For none of us liveth to himself, and no man dieth to himself." Among other things he said: "In the last decade there has been a pronounced change in the attitude of large business interests concerning the disclosure of facts and figures to the general public. Many now voluntarily and without the requirement of law make regular and complete reports so that any one interested may know the results of the business and the general policy of the company." Mr. Gary suggested a publicity tribunal which would serve the interests both of the business world and of the general public. "There is abundant evidence," he continued, "that at present the great general public is willing to meet halfway the individual or corporation in the consideration of all questions that affect private or public interests." The movement is unmistakable. Facts are becoming accessible. The use of such facts for the development of general enlightenment is becoming possible.

Surveys may discover the facts. But the organization of the materials for teaching purposes presents educational problems of great complexity. The direct fact-learning and recitation method, with which our profession is so familiar, is too primitive and inefficient for so large a task. Let us indicate some of the better ways that are being introduced into progressive school systems.

Each occupation is to be seen and vitally understood as *a group of men at work*. One learns the labors of a group by entering into their labors; by performing them actually; by performing them in play; by entering into them sympathetically through observation; by imaginative participation as they are reconstructed in well-written history, geography, literature, biography, etc. It is not by learning abstract verbal facts about a group, but rather by doing in one way or another what that group does that one comes really to understand it. The doing lays the interest-basis necessary for fact-accumulation and assimilation; and for right valuations and attitudes. Education must proceed by the active route not because we are aiming at fewer facts than formerly but because we must aim at far more; and must therefore employ effective methods.

1. *Concrete occupational activities*

Professor James, in his delightful essay, *On a Certain Blindness in Human Beings,* makes clear that one can understand and realize the experiences that make up the lives of others only as one has participated actually or sympathetically in those experiences. The detached and unmoved onlooker remains blind to the actual significance of life about him. Life must be lived in order to be known. "The right way of seeing each other's work" requires that we enter sympathetically and vividly into the occupational experience of others. The first step is to do the kind of work that they do.

Boys are given courses in woodworking in our schools, not because they are to become cabinet-makers or carpenters, but because they need an understanding of the hard and unyielding nature of the materials used in woodworking vocations; and a feeling of the arduous and monotonous toil necessary for shaping the materials into finished products. The woodworking is to give him the alphabet of experience in one wide field of human vocation. Its purpose is to open an experiential window out upon the world through which he can rightly see its labors.

For the same reason we give many practical activities: metal-working, leather-work, printing, bookbinding, arts and crafts, cooking, sewing, embroidery, millinery, school gardening, weaving, rug-making, dyeing, painting, varnishing, pattern-making, pottery work, poultry care, laundry work, banking, buying and selling, practical accounting, and others. These activities give to boys and girls a *sense of reality* as to the nature of labor and of the materials used in the labor. The development of this sense of reality is one of the most urgent of necessities, especially for boys and girls who grow up in our cities. When our population was mostly agricultural, the boy on the farm with hoe and rake and plough cultivated the fields; with axe and saw, he provided fuel for the family, built and mended fences, bins, barns, and other farm structures. He pitched the hay, husked the corn, cut the feed, milked the cows, in all weathers, heat and cold and storm. Thus he secured his necessary sense of reality; his understanding of the hard and unyielding nature of the material world that lies at the basis of economic industry. The girl in sewing, cooking, mending, washing dishes, laundry, general housekeeping, canning and preserving, in helping with the poultry, the gardening, etc., was equally favored. They were well-trained in the Great School.

But to-day in our towns and cities the boy has no spade or hoe, no axe or saw, no coal-hod, nor any other opportunity for performing a portion of the world's labor, and thereby acquiring a sanifying sense of reality. Except for his sports, perhaps, there is no call for him ever really to exert himself in any strenuous manner. The world moves visually before him; but on the vocational side, it is largely but a picture world like the motion picture on the screen. He sees men digging on our streets, but unless he has himself wielded the heavy tools of labor, and felt the burden that such men bear, he has not the experiential alphabet for understanding or appreciating the things that pass before his eyes. The deeper things of the situation are to be seen, not with the eyes, but with the sympathetic vision that has grown up out of like experience. Without this he may see the externals; he cannot, however, see the labor itself. Like one born blind who cannot know color, he is doomed to remain blind to the nature of actual realities.

Since the purpose of the practical activities is the opening of experiential windows out over the diverse occupational fields, obviously the range of activities should be as wide as conditions permit.

There should be work with wood — pine, oak, poplar, spruce, fir, hemlock, birch, maple, walnut, ash, cedar, mahogany, seasoned and unseasoned, straight and crooked, hard and soft, sapwood and heartwood, large rough work and fine accurate work. In connection with this naturally comes work with paints, oils, varnishes, stains, shellacs, alcohols, pumice, sandpaper, and other finishing materials.

There should be work with metals — iron, steel, copper, brass, tin, aluminum, nickel, silver, alloys, wire, sheet metal, forgings, castings. Pupils should become acquainted with metals in the form of ores and compounds. They should have an opportunity to reduce them, to refine them, to mould them in the foundry, and to shape them in the making of practical things.

There should be work involving the application of electricity to practical affairs — electric bells, wiring, toasters, cookers, irons, electric lighting, the telephone, the telegraph, clock controls, electro-plating, cells, dynamos, motors, with construction of these things.

There should be work in printing, composition, typesetting, presswork, copper-plate-making, applied art and design, bookbinding, cover-ornamentation, printing of bills, accounts, recipes, programs, invitations, supplementary material for classes, and the like. Closely related to this is cardboard construction, box-making, blotter-pads, desk-pads, etc.

There should also be work involving leather — the making of bags, purses, portfolios, bill-books, coverings of many kinds of balls, belts, satchels, suit-cases, trunks, handles, harness, upholstery, etc. All important kinds of leather should be used, as well as imitation leathers. Various kinds of dressings, finishings, preservatives should be employed.

There should be work with clay and allied earth products, plaster of paris, cement, porcelain, glass; the actual making

of brick and tile, of lime and cement, from the original
materials; pottery-making, cement-block construction, the
making and mending of cement walks, bricklaying, tile-
laying. The maintenance of the school plant affords excellent opportunities for practical labors of these types.

A large field is that of textiles — wool, cotton, linen, silk,
hemp, jute, Manila fiber, etc. So far as possible, the pupils
should come into contact with the fibers in their original
raw state; and understand through experience the kinds of
labor involved in bringing them to finished form. With
wool it should include the original washing, combing, carding, spinning, dyeing, weaving, fulling, shearing, shrinking,
and pressing. Flax can be grown in the school garden, the
fiber can be separated by the children themselves, spun,
woven, and bleached. Other work is sewing and garment-
making of every sort, with every usual kind of cloth —
garment-design, garment-fitting, embroidery, millinery,
laces, curtains, hangings, carpets, rugs, etc.

Closely related to this is work with straw, raffia, cane,
rattan, etc., in the making of mats, hats, baskets, trays,
cases of various kinds, chair-seats, chair-backs, and cane
furniture.

There should be work with foods. This should involve
cooking of all common kinds, canning, preserving, starch-
making, sugar-making, oil manufacture, pickling, butter-
making, cheese manufacture, condensed-milk manufacture.
Closely connected with this is the making of soaps, and
other cleansing agents.

Not only should one have experiential opportunities in
these fields of manufacture or transformation, but also in
the production of the original raw materials in farm and
garden. He should have an opportunity to raise corn, potatoes, vegetables, fruits, etc., in sufficient quantity and variety to learn the nature of the labors. He should have work

involving soil preparation, fertilizing, seed-testing, planting, cultivating, protection from insects, drainage, irrigation, adaptation to seasonal conditions, harvesting, storing, marketing. He should have an opportunity likewise to work with poultry, live-stock, dairy cattle, bees, and with such other agricultural matters as the administrative limitations will permit.

One's education also requires some participation in the activities of the commercial world, buying and selling, competition, salesmanship, bookkeeping, accounting, the handling of money, banking, savings banks, insurance, etc. The school buys much; it ought to buy more in order to take care of the wide range of activities here indicated. The school at present sells little; it ought to sell very much more. These activities will require much bookkeeping and careful accounting. They will require banking and the handling of money. So far as it is administratively possible, conditions should be so devised that students can participate in these serious commercial activities. This is now being done in many schools where the pupils of the domestic science classes conduct the lunch-room, the supply-store, or where they do contract work in the shops.

"All of these things?" the appalled teacher asks. In inclining toward the affirmative, let us point to the fact that practically every one of the occupations involved is already treated in our geographies. Now, what is the purpose of the book-study concerning occupations and products in the geography? Apparently it is an attempt to develop an understanding of the diversified human occupations. But how can this be developed through book-study if the children have not that alphabet of experience necessary for giving meaning to the words of the text? How can they appreciate the great cotton industry of the South, for example, as they read of it in their geographies, if they have never seen or handled or cultivated a cotton plant? How can they appreciate the process of ginning, as they read of it, if they have never had the experience of actually separating the fiber from the seeds? How can they appreciate the manufacture of cotton-seed oil, cotton-seed cake, etc., if they have never come into experiential contact with the cotton seed, and do not know whether it most resembles a mustard seed or a walnut? How appreciate the great cotton textile industries if they have never had anything to do with carding and spinning, weaving and dyeing? Without concrete experience with the occupational materials and processes, the students as they read the geographical treatment of occupations, but tread a hazy realm of verbal vagueness, lit here and there with chance flashes from their incidental daily experience, but in general obscure and dimly visioned.

Manual training throughout the elementary school and largely in the high school should have for a primary aim, not skill, not the production of a salable product, but an appreciation of the materials, processes, and products of a wide range of adult occupations. It is the most concrete portion of the home-geography of occupations. Combined with observation of neighborhood labors and products, we have the whole of home-geography on the occupational side.

The major portion of the concrete activities at all stages of maturity will be on the order of play — constructive, operative, and participative. It seems that some of them, however, as training continues, should be raised to the plane of work. Without actual work in an atmosphere of work, with the spirit of work alive within the participants, they do not sufficiently enter into work-experience. Their activities may have a commendable width and variety, but will be lacking in depth. In the later stages of the training, something more is required than manual training in a play-shop.

Since the end of the training is an understanding of the World of Work, this serious level must therefore be reached and explored in some degree. It is this that makes necessary a certain amount of skill; the production of a salable economic product; and a genuine shop-atmosphere. The work-level will be most fully reached by the student in the things in which he is specializing; and generally through part-time coöperative arrangements.

2. Observation

Having mastered the alphabet of experience, it is possible for a student to enter into the world's experience in more expeditious ways. The concrete experience gives the imagery and apperception materials; and the interests. The student is then equipped for understanding occupations through visit and observation. In cities opportunities are numerous. Many can be visited and viewed by young people in the course of their individual experience. Where inaccessible to incidental observation, in most cases managers are glad to arrange for systematic observation by classes or groups.

Observation of occupations must be a portion of the preparation for the reading experiences. It must provide a portion of the imagery, the apperceptions-mass, and the interest. In the school shops, students can secure basic experience with materials, processes, and products; but the world of occupation there developed is diminutive, primitive, fragmentary, and sometimes a very artificial and distorted representation of the actual industry itself. To revert to our cotton-study illustration, students in the textile room can get pretty accurate ideas of fibers, dyes, the basic elements of spinning and weaving machinery, and the nature of certain simple types of fabric. But the school shop as a whole bears little resemblance to a large textile mill with its great engines, its huge dyeing-vats and drying facilities, its countless spinning-machines and power-looms, and the bustle and whir of busy production. If for one's reading one has only the meager imagery supplied by the school shop, then one has but poor preparation for it. We find here the justification for the ever-increasing use of motion-pictures for greatly extending one's visual observation of concrete processes and conditions.

Observation of an occupation is greatly quickened if the observer can be a participant and carry a portion of the responsibility. There is nothing like responsibility for giving eyes to an individual; and especially eyes for values and relations. It is of immeasurably greater value for a boy to work for a season on a farm or in a store than it is merely to visit idly about the place. The observation through visit alone by classes or groups, and that for but a brief time, can give much valuable apperceptive imagery; but its limitations must be noted; and provision made, as far as possible, for actual participation in the labors of occupational groups. The pedagogy which sanctions the demand is simple and clear. The difficulty arises in connection with the administration of new activities that will not easily transfer to the schools. Present part-time arrangements are made only for specialized training. In time we may see our way clear for similar arrangements for some of the general training. Promise of this is to be found in the auspicious movement for promoting outside activities through giving credit for home work.

One important type of observation relates to the study of the products of industry. Social supervision of industries is designed, among other things, to secure from the specialized groups a type of product that fully meets human needs. In general an industry will be left free to use whatever materials and processes that it chooses — on condition that they result in the right type of product. Of occupations in general, therefore, the public will need no detailed technical understanding of materials and processes. *They need, however, as consumers to be competent judges of the products of industry.* Boys and girls coming out of our manual-training courses need not so much to be skilled in making furniture, tools, electrical appliances, garments, curtains, etc., as to be skilled in judging the quality of such things as they are offered in the market. Their shop-training is valuable for developing judgment. But if their ideas are limited to what they meet in the school shops in making things, then their ideas will be too primitive, crude, and meager for adequate judgment of the products upon the market. The latter are immeasurably more complicated in countless subtle ways.

One full department of training should, therefore, be the systematic and adequate study of the finished products of industry. Along with shop experience in making chairs, boys need to examine and discuss many types of chairs. They will be viewed in the light of principles of construction, of utility, of æsthetic design, and of economic costs. Along with the practical activities of girls in making curtains, for example, they need to refine and complete their powers of judgment through examination and study of many types of curtains in the light of general principles.

Carried to its logical limits, this means that in many fields we need a continuous exhibit of products which reveal all types of excellence and defect. Though startling at first glance, the conclusion is inevitable. We discover here another need that once was simple enough not to require the work of the schools, which has grown so complex that it can be adequately taken care of in no other way. Recognition of the educational task is really appearing a long time after the work should have been undertaken. As a people we have been deceived long enough by those who have been in a position to profit by ignorance of materials, qualities, and prices. *Just as occupational inefficiency needs to be overcome in the field of production, so also it needs to be overcome in the field of the consumer's judgment.*

But how can the schools have all the expensive things needed for such an exhibit of economic products? Where can they be stored? How is deterioration to be prevented? How are perishable products to be taken care of? How meet the problem of ever-changing styles, and of current improvements? Would not much of the exhibit be obsolete almost as soon as arranged? And how are obsolete but expensive things to be disposed of?

Such questions grow out of a type of educational thought that, let us hope, will rapidly grow obsolete, — a type that assumes that everything needed in education must be found at the school plant. As a matter of fact, economic products must be observed where they can be observed effectively and economically. This is generally where they are manufactured, stored for distribution, exhibited for sale; or where they are being used in home and street, in field and shop, and in the other places of the community. This constitutes a continuous community exhibit of the things. It permits them to be seen in their natural settings and relationships, taken out of which they lose half their significance.

3. *Occupational readings*

Occupations are to be seen in their nation-wide and world-wide distribution. The means must be mainly reading. This will be largely narrative in character. As one reads concerning any occupation, the aim will be the reconstruction in the imagination of the reader of an inner world of occupational experiences in which, lost to sense of time and place, he can participate, as a shadow-member of the group, so to speak; and thus enter sympathetically into the experiences with an intellectual and emotional vividness not greatly dissimilar to that which accompanies actual objective observation and participation. As one reads *Captains Courageous*, for example, one is for the time, so far as his consciousness is concerned, a fisherman off the banks of Newfoundland, almost as completely as if he were there in the flesh. Then as one reads *The Lumberman*, one's habitation is shifted to the wilds of Michigan in its early days, and one becomes an active and interested participant in the logging industry along the rivers. Let him again at another time read a spirited history of transportation in our country from colonial times to the present. One becomes for a time an early colonist, and travels and transports his goods in the primitive ways. Later he is a shadow-member of the group about Robert Fulton as he labors with the problem of applying steam to river nav.gation. A little later he joins the other group and participates in the experiment of applying steam to overland transportation. And thus the history, if concrete and vivid and full, reconstructs experience and permits him to be one with group after group and to participate in its affairs from early days down to the present. In the reconstructions of stirring narrative, one's experience can be as much wider than observation as the latter is wider than the circle of one's individual labors.

The readings concerning occupations will be of a varied character: history, geography, literature, biography, travels, current events, stories of inventions, etc.

Historical readings will be among the most vital for the purpose. It is true that the practical thing desired is a knowledge of the occupation in its present status. But history is one of the best methods of showing the nature of the present. It reveals the constituents of a situation by showing the influences that have produced it; and which are continuing within it. It is impossible to understand the railroad situation at present, for example, without a fairly extensive understanding of the influences of former years that have made it what it now is. The same is true of the steel industry, the lumber industry, the relations between capital and labor, the growth of labor unions, etc. Not only does history reveal the facts, but if the human element is kept foremost, it reveals them in assimilable ways. One can enter sympathetically into the labors of the human groups the story of which is being read. Such imaginative participation contains many of the factors of real participation, and more nearly approximates the nature of the latter than commonly supposed.

Public education has scarcely yet recognized the legitimacy of the purposes treated in this chapter. It is not surprising, therefore, that history is not used in our schools as a mode of revealing the growth and present nature of occupations. The little given in our historical textbooks is so minute, fragmentary, general, and vague, that it cannot be intended by the writers for the purposes mentioned. For example, taking a dozen textbooks in United States history commonly used in the elementary schools, and eight texts commonly used in the high schools, it was found that the average number of pages devoted to occupational topics was so small as to be negligible for training. The number of pages is shown in the following table: —

	Elementary texts	High-school texts
Inventions	5.3	3.3
Tariff and free trade	3.7	8.9
Railroads	2.7	5.2
Canals	2.5	2.7
Manufacturing	2.5	2.0
Foreign commerce	2.3	1.6
Mining	2.3	.5

Banks and banking	2.0	4.8
Relations of capital and labor	1.8	4.1
Agriculture	1.4	1.6
Roads and road transportation	1.2	.7
Telegraph	1.1	.3
Domestic commerce	1.0	2.4
Labor organizations	.6	1.9
Savings banks	.6	.2
Newspapers and magazines	.5	.7
Postal service	.5	1.6
Fisheries	.4	.4
Telephone	.4	.2
Wages	.2	1.0
Patents and copyrights	.0	.0
Child labor	.0	.3
Women in industry	.0	.2
Unemployment	.0	.3
Cost of living	.0	.2

If any one believes the average treatment of these topics to be sufficient, he can easily test the matter. Let him send the five pages on banks and banking to a list of prominent bankers requesting their judgment whether it presents an adequate revelation of the growth of banking in our country, and as its outcome, an adequate picture of its present status. Let him send the three or five pages on railroad development to prominent leaders of the railroad world with a similar request. Let him inquire of labor unions if the two or three pages devoted to them present a satisfactory account of the development of their present status and relations. It is not difficult to predict the character of the replies.

For each of these topics, and for many others, there is demonstrable need of a full historical treatment. Justice is not to be done to the railroad situation, for example, short of two hundred or five hundred pages. This should present in concrete, vivid narrative a reconstruction of experiences involved in the development of railroads, beginning with the early inventions and experiments, and tracing the expansion of lines and systems down to the present. The story should fully present the personal experiences of railroad leaders and groups: only as the "human element" is central in the story can the reader actually relive the experiences. But at the same time it should reveal fundamental processes and relationships of all kinds: the social influences that called railroads into being; kinds and amounts of service rendered to different regions; modes of organization, financing, regulation, wages, conditions of work, etc. The story should be so written that the reader can see and appreciate the valiant national service that the railroads have rendered in pushing back the frontiers and opening up the wilderness for civilization; in carrying the means of civilized life to every corner of our land; in breaking down isolation, provincialism, and sectionalism; and in promoting the general intra-national welfare. The story should be presented so vividly and sympathetically that the reader can enter whole-heartedly into the action. This provides right conditions for leaving large residues of information acquired through living rather than memorizing; and the materials and experiences out of which the abstract general principles are to be distilled.

Each vocation is also to be seen geographically in its nation-wide and world-wide distribution. One is interested in those portions that touch one's own affairs; but world-wide interdependency makes this the whole of the world's industry. The price of wheat, for example, in any community is determined, not by the amount raised in that community, but by the world-situation as regards wheat. Rightly to understand it one must read a long chapter on the geography of wheat — a chapter that changes from year to year. Likewise he must read similar chapters on all of the important occupations. Recent books are providing excellent materials for the purpose.

Lack of space forbids discussion here of the occupational illumination to be provided by literature, travels, biography, current events, popular technology, stories of inventions. Each has a large function to perform; and should find large place in the curriculum of occupational training.

4. *Generalization*

In the foregoing we have stressed concrete experiences. But each provides materials for discussion, problem-solving, abstraction of elements and relations, and generalizations. The work in the shops, sewing-rooms, kitchens, gardens, etc., will provide basic materials for generalized understanding of design, physical science, biological science, mathematics, economic relationships, etc. The history, geography, travels, current events, etc., will not confine themselves merely to a concrete construction of life in other ages and lands. These experiences are preparatory to generalizations. Pupils are to see the broad lines of influence that operate in human affairs; to see how some of them may promote human welfare, and how others may prevent or destroy; and to see how the influences have been and may be controlled for human good. It is in this connection that understanding of most of the economic and social principles required for effective social supervision is to be developed.

PART III
EDUCATION FOR CITIZENSHIP

CHAPTER XI

THE NATURE OF THE GOOD CITIZEN

EDUCATION cannot take the first step in training for citizenship until it has particularized the characteristics of the good citizen. The training task is to develop those characteristics. It is not enough to aim at "good citizenship" in a vague general way. As well aim at "medicine" in a large vague way in the training of a physician.

The citizen has functions to perform. We are to develop ability to perform those functions. But first we must know with particularity what they are. He must have certain social attitudes, valuations, criteria of judgment. We cannot effectively train for these, except as we have rather accurately defined them. He must have knowledge; but we must know how and where he is to use it before we can know what to give; or how much; or how to focus it.

The need of definite objectives is obvious. It will be a long time, however, before our profession can have any reasonably complete list upon which to base a system of training. And the reason is, citizens are not sufficiently agreed among themselves as to the characteristics of the good citizen, or his modes of thought and action. They agree so long as they talk mere vagueness; they disagree the moment they begin to particularize. And education must be built upon the particulars.

The primitive good citizen

We can best indicate the essential nature of the good citizen by first noting the situation in the small primitive tribes of our ancestors before the growth of complex institutions obscured the relationships. In those early times, the human race was broken up into innumerable small tribes. Each had little or no connection with its neighbors. Owing to the severe limitations upon the food-supply and other necessities, and to the tendency within tribes to expand, each tribe was usually hostile to neighboring tribes. There was always a state of active or slumbering war.

Continuing existence of the tribe demanded considerable social solidarity. In the common struggles with the enemy and with the hostile forces of Nature, each member of the tribe was expected to coöperate fully with the other members. He must deal fairly and honestly with his own people. He must lend assistance to those in need of it. He must be loyal to the group, and obedient to constituted authority. He must restrain his anti-social passions, and adjust his efforts to promote the tribal welfare. Without this solidarity, the group disintegrated and was destroyed by better-organized neighbors. So indispensable was group-cohesion and social virtues that man was endowed with powerful social instincts. Nature made sure of this type of social service.

On the other hand, for the tribe to survive under those hard conditions of primitive struggle, each individual had to be prepared to fight alien tribes. The rightful attitude of an individual toward members of alien groups was therefore anti-social, hostile, destructive. Toward the alien he was expected to exercise deceit, stratagem, treachery, and violence. He must despoil them of their property, enslave them, or destroy them. This exercise of anti-social attitudes toward the alien was as necessary and as virtuous as the exercise of the social attitudes toward the members of his own group. The tribe that would not fight was destroyed, root and branch. This resistance to the enemy was so important that Nature gave to man a full array of fighting instincts. In this manner, she set her seal of approval upon anti-social attitudes and action. She made sure also of this second type of social service to one's own group.

In his relations to other individuals, conditions forced upon primitive man two standards of conduct, two sets of attitudes, two sets of virtues. The good citizen of the tribe was the one who most vigorously exercised the social virtues toward the members of his tribe, and who most valiantly exercised the anti-social virtues toward members of the alien tribes. The bad citizen was the one who exercised the hostile virtues toward his fellow-tribesmen and the friendly virtues toward the aliens.

Intra-group virtues	Extra-group virtues
Mutual aid; social service	Injury; destruction
Fair-dealing	Double-dealing; treachery
Truthfulness; honesty	Deceit; stratagem
Loyalty; obedience	Hostility; opposition
Modesty; humility	Arrogance
Submission to group opinion	Defiance; antagonism
Courtesy	Incivility
Self-restraint	Unbridled freedom
Gentleness; mercy	Ruthlessness

In the table the two opposite sets of virtues are placed over against each other. The good citizen of the primitive tribe had to be active in the exercise of both. But he must exercise each toward its rightful object of reference. He must not reverse them. In so doing, he became guilty of the two sets of crimes. To exercise anti-social attitudes toward the members of his own group was to select the wrong objects for their reference and therefore to commit crime. On the other hand, to exercise the social virtues toward members of alien groups was to be guilty of rendering aid to one's enemies, the capital crime of treason. Whether an act toward another human being or group of human beings was virtuous or vicious depended not upon the nature of the act itself, but *upon the object of reference.* To kill women and children, for example, in that day was virtuous conduct, if they belonged to alien tribes; it was criminal conduct, if they were of one's own tribe. Any kind of human conduct toward another was good, or any kind was bad; it all depended upon the person toward whom it was exercised. Virtue or vice lay not in the act itself; but in the right social placing of the act. Virtues and vices were relative things, not absolutes.

The modern situation

As a result of the long-continued group-struggle of primitive days, the weaker tribes disappeared and the stronger tribes grew fewer in number and larger in population and territorial area. This absorption or destruction of the weak by the strong has continued down to the present day until there now exists over the habitable globe only some forty or fifty independent national groups. The situation with respect to the two sets of social attitudes, however, does not change with the size of the group. It cannot change so long as wholly independent competing nations exist. Within the large nation, no less than in primitive days, there still remains the need of inner solidarity and the exercise of the social virtues. Toward the alien nations, however, in the degree that they are felt to be alien, one is still expected to employ the anti-social attitudes. Between these larger nations there is, as of old, a constant hostility. This is not always on the surface. With war so expensive and destructive now, nations live mostly in a state of truce, — simply because anything else is suicidal in the end, and not because the world has developed the fundamental basis of peace.

The slumbering presence of extra-group hostility is revealed by the ease with which it flares forth at the slightest provocation, and the ease with which it bursts into the flames of war even in the case of nations that we have been accustomed to call civilized. The independent national groups still cling to the two standards of conduct and regard both as wholly justifiable, legitimate, and virtuous, if only exercised toward the right objects of reference. In times of international stress, when both intra-group and extra-group standards of conduct are fully aroused, and when the growing but yet feeble sentiment of membership in a world group is stilled in the strife, then the anti-social dictates become clear and unconfused. To kill the man who is not a member of one's own nation becomes a matter of entire virtue. It is not a crime. It is not a matter for reproach. It calls for decorations of honor. At the present moment it is the largest, the most expensively equipped and the most completely organized business in the world.

The nations have institutionalized their anti-social tendencies. They have developed laws, traditions, public opinion, military technique, organization, training, weapons, and other appliances for destroying aliens. And through newspapers, schools, churches, and public proclamations, they have arranged to make and to keep all people fully conscious of their anti-social duties, powers, and possibilities.

In relation to the wholly alien nation, then, who is the good citizen? It is the one who is ready and eager to fight the alien the instant called upon; who is ready to shed his blood to the last drop in service to his countrymen. It is the one whose thought and feeling and action are most completely anti-social — with these turned squarely against the hostile alien.

We may deprecate a world-situation which makes murder and destruction an inescapable part of social service; and therefore a necessary function of the good citizen. The situation is what it is, however; and not what we may wish it to be. The world is still young and in the green; and yet far from organized and civilized. An undesirable form of social service is not to be escaped by blinking it; but by so changing the world-situation that the noxious type of service is no longer necessary to continuing national existence and welfare.

Patriotism we say is a characteristic of the good citizen. But in our present state of world-division, there are two types of patriotism, wholly different, and both indispensable for national welfare. We are here referring to one of the types, the one that is built upon the anti-alien relations. It is the desire to serve one's own national group by restraining or injuring, or even if necessary destroying, alien groups. It is the aroused anti-social spirit. It is a state of mind that in the nature of things must persist so long as this whirling planet holds mankind-in-division.

But let us turn to the other and more agreeable side of the picture. The national groups not only institutionalize the spirit of world-division for their outside relations; but also build ponderous and stable national institutions upon the intra-social impulses of mankind-in-coöperation. For promoting the welfare of the group within, the more advanced nations — even though their hands now are reeking with the blood of alien human-kind — have been providing and developing the humanitarian institutions necessary to a superb state of civilization. They have been building schools and churches; and fostering within their boundaries the reign of intelligence and good-will. They have been providing hospitals for the sick, systematic state care for the weak, pensions for the aged and the incapacitated, workmen's compensation for the injured in industry, protection of women and children from industrial exploitation, eight-hour laws for workmen, the enforcement of sanitary living and work conditions; and a host of other human-welfare measures. And they have zealously promoted in a thousand ways those social institutions which perform for a people the basic intra-group services: industry, commerce, transportation, mining, agriculture, professional service, etc. Thus institutions growing out of the social virtues flourish profusely in nations that show no abhorrence to the most inhuman brutalities when exercised toward alien peoples. And press and schools and churches diligently foster this internal socialization; and the awakening of a sensitive social conscience that is keenly cognizant of intra-group obligation.

This brings us to the other type of patriotism—the aroused spirit of intra-group service. It is the desire to serve one's national group by promoting in every possible way those internal social adjustments and actions that make in maximum degree for the general national welfare. Instead of its being hatred of the enemy as in the other type, it is love of one's people, and of all of one's people; and positive. This type of patriotism is in need of greater emphasis since it is not so clearly conceived. It is coördinate with the other. But to most men the term refers only to the anti-social type. Men take great pride in self-sacrifice, and are willing to lay down even life itself, to promote the welfare of their people, so long as it is the anti-alien type of social service. Why should there not be equal willingness for self-sacrifice in the service of those same people when the service is social? And why should not the intra-group service be equally honored? Civic training should complete our ideas of patriotism; and develop attitudes of both types — so long as both are needed.

Functional differentiation

As social groups grow large territorially, they break up along functional lines into small groups again: commercial, manufacturing, agricultural, religious, political, professional, and others. The lower limit in size is the specialized individual standing alone.

With the appearance of the functional small groups, there arise naturally and inevitably the two standards of social conduct. Human nature is so made that without thought we adopt the social attitudes toward members of our own social group: our own political party, our own church, commercial organization, political ring, fraternity, club, trade-union, employers' union, school, college, or other organization to which we may belong. In the same natural way, without taking thought, we adopt the extra-group attitudes toward those who belong to outside or competing groups: the opposite political party, other financial, commercial, or manufacturing organizations, the churches of the other groups, the rival college, the close-fisted employers' association, or the striking labor-union.

One belongs to many overlapping groups and over all he belongs to the city, state, and national groups which include all of these. He has a conception of his membership in each of them. This complicated consciousness tends to soften and partially inhibit the workings of the anti-social attitudes in connection with one's small-group activities. Leaving aside this qualification, we must notice that as one's consciousness of membership within the small group becomes intense, he adopts the two standards of conduct and looks upon both as equally virtuous. They have been so regarded by mankind from the beginning of the world. Both are powerfully supported by instincts; back of each are powerful traditions. As a result both are considered equally right and necessary if only the one is exercised toward one's friends and the other toward outsiders.

A labor-union offers a good example. The members of the union extend mutual aid to all within the group. They aid in securing employment; in holding their positions; in the regulation of hours, wages, factory protection, sanitary conditions, etc. In times of sickness or loss of place, the necessary material assistance is extended. Toward each other within the union, after excepting the occasional wolf in sheep's clothing that preys upon ignorance, there is, on the whole, fair-dealing, honesty, truthfulness, loyalty, obedience, and submission to whatever regulations are necessary for the welfare of the union. However rough and ignorant the men may be, these social virtues grow up within the group in their relations toward each other about as luxuriantly as among the individuals of any social class. On the other hand, the union holds just as strictly to the extra-group, anti-social standard of conduct in their relations to the opposing employers' groups. Industry exists in division. Hence there is constant hostility. While active warfare flames forth only occasionally, the usual situation is one of truce, not of peace. The union stands ready to over-reach employers when opportunity offers. They combine to limit the output of each man. They tend to "soldier," to mismanage, to delay progress so as to extend the work. It is in times of acute trouble, however, that the extra-group attitudes reveal themselves most clearly. The union often strives to wreck or destroy the machinery and the materials belonging to the hostile employers. The labor strike is often a state of actual armed warfare. They will not work until their demands are granted, and others shall not work. Where persuasion will not serve, force must be employed. The unions justify the use of force by saying that it is class war. They use the term in its literal sense, not in a figurative one. It is a struggle for the group that grows out of adherence to the world-old extra-group standard of conduct. It has exactly the same kind of justification as any other kind of war. We shall not make headway in understanding the civic factors that enter into the situation unless we grant the warring union entire sincerity of conviction as to the rightfulness of adhering to both standards of conduct. They are acting as the race has always acted from the beginning of the world when divided into opposing and hostile small groups. To dispense with either of the standards so long as industry exists in division can result in but injury or destruction for their group. Even though they may wish to dispense with the extra-group attitudes, the condition of social division will not permit.

It is not that the men are vicious. It is the state of industry-in-division that is vicious. To say that the men are inherently ill-disposed and that they destroy simply for the love of destruction is to miss the whole secret of the matter. They are usually more rough and ignorant than their accusers, because they have had fewer educational opportunities; but they are not less honest nor less sincere; nor less virtuous when measured by the dual standard of virtue forced upon them by the presence of social division. They are using the same standards of conduct as their opponents. For it must be kept in mind that there are always at least two parties to a fight; and that when the fighting is fierce upon the one side it is no less fierce upon the other. The visible struggle of the labor-unions is proof of an equally strenuous opposition upon the part of the employing groups.

Let us reverse the illustration. The employers' groups have their same two standards of social ethics; and they live up to the standards forced upon them by conditions in the same vigorous and manly way. In their conduct toward each other, one sees revealed all of the social virtues at their best. They stand together and support each other in the promotion of measures designed to further the welfare of their groups, and in resisting injurious measures. They keep each other's counsels. They place opportunities in each other's way. They pass on information which can be used. They extend credit to each other on a more generous basis than that granted to outsiders. They fix prices, eliminate competition, make "gentlemen's" trade agreements, — and to each other their word is their bond. As a matter of fact, it is in the business world where one will find the highest examples of consistent and tenacious adherence to the social standards of group ethics. When one seeks an example of honesty that is unshakable, of fidelity to trust that is free from the breath of every suspicion, one will find it most frequently among the responsible leaders in the business world. This is, however, to refer to but one side of their dual ethical system. Opposed to them is the labor group and the great body of consumers. These are alien groups; and in proportion as they are conceived to be alien, the anti-social predatory standard rises strong and becomes the rule of action. Until recently they have had little care as to how much they injure or destroy the laborer. They have refused to install protective devices or to make factories sanitary until they are compelled to do so. They have refused to cut down hours and have been willing to work men in twelve- or even sixteen-hour shifts without care as to the effects upon them. They have given out false statements as to capitalization, costs, expenses of production, profits, and in other ways have sought to prevent the opposing labor organizations from obtaining their rights. They have circulated blacklists to keep out of their shops those who are especially strenuous in fighting the battles of labor. They have placed *provocateurs* in the labor camps to discredit labor in the eyes of the public. But in thus holding to one social standard in their conduct toward each other, and to a wholly different standard toward the laboring men, the employing class is doing what is in the nature of the situation forced upon them. Where such group oppositions exist, the rise of the two standards is inevitable. We must see the anti-social opposition to labor's welfare as a sincere and honest adherence to a dual ethical standard that the world has always accepted; and which it yet accepts. It is human nature in the face of social division.

Let the managerial groups lay down their oppositions under present social conditions, and grant all that opposing labor and consumer groups may demand, — and they but commit economic suicide. "Big business," no more than labor, is vicious or criminal. Our social problem is not a matter of dealing with "malefactors of great wealth," but rather with the maleficent results of society-in-division. The *dividedness* is the malefactor.

Illustrations are as numerous as small groups. Take the case of the corrupt political ring. Within such a group of gray wolves there is a tremendous social solidarity. One finds the social virtues blossoming as luxuriantly as they can be found anywhere. There is loyalty and obedience to the chief. Group secrets are kept inviolate. There is mutual service within the group in the getting of offices, political jobs, political contracts, access to the public crib, etc. One hears endless praises of the leaders because of their helpfulness and never-ending kindness toward the individuals of their class. In carrying forward these activities it matters not to them how much they injure the welfare of the other social groups. These are alien; and therefore legitimate prey.

In proportion as one's social vision and social consciousness are limited to one's membership in the small group, with ignorance of large-group existences and relationships, one will hold to the primitive dual standard of conduct. Though good to his friends, he is the undesirable citizen.

In proportion as one's social vision and social consciousness are widened so that one comes to have a vivid conception of one's membership in the large group, then the anti-social attitudes and standards tend to fade and disappear and to leave as the rule of conduct only the social ethics of civilized humanity. Of this type is the good citizen in a state of civilization.

Let one continue this line of thought and note the special attitudes and antagonisms among business groups, political parties, ecclesiastical organizations, medical and healing groups, etc., each with its own special dual system of ethics, and one can realize that in educating for citizenship we are to prepare to deal with some very obdurate aspects of human nature; and with intractable institutionalized small-group attitudes and traditions. If the training is to be vital, not merely some remote hearsay affair, students need to be brought into experiential contact with the realities themselves. That the training problems bristle with difficulties is easily evident. Every one of these small groups stands over against other small groups and equally against the large group. Its ethics not only demands that it fight competitor small groups, but that it also fight the large group when the latter refuses to let it pursue its group-ends without molestation. It therefore follows the dictates of virtue when it fights education for large-group valuations. And its blows have the vigor and persistence of sincerity; and equally the underhandedness that is fully sanctioned as a major virtue of the extra-group type.

Interdependence of specialized groups

We now come to the fourth level of our genetic story. The differentiation of the national group into small functional groups has as its obverse side the interdependence of the small groups. This again welds the small groups into a new and higher form of large-group solidarity. Each becomes dependent upon all the others; and the others dependent upon it. The oneness of the specialized groups becomes as clear as the oneness of the bodily organism with its specialized members. As this recognition rises clear, consciousness of membership within the large group becomes dominant in the members of all of the specialized groups and the extra-group attitudes of antagonism between constituent classes disappear. All come to accept the intra-group standards as the rules of civic conduct; the extra-group standards disappear; and good citizenship on the part of all is achieved. This level of social evolution, this subjective good citizenship which alone can bring the actual, has been but partially reached. The climb is yet a toilsome one. But the speed that we have recently been making, and the ease with which we have been responding to newly recognized social obligation promise great civic achievement in the years just ahead of us. And since the problem at bottom is one of creating subjective attitudes and valuations, it is mainly a problem for the educational profession. And the first problem — a most baffling one — is to draw up a curriculum that will with certainty forge an enduring and vitalized large-group consciousness.

CHAPTER XII

THE DEVELOPMENT OF ENLIGHTENED LARGE-GROUP CONSCIOUSNESS

THE problem of civic training is *par excellence* the development of large-group consciousness. If men understand the large-group social relations, and have right attitudes toward each other and toward the social whole, these automatically impel toward right action. Education will develop the emotional aspects of large-group consciousness for the sake of propelling power; and the intellectual aspects for the sake of guidance.

Let us first ask, How does one develop a genuine *feeling of membership* in a social group, whether large or small? There seems to be but one method and that is, *To think and feel and* ACT *with the group as a part of it as it performs its activities and strives to attain its ends.* Individuals are fused into coherent small groups, discordant small groups are fused into the large internally-coöperating group, when they *act together* for common ends, with common vision, and with united judgment.

Let us take for illustration that group-consciousness called "college spirit." The high-school youth who has not yet chosen his college is likely to have little or no interest in the success or failure of any particular college athletic team to which he sees reference in the daily press. But after he has entered a particular college, and has come to participate in its affairs, then the situation is altogether changed. His sympathies are with one group and with its team; and the more strenuously he exerts himself in promoting its welfare, the more keenly does he realize his common membership in the group, and the more willing does he become to sink personal self-interest for the welfare of his college group. "College spirit" is the flower and fruit of *action*. This action may be of other types than athletic; but action for common ends there must be or there is no healthy growth of the sentiment of solidarity.

Merely to find one's self a passive member of a group is not enough. The member of the college who does not participate actively in its affairs remains cold, aloof, unsympathetic. He does not fuse with the group. College spirit does not and cannot grow in such soil. And the principle is of universal application. The man who is passively made a member of a church or political organization, but who never does anything by way of promoting the common purposes of the group, will never attain any vital consciousness of membership in the organization. Like a piece of cold iron that cannot be welded, he remains detached, separate, apart. Man finds his normal social life only in action; and he attains a realization of his normal relationships only through action.

One of the arguments in favor of national wars is that more than anything else they cement national solidarity. This is because they represent group-action of the most strenuous and the most fully emotionalized type: actions and emotions that lie close to elemental instincts. The substitute for war that civilization is to find must have as its major ingredient group-action that is strenuous and emotionalized. Wanting this, there can be no effective and abiding national solidarity. The substitute need not equal war in its momentary power; for what it lacks in power may be made up in continuity of action.

Reconstruction of experience through language

The political groups of which one is a member are Statewide, Nation-wide. One's occupational or religious group is no less widely distributed. Clearly one can never observe his whole group directly; nor in his participation come into contact with more than a tiny fragment of the total-group labors. For width of vision and of contacts, therefore, one needs methods that are not so much limited by space and time relations. Hence, we must note the place of indirect or vicarious observation and participation through reading.

To resume our example, a college student may develop a large degree of college spirit and yet actually see and in the flesh perform but a very small portion of the common action. Kept away from it by other duties or by enforced absence, he may enter into it all through participative imagination as he reads the current happenings in the college paper. During such reading, he is lost to actual time and place, and for the moment dwells in the midst of the group-action. As a shadow-member of the group, he participates in all that is going on. He wishes and wills and hopes and feels and becomes emotionally heated like those actually in the fray — especially if he can also talk to somebody about it, and thus actively and socially stir the inner fires. By such means, his spirit is warmed and shaped, — his group-attitudes, valuations, and sense of solidarity.

Now, as a matter of fact, in a large institution most college students do not actually see or enter into much of the activity. They only hear about it through conversation and reading. In the case of one's national political party, or of the religious denomination to which one belongs, this remoteness of the individual and his dependence upon report is much more pronounced. And still more so is it in the case of the all-embracing national group. The normal mode of participation in the affairs of the very large group involves the doing of but a tiny fragment of the labors of the whole, and of seeing but little more with the eyes of sense. But as one sees and does the little, with his inner vision he sees the whole as he reads, and feels himself a member of the total group and performing a part of its action.

We must carry this thought one step farther. One's participation in the group-activity instead of being one per cent objective and ninety-nine per cent subjective, may, without noticeable change of character, be one hundred per cent subjective. Let one take, for example, a good narrative account of the Persian wars of the Greeks. This reconstructs subjectively the experience of the armies of Miltiades and Leonidas just as clearly as our current press reconstructs for our subjective participation the action of yesterday of our political party, our church, or our own national group. We can enter into the action with the same completeness and *abandon*. Language reconstructs the distant past with the same ease and clearness as the past of but an hour ago; action on the other side of the earth, as easily as that on the next street.

Language is preëminently the organ of social vision. With the eyes of sense one sees but a little way, and sees but fragments of group-action; even within one's own town. But language lifts the curtain upon all the earth. It enables one to see and know and relive all types of *human experience.* If the record is everywhere equally complete, the things are seen without the distortion of visual perspective which makes near things large and far things small. Civic education must, therefore, make large use of reading that is concrete enough to permit vicarious participative experience.

The creation of a large-group consciousness

Now, how do citizens act together in large-group ways? And how can children and youth participate in such action, so as to become fused in consciousness with the large group?

Let us begin with the national group, since the problems are in many respects simpler than in the case of the municipal or other local group. Our national group for some generations has had its separate identity in the always quarrelsome family of nations. For the maintenance of its political existence it has had to hold itself at least reasonably united against foreign aggression. Occasionally it has had to act. At the present moment the Nation is engaged in such a life-and-death struggle. For the promotion of its material welfare, it has had as a national group to compete with other aggressive commercial nations in the markets of the earth. For preventing schism and internal disintegration it has often had to array itself actively against States and specialized groups and to force them to subordinate their special interests to the greater good of the whole. It has had ceaselessly to keep a strong hand upon the activities of powerful special groups, always actively or potentially predatory; and in the nature of the case this must always continue. It has long fought, and is always fighting, at the gateways of our land, with the things that cause disease in man and beast and plant; and this warfare grows in intensity, and can never cease. In regions of flood, aridity, and obstructed navigation, upon dangerous reefs and shores, in the national forests, and otherwhere and in many ways, we are as a national group making war against the adverse forces of Nature. Within recent years our national group is seen to be girding itself for war upon national ignorance, national weakness, national inefficiency of many kinds.

When teachers are asked how to improve the teaching of our national history they frequently say, "Omit or abbreviate the wars." But in the above enumeration, it will be observed that most action can be expressed in terms of *conflict*. Life, whether individual or national, especially the serious part of it, is largely made up of *overcoming obstacles*. Man's serious life is mainly a battle with opposing forces. These may be men or animals, disease or ignorance, winter or famine, or powerful forces of Nature. But fight them he must; and he *lives* mainly in the fight, — so far as his serious moments are concerned. And even his best play is the mock-fight.

To participate actively in the wars of the national group is to act with it when its action is most strenuous and when its solidarity is most conscious. Let youth, therefore, mingle with the group at such times and they will then rapidly and effectively take on a vitalized nationalistic consciousness. For this reason, let youth continue to refight the colonial wars, the Revolutionary War, and the later wars with England, Spain, Mexico, and the Indian tribes. Let the accounts of these fights be so presented that youth can refight them in that spirited, intense, and whole-hearted way that is congenial to its hot blood; and which is necessary for firing the enthusiasms of youth and for indissolubly fusing the individual into conscious and acquiescent membership in the national group. The "man without a country" is the man who has never fought with his group for his group. Since the historical account is to be used primarily as a means of reconstructing the group *experience*, the reading must not be simply an abstract sociological and political analysis of conditions, of causes and effects, etc.; and dull chronological record of happenings. The purpose should be *living;* and *learning through living.* If the group-life of those stirring times is relived in the right way, there will be no dearth of proper learning.

This reconstruction of experience requires that the whole national fight be presented from the point of view of the participants upon one side. When one relives the fight, he has to be on one side or the other. If he is neutral, then he is not reliving the fight. He is an idle bystander. He will not be warmed by vicarious participation. His consciousness will not be effectively nationalized. He will remain a man

without a country. This need of taking the point of view of
the participants on one side or the other is intuitively
recognized by the writers of our textbooks and by teachers
in their discussion. Its purpose must be seen and the method
made conscious, however, because of the demand often
voiced that historical presentation, on even the concrete
levels, be coldly scientific, and look at the actions of all sides
equally and without sympathy. Our apparently contrary
suggestion does not imply any deviation from exact historical truth in the presentation. It is only to recognize the
principle of perspective; and the local and partial nature of
all active experience. The participants on one side in a battle, let us say, may see the whole action truly, — from their
side, — and yet have a different vision, different objectives and emotional experiences from those of their opponents. It is true, in entering sympathetically into the experiences of one side and not that of both at the same
time, the experience is partial. But no method has yet
been found of entering into the experiences of both sides
at once.

As a matter of fact, if the reconstruction of the actual
experience of the participants in the action is to be vera-
cious, then it must be partial. The incomplete vision distorted by perspective, the sympathies for the one side and
the antipathies for the other were just as much realities of
the period as the objective action. Their revelation must be
as adequate in the reconstructed experience or it will not
accurately reproduce the original conditions.

The preventive of exaggerated and intolerant nationalism
which might result from a disproportionate amount of
sympathetic experience upon the one side is not at bottom
to look with cold, impersonal scientific eye upon the nations;
but rather at different times to relive the experiences as
presented from *both points of view*. That is to say, let stu-

dents relive the experiences of the Revolutionary War as accurately presented from the British point of view; imaginatively traveling and associating with the British armies and unconsciously taking on its valuations and aspirations and seeing everything from its side. This was just as much a part of the actual experience of the times. Let the student read the history of the Mexican War as a shadow-member of the army of Santa Ana, and thus see the war through Mexican eyes. This is just as true a view of it as the one from the American side.

Not only can a sound nationalism be developed experientially, but also the corrective to exaggeration can be experientially developed. And in the two processes the experiential foundation is laid for a tolerant social consciousness that is wider than the national; and which *can* look equally and impersonally upon all sides.

Let the program of conflict, however, be no narrow one of military wars alone. Let there be far fuller experience on the part of youth in the Nation's economic struggle for the world's markets. This is going on at the present time. It has been going on these hundred years or more. Let youth read a spirited history of our American merchant marine; of the contest we have made in the markets of South America, China, Russia, Australia, the Philippines, etc.; and of our struggle to keep our home markets for our home producers as against foreign competition. Let the present aspects of this economic struggle be made to stand out clear by giving full space to the last decade or two. Naturally the student's participative experience in this economic struggle must come later in the course than the military struggles.

The corrective to vision so as to prevent distorted social perspective is to read also vivid accounts of British commerce from their point of view; of French commerce from their angle of vision; of Japanese commerce, etc.

A still larger program of experience should relate to the large-group conflict involved in its control of powerful internal interests: railroad corporations, manufacturing, mining, and commercial organizations, financial classes, capitalist and labor groups, political spoilsmen, etc. Students, perhaps on the high-school level, need to read, for example, the history of railroad regulation. This should reveal the self-seeking character in the past of those powerful organizations. It should present an extended story of the concrete ways in which they have tried, often successfully, to over-reach the public; and of the fight made by the public by way of resisting such powerful predatory attacks. Like all the rest, this, too, should be no dull sociological chronology and analysis, but a living reconstruction of spirited group-conflict. And it needs to be seen with the perspective of the large-group point of view. The purpose being the development of the wider community consciousness as opposed to that of the specialized group, this wider consciousness that made the fight originally must be reconstructed and reëxperienced in the youthful fighter. He will be thereby shaped for that continuing general community consciousness that must continue the fight in whatever form it may nowadays arise. Having thus fought the railroads in the past, he thus takes on the racial experience, so to speak, in the community handling of them.

"But the railroads perform indispensable services; and they have rights proportioned to those services," one says. "Therefore these matters should not be seen from just one side." This is all very true. And in chapter X we presented a part of the plan of training men to do full justice; namely, reading a sympathetic presentation of the history of railroad development and labors written from their point of view. Each type of account is then a corrective for the special perspective of the other. In either case the student is called upon to take sides. But not to take a side is not to enter the action; and therefore not to have experience — neither large-group nor small-group. To attain the large-group attitudes and valuations and understanding, he must fight the large-group battle, from its point of view; and strenuously. But to correct the distortion of perspective, he must at another time, in this vicarious way, also fight the small-group battle against the large-group; and with the same vigor and single-mindedness. The two sides are to be known, not by sitting on the fence and disinterestedly observing both, but by plunging in, first on one side and then on the other, and learning each side by *experiencing* it.

The problem is closely analogous to that of visual perspective. As one looks out on the landscape his image is a distortion. He sees near things large and clear and solid; and far things small and dim and unreal. The corrective is change of position. Let him go to the far things and renew his observations. He sees the things reversed. Observing from both points of view he arrives at true valuations as to all the things. An omniscient eye might see all things truly and without distortion from a single point of view. But human eyes cannot. Man's view is always partial view, to be corrected by change in the position from which he makes observation. We do not say a painting is untrue because it involves the visual illusion of perspective. Quite the reverse, it is untrue when it neglects perspective.

In arguing that the partiality of actual experience shall exist in reconstructed educational experience, the ends in view are justice and fairness and the balanced judgment. We are to recognize that we are dealing with two forms of bias, both inherently necessary, the maleficent results of which are to be avoided by developing both in the same minds in ways that permit each to correct the other. The experience also lays the foundation of concreteness needed for the problem-solving and scientific generalizations that involve seeing all sides clearly and impartially. Only those who have experienced all sides are provided with the materials necessary for sound generalizations. This alone can bring them into vital contacts with essential realities without which problem-solving is impossible and generalizations but empty verbalities. It gives them the substance and materials of thought before they are called upon to think.

Finally, there is another inspiring type of national conflict, namely, the ceaseless and ever-strenuous warfare with the hostile or reluctant forces of Nature. This is a battle that takes place mainly through the specialized activities of occupational groups. But the national story can be written so as to show these specialized groups as arms of the large group. Many things also have been undertaken in a national way: lighthouse and life-saving service, national forest service, the weather bureau, quarantine and health service, the flood control, river navigation, the fight upon noxious insects, etc. Let students read the full story of these important national undertakings, and they are further experienced in taking the national point of view. And the greater the width and intensity of this experience, the more intense becomes their national-group consciousness.

Large-group municipal consciousness

In one's city, for example, the good citizen is one who habitually looks to the general municipal good. He has a municipal consciousness, so to speak, instead of a special partisan one.

Now, education must use the same general formula for developing this type of mind. Participative experience must be the basis of it all. Youth must *act* as a member of the large municipal group. As he sees its ends from the large-group point of view, and helps in the fight against the opposing forces, he takes on the large-group consciousness and understanding.

Our first question must naturally relate to the things that a well-trained adult generation is supposed to be doing in its municipal civic capacity. Youth's best civic education then must come from *participation along with adults* in these activities. In the following unclassified list we have presented a few of the matters for which the entire body of citizens, old and young, adult and adolescent, are responsible: —

1. Keeping the city clean.
2. Making the city sanitary.
3. Making the city beautiful.
4. Care of the city's trees, shrubbery, and grass-plots.
5. Preventing the smoke evil.
6. Prevention of flies and mosquitoes.
7. Destruction of tree- and plant-destroying insects.
8. Care of insect-destroying birds.
9. Disposal of sewage, ashes, rubbish, etc.
10. Providing a clean and pure water-supply.
11. Providing suitable paving for all streets and alleys.
12. Cleaning and lighting all streets and alleys.
13. Providing for safe and rapid transportation about the city.
14. Regulating street traffic.
15. Providing play-opportunities for the children.
16. Providing adult recreational facilities.
17. Providing and maintaining a school plant.
18. Educating the children.
19. Providing for a sanitary milk-supply.
20. Seeing that all food production and distribution is sanitary.
21. Protecting the city from fire.
22. Protecting life and property.
23. Care of the incapacitated.
24. Regulation for the public weal of all public utility corporations, markets, factories, stores, trades, amusements agencies, etc.
25. Getting these and all other like coöperative activities done at a proper cost.

26. Securing from each a proper character of service.
27. Currently inspecting the conditions of each type of service.
28. Currently inspecting the results obtained.
29. Currently seeing that justice is done each specialized group: that it is supplied with all its needs, — not more and not less.
30. Current inspection of municipal or general community needs — so as to keep service always adjusted to actual needs.

The list is not exhaustive. It intends only to present types of coöperative tasks that the civic community is, or ought to be, currently performing. Some of the tasks are performed by all citizens. Some are delegated to specialized individuals and groups, the citizen's current duty being to supervise the labors; to make and to keep them effective. In some of the cases the citizen performs part, and he delegates part.

But whether he directly performs the functions or delegates them, he has his community inspectorial function to perform. It must be confessed that the technique of the citizen's civic functions has not yet been well developed. Citizens are actually doing all of the things mentioned; but often doing them badly, because they have never been taught or practiced in better ways. Much we hear nowadays concerning the technical inefficiency of workmen; but the technical inefficiency of the citizen in the performance of his civic functions is immeasurably greater. The workman knows what he is after, and has a good deal of technical knowledge as to what to do, even though but rule-of-thumb. But as a citizen, his ideas are very vague as to what he is after; and technical knowledge as to what constitutes efficient civic service and as to methods of holding his fellow citizens and their agents responsible for efficient performance is very small indeed.

Youth and adulthood need to act together in the performance of these functions — for the secure training of youth. But the problem is greatly complicated for educa-

tion by the fact that adulthood is almost as much in need
of training as youth itself. Part-time activity is a super-
lative training device in the occupational world; we need an
exactly analogous training method, in the larger civic field.
But when we look about to find men acting together consciously in performing their coöperative activities effectively
in ways in which youth may be permitted to mingle, except
for an occasional voting to-day, it is difficult to locate anything but haphazard and miscellany. Men seem to have
got the impression, and women, too, that the primitive art
of voting unintelligently is the major function of the citizen.
Naturally it is not advisable to organize part-time activity
in voting unintelligently.

The National Education Association Committee on the
Teaching of Community Civics expresses clearly the need
of participative or part-time civic activity on the part of
youth. The committee writes: —

> The pupil as a young citizen is a real factor in community af-
> fairs. His coöperation in many phases of community life is quite
> as important as that of the adult. He may help in forming public
> opinion, not only among his mates, but in the home and in the
> community at large.
> Therefore it is a task of the teacher to cultivate in the pupil a
> sense of his responsibility, present as well as future.
> If a citizen has an interest in civic matters and a sense of his
> personal responsibility, he will want to act.
> Therefore the teacher must help the pupil to express his con-
> victions in word and deed. He must be given an opportunity, as
> far as possible, to *live* his civics both in the school and in the com-
> munity outside.

It will be necessary for school people among others to
take the lead in developing the technique and the practice
of civic performance in our cities and other local communities. Just as it has been our educational institutions that
have taken the lead in improving both the theory and the

practice of agriculture and of many other occupations, so
must they also point, and in practice show, the way to civic
effectiveness. It is needed for the education of all the people, adolescent and adult.

To begin with, citizens of a given city must know what
they need. Do they need street paving that is twenty, forty,
or sixty feet wide? Or do they need one width in one portion
of the city and another width in another portion? And if
so, what widths, and where? Do they need one thousand
candle-power to the mile of street-lighting? or five thousand?
or twenty thousand? Should the city water system supply a
daily twenty-five gallons per capita? Or should it be one
hundred gallons, or three hundred gallons? In the play-
grounds furnished their children, should there be twenty
square feet per child, or fifty, or one hundred? In the city
health service, do they need twenty-five cents' worth each
year *per capita*, or a dollar's worth, or five dollars' worth?
In the maintenance of the fire department or the police
department, do they need the services of one man for each
five hundred people? or one for each one thousand, two
thousand, or five thousand people? If a large number is
needed, what are the reasons? If a small number, why is
the city so fortunate? Does the city need one high-school
teacher for each fifteen pupils, or each twenty-five, or each
thirty-five? How many food inspectors does the city need
per thousand places that require inspection? How many
school medical examiners and school nurses per thousand
pupils? For an effective performance of civic inspectorial
functions how many civic centers are needed for each ten
thousand population, and how many hours of regularly
scheduled community meetings are desirable? In the matter of public hospital facilities, does the city need one bed
per five hundred population? Or should it be one for each
thousand, or twenty-five hundred? A city cannot perform

any civic function effectively and economically until it knows what it needs, — and *in definite terms.*

Is it possible to find out what people need in these and all the other things? It is easily possible to arrive at approximations that can serve until more accurate standards are available. Take the matter of the water-supply. The accompanying table shows the number of gallons *per capita* used daily in a number of large cities in 1912.

Per capita daily use of water in certain cities of Europe and America, 1912

	No gallons
Buffalo	310
Chicago	225
Pittsburgh	218
Philadelphia	208
Boston	130
Baltimore	115
St. Louis	107
Cleveland	102
New York	100
Paris	63
Hamburg	42
London	40
Liverpool	38
Amsterdam	35
Copenhagen	27
Dresden	25
Berlin	20

There is nothing for beginning this type of study that is quite comparable in value to an array of *facts*. The table does not show conclusively just the amount of water-supply needed. But it gives one a few ideas to start with. All of these cities are reasonably clean and sanitary — on the basis of 1912 standards. But it will be noticed that New York does as well on a hundred gallons *per capita* as Philadelphia on two hundred, or Buffalo on three hundred. When one notes that New York's figures are corroborated by those of other large cities like Cleveland and St. Louis, it appears at least probable that a hundred gallons *per capita* is enough to meet human needs in large American cities, and that there was large waste in the four cities at the top of the list.

After a city has determined the amounts of things needed, the next question for the learning citizen, adult or adolescent, is: *What price should be paid?*

To take a specific case from another field, What price per thousand cubic feet should be paid for illuminating and fuel gas in our cities? The following table presents one type of facts needed: —

Price to families of gas per 1000 cubic feet, 1912

Jacksonville	$1.25
Charleston, South Carolina	1.20
Reading	1.10
Harrisburgh	1.10
Philadelphia	1.00
Omaha	1.00
Buffalo	1.00
Rochester	.95
Richmond	.90
Washington	.85
Pittsburgh	.85
New York	.80
Chicago	.80
Boston	.80
Cleveland	.75
Duluth	.75

Toledo.. .70
St. Louis..................................... .60
Milwaukee.................................... .60
Grand Rapids................................. .50
Detroit....................................... .50

A civic group, juvenile or adult, with such a table before them, will probably conclude that there is something that needs looking into. Conditions in different cities are different, and costs should be correspondingly different; but it is highly improbable that conditions demand such variety of prices as here exhibited. If Detroit is properly supplied, and the price just, at fifty cents, why must Buffalo pay twice as much? If sixty cents is correct for a city somewhat remote from the coal-supply like Milwaukee, why must a city in the coal region like Reading pay almost twice as much?

With such a table as a starting-point, those studying the problem in each city will get such facts as the following for their own city, and for each of the other cities that are used for comparison: —

1. The amount of investment in the plant per unit of gas delivered.
2. Interest, dividends, and taxes, paid per unit of output.
3. Cost of maintenance of the plant per unit of output.
4. Cost of operation per unit.
5. Percentage of cost returned from the by-products.
6. Price made to the large consumers.
7. Price made to the small consumers.

Some inkling can now be had of our meaning when we said that educational people need to lead in the performance of civic functions. In a representative democracy like ours the major function of the people as citizens is the performance of the inspectorial function. Most of their coöperative labors they will delegate to specialized employees.

But they can never delegate to anybody the function of examining the labors thus performed for them and pronouncing final judgment as to whether satisfactory. This they must do for themselves. But generally they have not the facts. They do not know where or how to get them. And not knowing the need of *facts* as the basis of all government, they have not even asked for them; and do not yet greatly appreciate their values, even when set before them. One never knows the value of a thing till he has tried it.

Citizens need to have such arrays of facts set before them in civic meetings, in bulletins, and in the public press. Their agents who are responsible for the labors need thus to render accounts of their stewardship. However presented the matters need to be taken up in civic meetings for discussion, comparison, explanation, justification, etc. Out of such discussion, clarified and enlightened public opinion grows; and this it is that lies at the basis of all effective performance of the inspectorial function.

Adults at present are not much more capable of discussing many of these matters than the young people in grammar grades and high school. They have less leisure for the purpose. And they lack the trained and paid intellectual and social leadership that is supplied the young people in their teachers. But adults are just as much in need of system, organization, and leadership for their thinking. Until society has evolved a profession of inspectorial leadership, — now in the making, as revealed in our bureaus of municipal research, etc., — this task falls naturally to the two professions of education and journalism. And in large part at least, perhaps chiefly, it must always remain with them.

Now, in ways which we shall explain more fully as we proceed, it is possible for teachers to interest the young people in these civic problems; to use them as fact-gatherers and fact-organizers for the total community; and to have them present the facts in the community meetings made up of both adults and young people. These students can search the reports of their own and other cities and draw up the tables of comparative and other facts. They can prepare charts, maps, diagrams, exhibits, etc., that will reveal a wide range of well-organized facts for the topic under discussion. They can make systematic surveys of their own town by way of bringing a wealth of concrete facts to the discussion. They can make surveys of sanitary conditions, street-cleaning, street-paving, garbage disposal, breeding-places of flies, the city's trees, billboards, smoke, fire protection, distribution of police over the city, distribution of public recreational opportunities, the milk-supply, water-supply, etc.

In connection with such surveys no finer practical task can be devised than the making of survey maps — each one carrying its information and its lesson to the public-spirited citizen. They can make health maps, recreation maps, street-paving maps, street-cleaning maps, street-lighting maps, crime maps, tree maps, maps showing breeding-places of flies and mosquitoes, etc. Along with the map-making they can make exhibits, models, diagrams, pictures, statistical charts, etc.

They can do it all for the practical purpose of rightly forming and influencing public opinion on the basis of objective evidence. This is the most fundamental and practical civic task involved in the citizen's major function of inspectorial supervision. In doing this the young people are engaged in civic part-time work. They are dealing with actual things. The motivation is not make-believe. It is that of real life. They are bearing responsibility for actual labors that they can see need to be performed. They are working in conjunction with adults, under their leadership and direction. It is real work. It is not play-civics of the mock-court, mock-congress type. The motives are the same as those that control adults — in the fact-gathering, the fact-presentation, and in the judgments arrived at.

But the facts are inaccessible? Often they are; specialized groups like to keep them hidden because they know the bludgeoning power of facts when applied to the inspectorial supervision of themselves. But at the present time there are huge quantities of accessible facts that are not being utilized. But they lack significance, we are then told, unless we have similar facts from other cities for tables of comparison. And they say that while school people may get the facts relative to their own city, they cannot secure them from other cities. The objection is but the voice of inertia. Let a wide-awake body of teachers in each of fifty cities gather pertinent facts for their own city. Let them send these facts to each of the other forty-nine cities. Then all will have the facts for the fifty cities. Most of the actual work of collecting the facts can be performed by the students themselves. They can do the sending, the receiving, and draw up the comparative tables. Better educational experience for them cannot be devised. It is a continuing task to be done year after year.

Civic training in the schools can be healthy and virile only as it involves the things that are being striven for by the community. It must be an organic part of the total civic striving of the community. In proportion as the school isolates itself from the community and finds mere textbook matters of study that are in no wise related to the conditions within the city, the school work drifts from its proper moorings and loses its educational effectiveness.

In addition to the ways mentioned, another method of keeping the school civic work grounded in reality is to make the schools, as fully as possible, the civic forums of the city — especially the high school. For example, when the topic of street-paving is being considered in the high-school civics class, the chairman of the committee of the city council which has charge of this particular work, the commissioner of streets, or the chief of the bureau of public works, should be invited to discuss the situation before the high school. When the subject of taxes is taken up, the chairman of the finance committee of the city council, the tax collector, or the chairman of the finance committee of the school board, should be invited to discuss the problems of taxation. When the topic is community sanitation, then it is the board of health and its inspectors who have an opportunity of disseminating the necessary sanitary information. Nearly all civic functions are delegated. The man to whom any function is delegated is the one who should feel responsible for keeping the public enlightened as to his work. It is necessary for his own effectiveness, and for the success of his labors in the community.

This plan is incomplete if the report is to be made only to the high-school students. The information that these men have should be for the whole community. Yet here within the school we have segregated only the children and youth of the community. Those to whom the information should primarily be given, namely, the adult leaders of the community, are not present. The officials are reporting, not to the men who hold them responsible, but only to the children; and in a comparatively artificial situation. They cannot talk to the youth of the city in normal fashion if they are talking only to youth in isolation. They can talk normally only as they are addressing the adult leaders of the city, their peers, those to whom they owe their responsibility. The children can then hear and learn in normal fashion. Youth must learn in large measure, not from being addressed directly, but from listening to adulthood talking to adulthood. It is for youth one of the normal modes of participation in adult affairs.

It may be objected that youth has a right to its own life at this age, and ought not to be caught up in the wheels of serious adult responsibilities; that it has a right to a long season of rosy-hued irresponsibility before being condemned to these things that belong to the somber gray of the adult world. In reply, let us say that it is in mingling in the full life of the world as made up of childhood, youth, maturity, and old age, in which youth finds its fullest and best life. They have not only the right, but the duty, of play of an abundant and varied character. This we emphasize fully in other portions of our discussion. But youthful participation in adult activities from infancy onward is really one of the most satisfying and most beneficent forms of play. They do not give up life in having something in it besides the purposeless. Rather do they find it.

Other concrete civic activities

The chief part-time civic work of youth will be participation in inspectorial activities; because this is also the adult's major civic activity. But there are certain other community activities not yet placed entirely in specialized hands. And of those so specialized, there are certain ones in which youthful participation is possible.

Children can aid in tree-planting and in tree-care — an extension of the Arbor-Day spirit to three hundred and sixty-five days in the year. They can study intensively the kinds of trees and shrubbery best suited to the city's needs and conditions in its various portions — modes of securing them, of planting them, and of protecting them from drought, insects, and other enemies. They can be organized to carry out the various steps of the labor in both the planting and the year-long protection.

"Clean-up week," like Arbor Day, is being institutionalized for the training of children. While this annual spring renovation is an excellent civic opportunity and should be vigorously carried on, even better training comes from year-long interest and attention to the need, by way of preventing a goodly portion of the accumulated rubbish.

As conditions change, as work becomes specialized, and as groups grow large, this "community chore-service" is coming to take the place of a portion, at least, of the family chore-service performed by children in past generations. In our professional literature nowadays we read of a considerable variety of possible community activities: —

1. City beautification.
2. Care and protection of birds.
3. Anti-fly campaigns.
4. Anti-mosquito campaigns.
5. The fight on weeds.
6. Cleaning up vacant lots.
7. Patrolling railroad and street-car crossings at the hours when kindergarten and primary children are going to and from school.
8. Constructing community property: ice-boxes for poor-relief; tables, cabinets, book-cases, work-benches, desks, stage scenery, printed helps, textbooks, etc., for the school; bird-houses for parks and streets; rubbish-receptacles for streets; playground equipment and apparatus for school and park systems; etc.
9. Making minor repairs on public property.
10. Fighting fires in villages where there is no specialized fire department.
11. Raising and delivering flowers to the sick and the aged.
12. Looking after the sanitary aspects of schoolrooms, recreative places, etc.
13. Decoration of school-buildings.
14. The community labors of Boy Scouts, Camp-Fire Girls, Juvenile Civic Leagues, etc.
15. Clearing the snow from sidewalks and paths; and sprinkling sand or ashes on icy sidewalks.

By way of showing the practical man's attitude toward

this problem we quote the following words from an editorial in one of our metropolitan newspapers, entitled "Citizenship and the Schools ": —

The public school has been less effective than it might and should have been. It has laid most of its emphasis on information, little or none on will and moral relations. In short, the public school needs drastic modernization to make it a practical and efficient instrument of at least rudimentary good citizenship. . . . It must take upon its broad shoulders a large burden. *It must make itself rather a civic gymnasium, a social drill-yard for soldiers of peace who march forward.*

These civic labors of youth, like the inspectorial ones previously mentioned, must not be things detached and isolated from the life of the general community. The children must see and feel their labors to be but a delegated part of a serious community responsibility of which the adults are carrying the major portion of the load. Otherwise their efforts will be but irresponsible make-believe; and soon degenerate or disappear. If the civic responsibilities are such that they are conceived to rest only upon children, then they rest upon nobody; since they are not real community responsibilities.

But this is only local participation by way of developing municipal-mindedness. Can the plan be extended for training purposes to practical state and national service? Under present conditions of war it is being done: both by those students who have entered active military, naval, aerial, Red Cross, or other service; and by those at home who are striving along with adults to augment production and to facilitate just and economical distribution and consumption The consciousness of solidarity and the spirit of service thereby engendered is one our Nation cannot afford to lose in time of peace. It can be kept, however, only if there is actual and genuine and necessary service to be rendered.

Make-believe service will not accomplish the purposes. The largest field of active peace-time service is that of the specialized occupations. As industries grow, this service tends more and more to be national. A major social problem is not to make it service, — it is already that, — but to make it *seen as service*. The educational problem here is largely so to train occupationally that the workers can realize the social implications and relations of their labors; so that they will see their peace-service to the nation on a plane no less high than their war-service to the same nation.

Professor James was of the opinion that this should be prepared for by some years of general occupational service He writes:[1] —

If now — and this is my idea — there were, instead of military conscription, a conscription of the whole youthful population to form for a certain number of years a part of the army enlisted against Nature, injustice would tend to be evened up, and numerous benefits to the commonwealth would follow. The military ideals of hardihood and discipline would be wrought into the growing fiber of the people; no one would remain blind, as the luxurious classes now are blind, to man's real relations to the globe he lives on, and to the *permanently solid and hard foundations of his higher life*. To coal- and iron-mines, to freight-trains, to fishing-fleets in December, to dish-washing, clothes-washing, and window-washing, to road-building and tunnel-making, to foundries and stoke-holes, and to the frames of sky-scrapers, would our gilded youths be drafted off, according to their choice, to get the childishness knocked out of them, and to come back into society with healthier sympathies and soberer ideas. They would have paid their blood-tax, done their part in the immemorial human warfare against Nature; they would tread the earth more proudly; the women would value them more highly; they would be better fathers and teachers of the following generation.

Such a conscription, with the state of public opinion that would have required it, and the moral fruits it would bear, would pre-

---

[1] "The Moral Equivalent of War." By William James. In *McClure's*, August, 1910.

serve in the midst of a pacific civilization the manly virtues which
the military party is so afraid of seeing disappear in peace. We
should get toughness without callousness, authority with as little
cruelty as possible, and painful work done cheerily because the
duty is temporary. . . . I spoke of the "moral equivalent" of war.
So far, war has been the only force that can discipline a whole
community, and, until an equivalent discipline is organized, I
believe that war must have its way. But I have no serious doubt
that the ordinary prides and shames of social man, once developed
to a certain intensity, are capable of organizing such a moral equivalent as I have sketched, or some other just as effective for preserving manliness of type. Though an infinitely remote Utopia
just now, in the end it is but a question of time, of skillful propa-
gandism and of opinion-making men seizing historic opportunities.

Whether any of the features of this proposal are practicable or not, it reveals a real educational problem of large
proportions and complexity. Upon our profession rests
responsibility for proposing and effecting a practicable
solution.

The international situation

Thus far we have discussed local and national civic problems. In the knitting-up of the world's social fabric politically, the national group is practically the ultimate group.
In the world of productive industry, however, whether
agriculture, manufacture, mining, or other, it is clear that
the peoples of the world are interdependent; that on the
side of production we are really a world-community, each
region producing for all. When this is the case, naturally
in the distribution and consumption of commodities we are
a world-community. Whatever the political situation may
be, it is clear that we have already largely achieved economic
cosmopolitanism. On the side of art also we are a world-
community; and also in the fields of literature, and science,
and technology, and invention, etc.

But in our social-group or political consciousness, we have — until the last few years — scarcely even looked beyond the boundaries of nationalism. To look upon other peoples as members of a world-family, to look with friendly eye upon other nations as equal neighbors having rights similar to and equal to our own, even to contemplate common action with such neighbors in the coöperative promotion of world-welfare, — such attitudes we had felt to border dangerously upon mild treason to our country. Politically we have been essentially parochial-minded.

The present World-War is revealing the interdependencies of peoples. We now see that no nation can live to itself. We are coming to realize that just as the States of our Union form one national family, each of which is necessary to the highest welfare of all, so the various countries of the world are members of a planetary family and each necessary to the highest welfare of the others. We see that nations have rights equal to our own; that nations have duties also to the others that are proportioned to their rights. It has been demonstrated that unbridled nationalism is a peril to the world. In our previous discussion we have tried to show the inevitability of the ethics of aggression as a component part of the nationalistic consciousness. In proportion as nationalism is strong, the dual standard of social conduct arises. In such case the nation sees its own rights large and sees its duties small. In mind and heart, in ambition and in action, such a nation becomes parasitic upon the rest. When not held in check by a cosmopolitan consciousness, such a nation, if it feels strong enough, goes ruthlessly abroad to rob and plunder the others. Of this we have sufficient practical demonstration. In the present World-War we are but reaping the natural and inevitable fruits of exaggerated nationalism.

We are not here condemning nationalism. We have already said that the large-group consciousness exists upon different levels. A wide and generous municipal consciousness is the cure for the evils that result from the petty consciousness of self-interested small-groups within the city. A county or congressional district or state consciousness that looks to the welfare of the total group specified is that which for that region eliminates the parasitism and other evils resulting from the small-group consciousness. Rising to the next level, it is then a broad, generous, and vitalized national consciousness which alone can provide a spirit of mutual service on the part of all of the constituent portions of the nation. Within the nation this national consciousness is in all respects most beneficent. Without it the nation disintegrates into internal warring and parasitic groups, bringing all the evils of social chaos in their train. Because of its intra-national aspect, we must emphasize the fullest practicable development of the national consciousness.

In insisting that we also develop an international consciousness we are but arriving at the next and inevitable logical step of the same argument. The national consciousness at the present time needs to be huge in order to take care of the difficult intra-national problems; but if it is not tempered by a large-group consciousness that takes in all of the rest of the world, the extra-national attitudes thereby developed threaten the rest of the nations; and in reaction, the nation itself. The cosmopolitan consciousness alone can bring about that wise coöperation of the various nations of the earth for the more adequate promotion of the general world welfare. Just as nationalism will temper the spirit of strife that tends to arise within the nation, so will internationalism temper the analogous spirit of strife that tends to arise among the members of the planetary group.

We are not here referring to an international political organization. That has not yet come into being. If it ever arrives, it will *grow* out of a widely diffused cosmopolitan consciousness. This is prerequisite to, and must precede, any organization. Our educational problem relates only to the development of this cosmopolitan consciousness. The state papers of our President have recently breathed the spirit of this high consciousness which is rapidly transfusing the minds of all peoples.

Turning now to the educational problem, How are we to develop this cosmopolitan consciousness? We have already referred to the place of action, observation, participation with a group, as a mode of developing an understanding of that group and sympathies with its purposes and its labors. We referred to the large place of reading for the sake of vicarious action in the case of the large groups. What is true of reading in the case of the nationalistic spirit is even more true of reading in the development of the cosmopolitan spirit. There is needed for the world as a whole, and of the separate nations that make it up, readings that will permit children and youth sympathetically to enter into the actions of men in the various regions of the earth. Let one in his reading live imaginatively with a nation for a sufficient length of time and he will come to feel himself one with it, in much the same way as though he dwelt among them for a time.

The readings for the purpose will be history, biography, travels, geography, and literature. With any of these the primary aim will be the reconstruction of life within the various lands; so that the reader can relive it. In proportion as it is vivid and stirring so that the reader can become warmed, can lose himself to actual time and place, can become enveloped in the action of which he reads, it will be effective for the purpose.

The ends in view demand catholicity in the choice of the readings. Schools need to gather of each type readings that reveal all important present-day nations and peoples; Canada, America, Mexico, Central America, West Indies, Brazil, Argentina, Chile, Australia, New Zealand, Japan, China, India, Turkey, Russia, the Balkans, the Central Empires, Italy, Switzerland, Spain, France, Belgium, Netherlands, Scandinavia, England, Ireland, Scotland, North Africa, Egypt, Central Africa, and South Africa; at least these. This is to choose the history of grammar grades and high schools on a basis that has not hitherto been employed; and the literature; and the biography. This basis has been employed, however, in the case of geography which actually does reveal in some degree all of the nations of the earth. The principle that is applicable to geography appears to be equally applicable to history and literature.

Another type of social reading belongs, then, on the later levels of education. After developing understanding and sympathetic attitudes toward the various individual nations, students are prepared to read, not the particular histories of nations, but world-history: that which looks in a unitary way to the entire world-situation. Thus the student will read the history of world-commerce; history of world-industry; history of transportation; history of agriculture; history of political institutions; history of finance; sanitation; recreational activities; municipal government; etc. In each case the history of the last decade or two should probably be as voluminous as that of all of the previous centuries combined. This will then introduce all of the needed geographical and economic elements. Through problem-solving, discussions, etc., students can be brought to an understanding of the general principles involved.

The thing demanded is not a new program. It is rather a definition of social purposes on the basis of which present programs can be rectified and further developed. As a matter of fact, in our supplementary readings, especially in the elementary school, we are tending more and more to

give width of world-understanding both historical and
geographical. High schools and colleges of liberal arts have
been more enmeshed in tradition, and in the task of training
specialists. On the levels, therefore, where most of this
training should be accomplished, it has scarcely been begun.
But in their recent inclusions of industrial history, commercial history, industrial and commercial geography, history
of civilization, a fuller emphasis upon modern problems, etc.,
we discern the ferment at work upon these levels also.

"The program is impossibly large," it is objected. "An
impossible task cannot be the right solution." The objection
shows the need of referring to the methods to be employed.
It will be noted we have nowhere said that these histories
are to be *learned*. We have only said that students need
experiences of certain kinds; and that these experiences are
to be had in part by reading vivid historical accounts. The
history of a nation is to be read rapidly. This is necessary
for warming the personality and making one for the time a
member of the group. If a four-hundred-page book is not
devoured in ten or fifteen days the experience is likely to be
anæmic and relatively ineffective. If the experience is vivid
and stirring, it will leave its normal residues in memory.

It must be kept in mind in considering methods that
knowledge is not the most fundamental thing aimed at; but
rather social attitudes and valuations. For these, it is living
experience, not memorizing experience, that is the all-
important thing. And even in the matter of knowledge it is
not a remembrance of specific facts that is desired; but
rather a knowledge of general social principles. Let the
reading experience be of the type suggested, and the proper
materials are provided for problem-solving and generalization. Right accomplishment of these latter requires not
merely batches of pale facts, but all the emotionalized
attitudes and valuations that can arise only out of emotionalized experience.

CHAPTER XIII

MORAL AND RELIGIOUS EDUCATION

MORAL education has always been and must always be looked upon as fundamental in the training of youth. In our schools we have attempted it through direct and indirect methods; in our churches through direct teaching, persuasion, and the fear-motive. It is probable that most actual training has been accomplished within the Great School of practical social action and reaction.

Those who live as members of the small social group, and from year's end to year's end breathe its social atmosphere; naturally and inevitably take on its attitudes, valuations, and dual standard of ethics. Direct ethical instruction by school or church seems relatively ineffectual in the face of these powerful experiential influences. On the other hand, those who grow up in vital contact, direct and indirect, with the large social group, and who breathe its humanizing atmosphere, naturally and inevitably take on the large-group attitudes, valuations, and tendencies to social reaction. In such case, church and school may well reinforce the process by giving supplementary training. Their efforts are likely to be efficacious, however, not in proportion to their direct teaching or persuasion, but rather in proportion as they are actually able to provide the conditions of large-group living experience.

A frequent conception of moral training is well expressed in the report of the National Council Committee on Moral Education: —

If we would have strong and beautiful characters in adult life, certain elemental virtues must be inculcated in childhood and youth. These the teachers should have as definitely in mind as they do the nouns and verbs in grammar or fractions in arithmetic. They must know, not only what virtues they would implant, but how they would develop them. Among these elemental virtues we would include those which are generally accepted as forming the very basis of character, such as obedience, kindness, honor, truthfulness, cleanliness, cheerfulness, honesty, respect for self and for others, helpfulness, industry, economy, power of initiative, justice, usefulness, patriotism, courage, self-control, prudence, benevolence, system, neatness, politeness, fortitude, heroism, perseverance, sympathy, consecration to duty, unselfishness, comradeship, patience, temperance, hopefulness, determination, and fidelity. Pupils should not only have some idea of the meaning of these virtues, but they should be trained in the practice of them until they become fixed habits.

According to this widespread conception, the task is to give information concerning the abstract virtues and to drill the pupils in action that involves them. They are assumed always to be virtues. This, however, is far from being the case. Take, for example, perseverance. This may characterize the conduct of a statesman, burglar, mechanic, farmer, housewife, political grafter, assassin, or anybody else engaged in any kind of action good or bad. Clearly this abstract aspect of human action is not a virtue in itself. Quite true, where it is exercised in right directions it produces increased human good and is then an aspect of virtuous conduct. It is equally true, however, that where it is exercised in wrong directions it may produce the most disastrous human results; and is then an aspect of vicious conduct. Obviously the virtue or the vice is not in the perseverance itself.

It is urged that while the perseverance itself is always a virtue, it may be a virtue of either good or bad conduct. This is but a verbal quibble. Perseverance may be a *characteristic* of either good or bad conduct. But its characterizing bad conduct does not make the latter good; it only makes it worse. And what increases evil is evil at the time.

If, now, we look at obedience, courage, industry, loyalty, and most of the others, we can see that they may be characteristics of conduct within any kind of social group. They are sometimes characteristics of virtuous conduct; and sometimes of vicious.

Obviously these so-called "virtues" are not the moral ultimates. They are but aspects of human conduct which must be judged good or bad on quite other standards. Good moral conduct is that which increases the total sum of human welfare. The more efficacious it is in producing beneficent results, the higher is the type of morality. It springs from an intelligence that discerns equally the things which promote human welfare and the things that are injurious. It is rooted in large-group sympathies, love of human-kind, large-group vision, attitudes, valuations, and tendencies to behavior. Whatever will produce and intensify large-group consciousness and expand social intelligence will develop high moral character.

Bad moral conduct is that which increases the total sum of human woe. One of its basic conditions is an ignorance of the things required for human welfare. A second is small-group consciousness. Members of small groups hold to the dual standard of conduct. Virtuous action for them is that which promotes welfare of their little group through (1) the exercise of the social virtues toward each other, and (2) the exercise of the anti-social virtues toward society in general. Since such action tends usually to be parasitic rather than efficiently productive, they force others not only to carry their own share of the total load, but also the share that should be properly borne by the parasitic group. Their action results in social injury in the degree in which they are actually parasitic; and in the degree in which they employ anti-social action in effecting their parasitism. The problem of education is to develop within them the large-group consciousness, valuations, and sympathies; and a clear intellectual appreciation of the forces and influences that are to be controlled in the interests of all. The problem of moral education is not to develop within them the various virtues of industry, obedience, courage, loyalty, etc. These exist within those possessing small-group consciousness as abundantly as in those having the large-group consciousness. Simply they are wrongly directed. The central training task is a transformation of their group-consciousness.

Quite clearly the central problem of moral education is identical with that of civic education. The humanizing and socializing training discussed in various chapters, in so far as it can be made to promote width of social vision, and breadth and intensity of social sympathies, will provide the taproot of morality. And there can be no substitute that will accomplish this training. It is not done by giving information about the virtues, as in ethics; not even by drilling in the practice of the specific virtues. It grows from deeper roots. And it must *grow;* not be grafted.

If the foregoing statements are true, why is there so much insistence upon religion as the necessary sanction and support of morality? In reply we must say that it is because religion is the taproot of morality. The religious vision is but a further widening of the large-group civic vision. The religious sympathies are but further widening of the social sympathies. We are not to stop with a mere present-day planetary consciousness. We are to go on to that wider cosmic consciousness of man as a member of a universal order that is not limited in time or space. It is to conceive one's membership within an order that includes all things that are, and all beings that are. It is to see one's self as a member of a social group that is not only as wide as the municipal or national or world-group of to-day, but which is also wide enough to include the members of the generations that have preceded us, and those that are to come after; and which includes all benevolent and beneficent non-earthly beings so far as we can know of them or reasonably conceive them. Individuals differ as to many things that lie beyond the realm of sense; but the essentially religious-minded seem to agree upon the central conception as here stated. What social science calls interdependency, coöperation, community of origin, and group-consciousness, religion calls the brotherhood of man.

It is often said that our public schools cannot train for religious thought and springs of action. If what we are saying is true, the highest function of our public schools is the development of the social attitudes and valuations and knowledge that are equally central in conceptions of social interdependency and of human brotherhood. Naturally in our schools we shall hold to the terminology of social science; to the non-controversial and therefore fundamental portion of the field. This is not to attempt the whole; but it is to assist in laying the solid foundation for the whole; without which little else worth while can be done. The churches need such solid ground as the starting-point for the extensions that they would rear into the infinite.

PART IV
EDUCATION FOR PHYSICAL EFFICIENCY

CHAPTER XIV

THE FUNDAMENTAL TASK OF PHYSICAL TRAINING

THE human organism may be conceived as a *reservoir of energy,* which is continually emptying itself through various channels of expenditure, and which is being continually refilled through other channels of inflow. The analogy is an old one, used by Descartes; but in the light of modern science there is none more exact nor more fruitful.

The outflow of energy is through many channels, accomplishing many types of result. One portion is consumed in the production of bodily heat; another in secretion and the involuntary muscular actions of respiration, digestion, circulation, etc.; a third portion is consumed in the elimination and neutralization of poisons generated in the system; a large amount, in voluntary activity; and finally, there is the portion that flows out through the nerve-channels underlying thought and feeling and emotional excitement. The expenditure is unceasing; but in amount it varies according to conditions of temperature, of work and play, etc. One's waking hours constitute mainly a season of outflow.

The inflow of energy is through the channels of nutrition. The process is continuous, occurring at all times, but proceeding unequally. The chief season of inflow is during the hours of sleep. Without this restoration of supply, the level of the reservoir is rapidly lowered.

In an individual of invariably robust health, living under normal conditions, the level of the reservoir is high, — in the neighborhood of one hundred per cent of potential. The daily income of energy just about equals the daily outgo. If he is doing light work with light expenditure, the inflow will be light. If the daily expenditure is heavy, — but not abnormally so, — the return inflow is correspondingly abundant. Thus, barring accident, he may go through life near one hundred per cent physically efficient. His condition in this respect may be roughly represented by A in the accompanying figure.

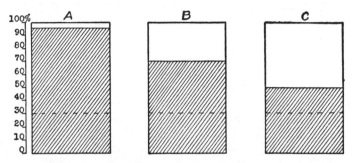

FIG. 3. To represent different possible levels in the reservoir of one's vitality

If, however, the daily expenditure through channels of work, play, worry, struggle with body-poisons, mental excitement, etc., is greater than the daily income, the level is lowered. His energy-supply may come to be such as represented by B or C in the figure. The level of his vitality may stand at seventy per cent or fifty per cent of potential instead of at the normal one hundred per cent. The lower the level, the nearer he approaches the danger line.

An equilibrium may be established at one of these lower levels. Daily income and daily outgo may again be equal. In this case, the level of vitality does not sink lower; neither does it rise. Such a devitalized individual may go through life with his vital reserves at fifty per cent of what they ought to be. The original causes of the lowered vitality may continue, physiological habits may become established, and the individual is held down permanently. If, however, he can discover and remove the original causes, and carefully regulate income and expenditures, he may — usually slowly, if habits have been formed — raise the level of his reserve vitality again to something near its old level.

Relation to vocational efficiency

It makes a large difference whether the level of vitality is maintained at fifty per cent of potential, or at one hundred per cent. The vocational demand for efficiency when reduced to specifics is a demand for forcefulness, for accuracy, for speed, for endurance, and for consistency or uniformity of good work. And these are all fruits of a full vitality. While the nervous, under-vitalized individual may present a great show of energy and may in fact put forth large effort for a short time, he cannot be consistently forceful, day after day, and month after month. He lacks resiliency. When expenditure is large, it is not restored sufficiently rapidly. The daily oscillation must not be large, if he is to be consistent. On the other hand, the fully vitalized individual may make large effort and large expenditure day after day over long periods of time. The return surge is equally prompt and vigorous. Even after strenuous exertion, each new day finds the level of the reservoir at its previous high level. With him the daily oscillation may be wide. He alone is prepared for forcefulness, endurance, speed, and consistency of work. He also is accurate. His nerves are sound, his movements under secure control, his inhibitions prompt and certain. The devitalized individual is nervous, incoördinated, uncertain in his movements and inhibitions. The range of his mental life is narrowed. He does not see so many things at one time, and his failure to observe all of the things related to his work involves him in mistakes and accidents. He is the type of man that industry nowadays is trying to eliminate.

There is the further need of joy in one's work. The forceful, well-poised individual does his work with ease, with confidence, with accuracy; and without taxing himself, obtains the results that he desires. He does not "live upon his nerves." He does not drive himself to his work. He is not in that state of nervous irritability which makes steadiness and accuracy so constraining as to be maddening.

Training for a high level of physical vitality is thus one of the most fundamental aspects of training for vocational efficiency.

Relation to morality

The physical condition of an individual or of a nation is intimately related to the moral and civic character. On the positive side, morality in our complicated age is rooted in width and clearness of vision of human affairs in community, nation, and world; and in permanent sympathetic attitudes toward all individuals and social groups; and in the disposition so to act as to promote without mistake or accident the general welfare. On the negative side, morality consists of inhibitions which restrain tendencies to anti-social or other injurious conduct.

The state of one's vitality is intimately related to both the positive and negative sides. Psychologists tell us that when we examine a state of momentary consciousness, it is found to consist of two portions: the focal idea to which attention is being for the moment given, and which occupies the center of consciousness; and the marginal ideas, sensations, etc., many in number, of which we are at the moment aware, but to which we are not giving attention. Now in individuals of different degrees of vitality, the focal idea may be about equally clear to all. The difference is in the character of the marginal consciousness. In the man of full vitality, there is a width and richness of marginal life.

He holds many things in mind at once. Consequently he is the man of wide mental horizon, and of far vision. Since the subtler and more complicated social relations are those that involve seeing many things at once and in wide perspective, he alone is in a position clearly to see and appreciate the existing social relations and demands in our modern society. Seeing the relations, he is in a position to act wisely and justly and for the best interests of all concerned. He is morally responsible.

In the case of the semi-vitalized individual the marginal life is much narrowed. He holds fewer things in mind at once; and therefore less adequately sees the relations; especially the subtle complicated ones. These he must see if he is to visualize modern society, his place therein, and his rights and responsibilities. But his physical condition shuts out much of the needed vision. Morally he is but semi-responsible. Even though he be richly endowed with good-will, he cannot hold to action of the highest moral type because he cannot see what it is.

For the man of a very low level of vitality, the curtains are still further drawn. There is little margin to his consciousness. His stream of thought is little more than a succession of focal ideas. He has but little power to hold the many things in mind at once that are needed for seeing complex social relations. As a consequence, he is morally incapacitated, irresponsible. He misses the road largely because he cannot see where it lies. He falls back upon the guidance of instinct, passion, and other crude impulsions. He may be entirely well-meaning, and yet thoroughly criminal in his conduct. His irresponsibility, however, is but a symptom of illness. Even if criminal, the treatment he most needs is the hospital.

In the preceding discussion we have been noting the positive propulsions to right moral conduct. There is also the matter of inhibitions. In the man of full vital reserves, these are full and strong and certain in their action. In proportion as reserves are depleted, and the marginal life narrowed, the inhibitions grow weak and uncertain. The same thoughts of possible action may pass through the minds of the robust and the devitalized. Some of these are anti-social, and refer to acts that are undesirable, or even criminal. In the case of the man of full vitality, however, when the idea of the harmful act arises, even though prompted by strong instinct, the marginal ideas of the results arise at the same time. He sees the undesirability and dismisses it without effort. With the man of low reserves the same idea may arise with the same degree of clearness and with no greater instinctive propulsion. But there does not arise the same wealth of marginal ideas as to the consequences. He does not see the harm of it. He has little or nothing to restrain him. The anti-social idea, therefore, discharges itself into action, and he commits the criminal deed. In original nature and training the two men may be of identical disposition. The difference in their acts is due simply to a difference in the levels of their physical vitality.

Needed for civic control

A state of democratic government is one in which each individual is largely free to shape his conduct according to the dictates of his best judgment. And yet the democracy of to-day is such a concatenation of mutual interdependencies that if we have both democracy and organization, the dictates of judgment on the part of all must largely be identical. Each must, therefore, see the whole of the social mechanism, and his individual part within the coördinated labors of the whole. No other plan can possibly bring community of judgment. But the plan requires that the citizens have the power to hold a large number of things in mind at once so as to see the innumerable and complex relations. This is possible only to a citizenry of large vitality. A wise, vigorous, and beneficent democracy on the part of devitalized individuals is impossible. The uncertainties of our inchoate and wobbly democracy are due, not entirely to ignorance and small-group consciousness, but in some degree also to a general depletion of physical vitality with its consequent nervous irritability, narrow vision, and lack of inner restraints. There can be little question but that the instability of democratic governments in certain tropical states is partially due — the degree none can say — to the lowered vitality of a European population in tropical countries.

A problem of first magnitude in training our population for efficient citizenship is the training at the same time for the indispensable basis of physical efficiency.

Needed for leisure occupations

In other chapters we have tried to indicate the large place rightly occupied in human life by leisure occupations. For a number of reasons we need to develop appreciations of art, literature, music, science, philosophy, and religion. We feel that these are necessary for a stable and continuing form of civilization. But in a world where there are so many serious things to do, we cannot have them unless there is a surplus of leisure time and liberated energy that can be used for the purpose. But if physical efficiency is low, then productive efficiency is also low; and there are the further wastes of time and energy in correcting mistakes, in fighting, and in dissipation. There is no surplus for the humanistic activities. And further, things like literature, or science, or religion, on their high levels, are not to be appreciated without the richly irrigating streams of consciousness characterized by the wide margins; the types of those with the high physical reserves. The individual of narrow conscious-

ness can have but restricted glimpses of these wider fields;
fails to see things in proportion and relation; finds them
meaningless and therefore uninteresting or wearisome; or
perplexing, baffling, irritating. He leaves them and goes to
pleasures of simpler and lower nature. A high humanistic
civilization is not to be built on foundations of physical invalidity.

One aspect of humanistic education must be the development of that degree of physical efficiency without which
such education lacks a fundamental condition of success.

Need for "keeping well"

One's major health ambition usually is to "keep well";
that is to say, to avoid acute illness or physical collapse.
One can, however, keep well in this negative sense with his
reserves of vitality at a low level. Through regularity he
keeps out of the sick-bed and goes about his work. He becomes used to the conditions, physiological habits are formed,
and he does not know that the volume of his life might be
doubled. Standards of vitality are lacking; modes of measuring have not been developed or applied. Everybody else
is in much the same condition. Neither industry nor citizenship has accurately defined the standards of physical efficiency necessary for consistent success. One therefore
"keeps well" upon a low level: but is not physically efficient.

The result is that he is easily susceptible to attacks of
acute diseases, like colds, grippe, bronchitis, tonsillitis,
pneumonia, rheumatism, and a host of others. On the other
hand, the man of large physical reserves, who almost of
necessity has good physiological habits, finds himself, barring accidents, practically immune from most of these
troubles, and relatively immune from all.

The latter is equally fortunate also in his physiological
inhibitions. The nervous individual of depleted vitality

often presents a great show of energy because of the multitude of excess movements, of emotional excitement, and of other needless wastes of energy. The man of high reserves, however, tends to be calm, poised, direct, and accurate. He does not waste himself in useless ways. He therefore retains himself upon his level with greater ease than one retains his position upon one of the lower levels.

And there is also the latitude of resiliency. The man of large reserves may, in case of stress and strain, greatly increase his daily task through weeks or months without undermining himself. Though work is unusually strenuous, the daily restoration is unusually large. On the lower level, however, lacking this same resiliency, a man cannot go far below his normal without finding himself the prey of acute illness, and of tedious recuperation.

Training, therefore, for the ideal of keeping well, if it is to be done at its best, involves training for high levels of reserve vitality. It presents a positive program, not a mere negative one.

CHAPTER XV

PHYSICAL TRAINING

PERFECT physical training for child or adult is that which brings him to the one hundred per cent level of possible vitality and which holds him there. Since perfection is scarcely attainable, education will aim at the highest practicable levels. This definition appears desirable because of the frequent limitation of the term to muscular exercise. Naturally physical training must always include a generous amount of muscular exercise; but there are other things just as important, such as proper sleep, food and food habits, air, temperatures, sunlight, balance of all physical expenditures, protection from micro-organisms, the elimination of wastes, healthful mental states, etc.

Physical training has long been on the school program. One has, however, only to glance over the statistics of physical deficiency among school children, army recruits, or the population in general, to realize how lamentably this physical training has failed to accomplish the essential purposes of abundant vitality and freedom from physical imperfection. Our physical training has relatively failed because it has lost sight of most of the vital factors for such a program. There has been and still persists the conception that education is a classroom affair; that only what can be taken care of at the school-building is to be done; that educational specialists are not to lead or direct or be otherwise concerned with experiences which must be had in other places within the community. The present topic more than any other discussed in this volume reveals the limitations of such primitive educational thought and practice.

Good physical training can result but from one thing; namely, *right living*. One must actively do the things that enhance vitality and actively avoid those that waste it. Learning the facts of a book will not accomplish it; nor good recitations; nor good marks upon examination. Nothing will serve but right living twenty-four hours in the day, seven days in the week, and all of the weeks in the year. Naturally pupils must have preliminary ideas as to what to do. These they will secure from books, teachers, nurses, physicians, physical trainers and personal observation; but getting such ideas constitutes only the preliminary step in the series of activities that constitute the physical training. It is not even the preliminary step unless there is the conscious intention on the part of those securing the ideas to put them to work. Let a student have any quantity of ideas as to what constitutes right living, if he does not put them into operation they do not acquire vitality nor result in physical training. The curriculum must be *living* — with learning only one of several steps.

Since muscular exercise is the part that has been most completely institutionalized, let us begin with that. The first thing to be noted is that it is mainly taken care of in the general out-of-school experience. Pedometers on six-year-old boys not in school have shown that they travel more than ten miles a day in their play; and the other portions of their play are probably the muscular equivalent of another ten miles. Since children have four waking hours per day out of school for every one in school counting all of the days of the year, if equally active in the two cases, they will be getting four fifths of their muscular experience outside of the schools. In general, however, the out-of-school experience is the more active; so that most of the developing experience is not directed by teachers.

There are two general types of training. One is systematized gymnastics, variously called calisthenics, Swedish gymnastics, German gymnastics, etc. It is usually taken indoors. It involves wands, Indian clubs, dumb-bells, etc. Usually there is no spontaneity in the exercise, but it is all done at the arbitrary word of command. It is not play because the children are not actuated by the play-motive and it is not performed in the play-spirit. So far as it is work it is of the unhealthy taskmaster type. The fear is often expressed when "supervised play" is recommended that the supervision will injure the play by depriving it of its spontaneity. The formal gymnastics, however, represent a type of systematization and supervision that has been carried to such an extreme that the play-spirit has completely departed, and not even a memory of it remains. It is the antithesis of normal living. It therefore cannot adequately serve for education.

The other type of physical training is an institutionalization of children's play which retains the play-spirit. The leaders of the movement have been assembling a great repertory of plays and games for indoors and outdoors, for boys and girls, and for all ages and stages of development. These include ball-games, running-games, catching-games, athletics for all, rhythmic dances with and without music, folk-games and dances, — as pleasurable as they are effective for training. They represent real child-life at its best transferred to the schools with as little change as practicable. It is the type to which schools are turning.

To these play-activities must be added an increasingly active type of general school life. Experiential education is introducing more activities of the laboratory, the shop, the kitchen, the school garden, community observation and survey, active participation in practical community affairs, chorus singing, playing of musical instruments, field work in the country, etc. In normalizing education in general, excellent physical training is also provided for.

Perhaps it should be mentioned that where one is abnormal and is in need of corrective orthopedic exercises, like medicines for the sick, systematized gymnastics may often have a legitimate place. But it has no more place in the normal muscular development of normal children than have medicines for the well.

Perhaps chiefly because of tradition, teachers seem to prefer the formal gymnastics. The writer had occasion to ask a group of elementary teachers as to the type of physical exercises which seemed to them most beneficial for their pupils. Out of sixty-eight teachers who replied, forty-eight preferred the formal gymnastics; twenty, the plays and games, especially when outdoors. When asked which type the children preferred, they were all agreed that the children preferred the games. The majority of the teachers, therefore, said that in their judgment the instincts of the children placed there by Nature are wrong; that the children's normal appetites in the matter of physical exercise are unsafe guides; and that a type of muscular experience so foreign to human nature that children never indulge in it in their spontaneous play is the thing needed for proper development of their physical natures. It is safe to presume that instincts are safe guides until the contrary is proven.

In the elementary schools, especially, the calisthenics is urged because of the relief it brings to pupils after an hour or so of concentrated mental work. The children need relaxation of attention and lowering of nervous strains. The need is real; but the method is not very effective. While five minutes of vigorous exercise in a classroom with the windows open may be made to serve the purpose, yet it is certain that the same amount of time devoted to running around the block would be worth immeasurably more. The run is a normal type of exercise. It possesses a social aspect and permits a degree of spontaneity lacking in the calisthenics. It is vigorous. The slackness characteristic of calisthenics is impossible. Children return with flushed faces, deep breathing, and circulation vigorously irrigating the tissues. It gives them real relief from concentrated attention; and real exercise.

With this compare the calisthenics, where every movement is at word of command. To quote one of the manuals: "Strict attention is very essential. The commands must be given in a commanding spirit, with expression of voice such as to convince pupils that they must obey and move promptly. The quality and the value of the exercise depends almost entirely on its execution at the command. The latter is the signal to perform and must clearly indicate that we expect accuracy and promptness." In other words, this exercise is not intended to afford relief from concentrated attention. Quite the reverse, they insist that attention be absolute.

And what is more, relief is not given through the vigor of the muscular exercise. Too often it is but a series of formal posturings, perfunctory and lifeless. One manual quaintly remarks: "It should be work in the garments of quiet pleasure and tranquil delight." But when pupils are to be given relief from mental tensions, the negative things of quietude and tranquillity are not the most effective. They need a type of exercise that will permit the vigorous discharge or even explosion of pent-up energies. But spontaneous outbursts of activity are the last things desired in the formal gymnastics. "Pupils should stand still during position and while exercising; laughing, smiling, whispering are acts and motions not favorable to good work." They are tranquilly to go through with their posturings with the faces and mien of wooden men. Those who know children know that their play cannot be normal, and that they cannot obtain proper relief from their study-tensions without laughing, shouting, and running about as whim impels. Such physical-training instructions as those quoted read like an educational fantasy instead of being things actually prescribed in many systems of training devised for the second decade of the twentieth century.

A major advantage of the play-exercise is that it can fix habits for life. Adults in a sedentary age need physical exercises as much as children and adolescents. The training should prepare them for this. But adults in their recreations refuse the taskmaster and all his ways. They will have spontaneity or nothing. If their training has given them command over a variety of sports, games, and athletics, and has developed appreciations and habits, they are prepared for types of exercise that they will gladly continue. But they will not continue formal gymnastics. Even though it may have accomplished the development of youth, it fails to meet the continuing needs of adulthood. We are prone to forget that education is for adult life; and that it cannot be accomplished once for all time, but must be a lifelong continuing affair.

Let us turn now to other factors concerned in any adequate program of physical training. In bringing children and youth as nearly as practicable to the one hundred per cent level of physical vitality and in keeping them there throughout school-life, food, air, sleep, etc., are just as vital as muscular exercise. And for the self-directed activities of adulthood for which education is to prepare, proper food habits, ventilation habits, sleep habits, etc., are just as important as lifelong habits of physical exercise. Education has institutionalized the factor which will easily transfer to the schools. It has not institutionalized the factors which will not so transfer. Yet food violations and wrong food habits are just as frequent and deleterious as wrong muscular habits. And there are also violations in ventilation, sleep, the elimination of wastes, mental states, etc. The physical-training inefficiency with which education is often charged and which is substantiated by facts is mainly due to the woeful incompleteness of its program.

Most of these activities cannot be transferred to the school-buildings. Food-activities under normal conditions, except possibly for the noonday luncheon in high schools, will not and ought not to be transferred. Sleep-activities will not transfer in any degree. Ventilation-activities must be taken care of fully at the school plant, — and this should be done by pupils for the sake of their training, — during the hours of their presence there; but it is to be taken care of elsewhere during their out-of-school hours. Experience in protection from micro-organisms can be had at the school during school hours, but it is an experience that is to continue during the rest of the twenty-four hours at home and throughout the general community. The regulation of temperature by means of clothing and the heating of rooms can be only partially transferred to the school, the major portion of the experience taking place outside. The experiences involved in the elimination of wastes and in bodily cleanliness are only partially transferable; the training should mainly be the general living experience.

In some things, as, for example, the bath for cleanliness, there is occasional tendency in congested poverty sections of our cities to introduce at the schools bathing opportunities actually needed in the homes, but which are not to be found there. This is in obedience to the educational principle that where community experience is seriously inferior, substitutionary opportunity should be provided at the schools. Under present conditions, therefore, we shall occasionally institutionalize types of experience which normally ought to be taken care of in the homes. This should be but a temporary educational expedient to be dispensed with as quickly as improved community conditions will permit. In introducing substitutionary opportunities, the schools are conscious agents of community progress. In proportion as they are successful, they reduce their portion of the task and turn it back where it belongs.

We appear here to be confronted with a startling addition to our professional responsibilities. Progressive school systems, however, have for some time been working on the program. The first step is the accurate determination by physicians, school nurses, and physical trainers of the physical condition and habits of each pupil; to find wherein his physique and habits are already good, and training not required; but more particularly wherein he is physically deficient, and given to wrong habits. The training problem is to make him and his parents conscious of his shortcomings; to give him the information needed for self-guidance; to assist him in the antecedent planning for the right activities; to encourage and stimulate and see that the opportunities are provided in the homes and the community. The pupils are then to be trained through self-directed but supervised experience in putting their ideas to work.

Full and right performance of these activities on the part of the children requires the example and leadership of the adult generation: parents, associates, teachers, nurses, and physical trainers. These specialists need to be as fully in contact with the community experience of the children as they are in contact with the school portion. Educationists can no more perform their services long-range than can physicians or farmers or blacksmiths. They must be in contact with the material which is being shaped during the time of its shaping. Naturally this statement must be interpreted in the light of the fact that both teachers and children have memories; and that this permits influences to be continuous without continuity of contacts.

The program requires that teachers and other trainers of youth be primarily members of the adult community, associated with the parents and leaders of that community. It is to get them out of the schoolroom into the larger life of affairs. It is to give their schoolroom labor its proper place in the total scheme of community affairs. It is to bring them to see education as living; and to see learning in its true relation to living. It is to make men and women of a profession that has all too often been dwarfed through living primarily within a child-world. Those who are to lead children to the high levels of adult performance, who are to confer the wide outlook of the adult world upon the new generation, are to be those whose associations are primarily with the mature members of the community; and whose outlook and valuations thus remain those of the adult world. Naturally teachers long accustomed to the easy grooves of academic tradition and the cloistral isolation in which they have been spared from grappling with the knotty problems of the full-grown world will be fearful of any such emancipation and increase of responsibilities. But the present is an age of swift change. We emerge into a new and humanistic world. Our profession is being called upon to bear a large responsibility in making the adjustments. Along with all the world, as fully and perhaps more so, our profession must readjust its ideas and its practices. The things are not to be feared; but welcomed. It is the new day of our professional opportunity.

CHAPTER XVI

THE SOCIAL FACTORS OF PHYSICAL EFFICIENCY

In an age of multiple interdependencies and contacts, one cannot alone determine the conditions upon which physical welfare depends. These are determined by the social whole. His food-supply, for example, comes to him from a thousand hands and through a thousand channels. Properly to serve its purposes it must be genuine, not an adulteration or imitation. To be pure and wholesome, both sources and channels of transit must be uncontaminated. Care of the food-supply is not merely a matter of personal hygiene; but a coöperative task of the entire community. For this, social training with definite objectives is imperative.

There is the same dependence of each upon all in the management of the water supply; sewage disposal; the ventilation of street and railway cars and public buildings; the provision of pure air in cities, not contaminated by excess smoke, dust, and gases; the prevention and destruction of harmful micro-organisms; the prevention of flies, mosquitoes, and other carriers of disease; protection against accidents in factories, mines, non-fireproof buildings, and street traffic; the hours and sanitary conditions of labor; provision of community play-facilities; elimination of noises; the social control of the liquor, drug, and proprietary-medicine traffic; the sanitation of schools, hotels, restaurants, stores, theaters, churches, hospitals, jails, public institutions; arranging right community relations with the medical profession; the suppression of public nuisances; the promotion of the social, economic, and political relationships that are conducive to mental serenity; adequate support of the health department; the gathering, presentation, and use of health facts; the elimination of poverty as a potent, widely ramifying cause of physical invalidity; setting up of standards of living which recognize the physical-efficiency factor; and finally, the general diffusion of the knowledge, attitudes, and valuations needed for the coöperative performance of these things.

The training is to be for practical performance. It is therefore to use the technique of training upon the work-level, in which training for action is to be accomplished through action; in which knowledge, habits, and valuations are to guide, impel, and facilitate right action.

It is difficult to arrange for practical training except in the Great School of community affairs. Pupils must, therefore, under the guidance of teachers mingle with the adult world in their performance of the coöperative activities. They will look on; serve as helpers; in places bear a little responsibility; in other places, larger responsibility; and they will talk with those performing the responsible labors. They will also look out upon a wider world of health relationships through varied reading; and discuss the problems in their classes in health-science and civics, and with school physicians, nurses, and physical-training directors. Along with these they will antecedently plan; and with the stimulation of the adult leadership, they will perform the part that can legitimately be given to youth for their social education.

Coöperative provision of play-facilities

We can best explain by illustration. Let us take first the coöperative task of providing and maintaining adequate physical play-facilities for children and adults. One's first reaction is that this task does not require training. All that adults have to do is to vote the money and have their officials purchase and maintain the facilities. This is true. But it is like saying that one does not have to be trained for spelling because it is only the simple task of putting the letters in the right order. However simple this task, men cannot do it until they value it, want to do it, and know the right order of the letters; and all admit that these require training. Now, voting money for sufficient purchases and for adequate maintenance, delegating the authority wisely, and holding agents responsible for effective service, — these more complex things require that men value physical play for themselves and for their children, that they want it, and that they know how to get the things done with certainty, effectiveness, and economy. They need training first, for valuations, appreciations, attitudes of mind; and second, for knowledge of means and processes. Of the two the first is the more vital. It is prerequisite to the second. It requires that men know play in its essences; know the soul of play through having long experienced it. It requires also that education aim definitely at something deeper than knowledge — an unaccustomed task. With the soil thus prepared, the knowledge factor can be taken care of with ease.

The valuations can be developed only where children and adolescents have an opportunity *to live the necessary play-experiences* — tennis, baseball, skating, basket-ball, football, running-games, folk-games, and dances, and all the rest — *for all of the pupils.* To read books about the topic, to present reports in class, and to listen to talks by the teacher, however fervent, is not to know play in its essences, not to arrive at the valuations; and therefore never to attain these ends of the training.

But participation alone is not enough for the social valuations. The experiences of any individual are limited and partial. He needs also to observe widely; and to read for width of social vision. In this way he should view the recreational life not only of his own region, but usually indirectly that of various cities and regions of our country, and of other lands and ages. One does not realize the fundamental place of play in human affairs until one observes the large place that it has always occupied and still occupies in the lives of peoples over the entire earth. Pupils need, therefore, to read an adequate history of human recreation which will reveal concretely the large place of physical (and at the same time usually social) play among primitive peoples both ancient and recent; to read the history of play in Greece, Rome, Persia, mediæval Europe, Spain, England, Germany, Japan, America, etc. In each case the chapter dealing with recent history should be full.

As the participation, observations, and readings develop valuations, it is easy to introduce the knowledge aspects: the physiology of play, the simple concrete psychology, and the social and economic aspects.

The coöperative fight on disease

A second coöperative task requiring practical social training relates to the prevention or limitation of diseases. This problem is considerably more difficult for education. There is not the same strength of propelling instinct. The tasks, therefore, are less congenial. The problem is rendered more difficult since pupils are not often to be brought into direct contact with diseases and disease-producing conditions because of the dangers. In the vocational or civic education, one aims to bring children into as vital contact with the realities as possible; but here the demands of the usual pedagogy are reversed by the conditions. Pupils come to appreciate work by working, and play by playing; but we do not think they should become acquainted with the nature of disease through having the diseases. This brings forward the educational problem of how to develop understanding without the direct experiences. As in history or foreign geography, it is simply to fall back upon the indirect experience of concrete reading and lectures, making these full and vivid enough to serve in lieu of direct experiences. It is to use the language-avenue of contact with essential realities when the direct avenue of sense-contact is barred by distance or lapse of time or danger.

The reading should be largely historical. This can reveal the nature, seriousness, and gigantic proportions of the human struggle with disease and disease-producing conditions. To illustrate, the accompanying Figure 4 shows

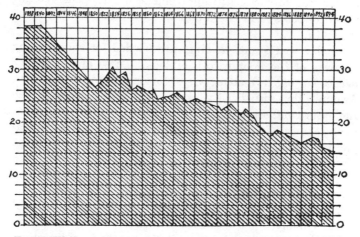

FIG. 4. Death-rate from pulmonary tuberculosis in England and Wales per 10,000 population, 1838–1894.

graphically the mortality in England from pulmonary tuberculosis from 1838 to 1894. The amount was great at the beginning of the period; at the end, much diminished. The decline shows a winning fight; and suggests the possibility of making further gains.

Along with the chart there should be concrete vivid reading which reveals the action of the factors concerned in the struggle. The story should present biographical materials from the lives of men and women who were leaders in the movement. These should show the nature of the things upon which attacks were made, the modes of attack, and the degrees of success. The story should reveal the attack upon bad housing conditions, uncleanliness, bad ventilation, and the lack of sunlight; the rise in the general standard of living; the changes in wage-standards that permitted better sanitation and higher standards of living; improvements in the care of the milk-supply; improved methods of treatment; segregation of the sick; improvements in the general sanitation of cities; and the labors of local and general boards of health.

Similar charts and readings are needed for showing the progress of the fight in other lands. These are especially needed for our own country and for one's local community. As pupils thus visualize the experiences, they come to realize the nature and seriousness of the struggle, their sympathies are awakened, and they are impelled toward active participation. Along with the concrete readings, there should be discussion, problem-solving, and more general readings by way of generalizing their information as to the factors. As these social interests awake, — and they must precede, — it will be possible to awaken interests in the more technical matters involved in the causation of tuberculosis; the nature of the bacilli, modes of transmission, methods of infection, physiological conditions conducive to infection, physiological and anatomical results of infection, etc. The technical science can largely be presented through reading and the lectures of physicians, nurses, and science teachers; and through the use of well-prepared anatomical and bacteriological charts and diagrams. At some point in the course the microscope and bacteriological laboratory will reveal certain of the factors as concretely as practicable. Children must be given the concrete imagery needed for substantiality in their thinking. This is a primary condition of sanity of thought in this field.

Other social studies of a comparative character for students of high school and later levels should reveal the geographical, occupational, social, and other distributions of tuberculosis. The studies will be largely statistical and graphical with interpretative discussion of causes and relationships. These studies will reveal the differences in different portions of the earth; the differing immunities to the disease on the part of different races; differences due to higher and lower standards of living; to different occupations; and to variations in any of the other major factors.

If the early levels of study in this general field are concrete and experiential, it can be made as interesting to childhood and youth, as any other. The human interest in a fight is perennial and universal. The fight upon disease is likewise perennial and universal; a never-ending struggle with hostile forces. It is in literal fact a more sanguinary conflict than any military war ever waged: the major number of all human beings are killed or seriously injured long before their allotted years are run. If the readings can be so drawn that one can visualize and realize a struggle which is so largely invisible to the eyes, it can be given an educational vitality hitherto little realized.

Figure 5 shows in general outline the history of diphtheria in Chicago from 1875 down to 1916. Injection of antitoxin was instituted in 1896. The figure shows the fight to have been a winning one before that time; but that since then, through the use of this new weapon, the battle is largely won. Let young people read a well-written history of the movement in this and other cities and countries. Let them

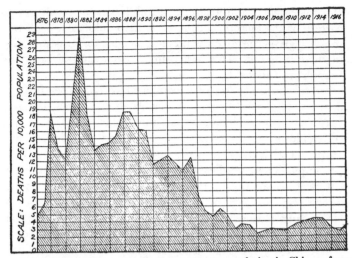

Fɪɢ. 5. Deaths from diphtheria per 10,000 population in Chicago from 1876 to 1916. (From the Bulletin of the Chicago Department of Health for January, 1917.)

understand the physiological and bacteriological causes and conditions. Let them understand the technology of the antitoxin. Let them have the charts showing the historical trend, — and with these things before them they cannot fail to see the whole situation and its factors in perspective and with perfect sanity. The major cause of the great abundance of irrational thinking in this field is that individuals have never been supplied with the necessary materials of thought.

Not every fight has been a winning one. Figure 6 shows the history of cancer in Chicago from 1871 to 1910. It has increased steadily and apparently irresistibly. Other maladies like Bright's disease, heart disease, pneumonia, etc., have been increasing in the same way. With them the fight has been a losing one. This is the case in our coun-

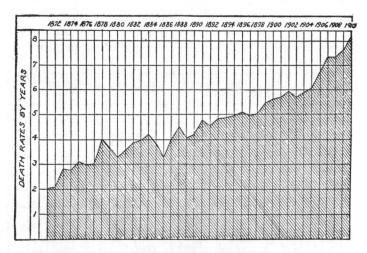

FIG. 6. Deaths from cancer per 10,000 population from 1872 to 1910. (From Report of the Chicago Department of Health, 1911.)

try at large and in all civilized countries. These foes of human welfare appear to be gaining an upper hand. In connection with such matters as these, where the fight is being lost, it is even more important that there be fullness of reading, fullness of direct observation so far as practicable, and fullness of related scientific studies by way of developing an understanding and realization of the causes and conditions of these more deadly enemies.

The history to be used is not always that of one's own country; but rather that of any country where effective work has been done. Figure 7 shows the history in graphical form of smallpox in Germany since 1846. It shows that previous to the Franco-Prussian War, when there was no compulsory vaccination, the average annual death-rate per 100,000 of population was above 24. During the disorganization of the Franco-Prussian War, the rate rose to 262, or more than ten times the normal average. This brought compulsory vaccination. The result was that the average mortality from 1875 to 1886 was only 1.5. Since 1886 the

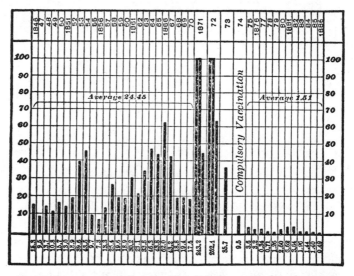

Fig. 7. Progress of smallpox in Prussia before and after the enforcement of general vaccination. Death-rate per 100,000 population, 1846–1886. Courtesy of W. B. Saunders & Co.

rate has been less than 1, or less than one twenty-fifth what it was during the years previous to compulsory vaccination. It is possible to discuss the pros and cons of vaccination with the negationists without accomplishing any great result. This is a normal mental phenomenon, and not mere intellectual perverseness. The individual negationists are not to blame; but rather an education that failed to give them the materials of thought. Let youths have an adequate history of smallpox; comparative figures such as shown in this chart; the technical information relative to the disease; the theory of the vaccine, the mode of preparation, the theory of its action within the human system, etc. Having this information they cannot be negationists, even if they wish, since the conditions requisite for mental negation have been removed.

For the entire health field, nothing is so much needed as incontestable historical evidence as to the past ravages of diseases, and as to the beneficent effects of modern sanitary and medical procedure. It is now a field of much vague and often bizarre thinking. Let men have the genuine materials of thought, and they can come to think sanely.

Because of past neglect, before leaving these topics we wish a little further to urge the need of vivifying reading. A spectacular engulfing of human life, like a Collinwood School or Iroquois Theater fire, an Eastland or Titanic disaster, under normal world-conditions, catches our attention and fills us with horror for days and weeks. But here in the city of Chicago where these words are written, to take a near illustration, at the present rate the lives of 12,000 children now in the schools of the city will be snuffed out unnecessarily before their school days are over because of evil and uncorrected health conditions. This is the equivalent of more than sixty Collinwood School fires, — and but few take notice. It is equivalent to twenty Iroquois Theater fires, — but not even the city, much less the Nation, is aroused. It is equivalent to six or eight Eastland or Titanic disasters, — and we let it pass unheeded. No spectacular official investigations are begun. Unlike the catastrophic engulfing of human life, although they were small as compared to this, it does not fire legislatures, city councils, and school boards the country over to zealous correction of dangerous conditions. The causes are so omnipresent, disease and death so diffused, everything so undefined, it is so distributed over the whole community, over the entire year, it is so much behind closed doors, the foe so invisible, the fight so secret and insidious, and men are so used to it all, that they simply accept it as a portion of the inescapable human lot. The ignorant are apathetic and their imaginations are dull. They lack the apperceptive ideas for realization of such chronic, non-striking conditions. They lack the imagery necessary for conjuring up the horrors that invisibly surround them. Fullness and vividness of reading experience which effectively reconstructs and reveals the situation, is the remedy for such indifference to needless suffering and premature destruction.

Readings should present a history of the human struggle with micro-organisms: the history of the fight with smallpox, yellow fever, Asiatic cholera, bubonic plague, typhoid, tuberculosis, diphtheria, pneumonia, malaria, and the others of the list. It should present a history of city sanitation, the sanitation of dwellings, schools, theaters, street and railway cars, etc. It should show what history usually does not show, namely, the large place that disease has played as a factor in human history, as in the disappearance of the virile Greek and Roman races; the obliteration of the Vandal Kingdom in Africa and Italy; the disappearance of every German army that during the period of the Holy Roman Empire descended into Italy; the disappearance of the American Indians of North America, not before the guns, but before the diseases of the white invaders; the retardation of the civilization of the tropical regions, etc. Pupils should read vivid accounts of the history of sanitation in Panama under both French and Americans; the story of Gorgas in his sanitation of Cuba and in his clearing-up of the typhus epidemic in Serbia; the story of the obliteration of Asiatic cholera in the Philippines; of the fight of the Japanese upon disease before and during the Russo-Japanese War; and so on through an extended list. It is most remarkable that the historians in drawing up lists of influences that have controlled the mutations of human affairs should, except in occasional instances, have overlooked the fundamental influence of this biological factor.

As a profession we have not yet come sufficiently to value reading as a mode of experience. We have valued it for securing systematized information which can be recited and examined upon. We have not, however, sufficiently looked upon it as formative experience which flows through the consciousness, leaving its effects in the general mental cast, in perspective, in valuations and attitudes, and in a rich background of conscious mental life. Most of such experience is forgotten and should be forgotten in the sense that most details are not recallable. Forgetting is as normal a mental function as remembering. The human mind can hold only a limited quantity of memories in recallable form. In order that this little be of the right sort, it must be the residuum from a wealth of mostly forgotten experience. This residuum is largely a texture of generalizations from one's concrete experience in which are intermingled concrete memories of some of the more striking, more frequently repeated, or more recent experiences. These remembered concretes are usually partially digested matters that have not yet lost their identity in their assimilation into the general.

We are not recommending readings that are to be learned or memorized any more than those of the morning newspaper. If the experiences are of the right sorts, if they have depth and warmth and emotional potency, the foundation will have been laid for the desirable generalizations. These latter are the things that most need to be remembered; and fortunately nature has provided for them in the process of generalization through natural assimilation of the concrete details. They need not be memorized after the plan of the old-fashioned textbook method. They are the natural fruits of experience if it can be made normal and full. And there are also the other fruits of this experience: right attitudes of mind, standards of judgment, valuations, emotional sympathies, dynamic tendencies of the will, etc. These latter are just as important as the intellectual generalizations. They are, however, practically neglected in their entirety where education consists of textbook fact-memorization.

Practical activities

What can young people *do* by way of putting their social health-ideas to work, and their attitudes, valuations, and social sympathies? To begin with, there are certain non-specialized labors related to the public health which they can perform. They can engage in anti-fly campaigns. They can make accurate surveys of every city block by way of locating and mapping every fly-breeding spot. In places where they can have control, they can eliminate the fly-breeding conditions. They can make effective public report on places where they have no control. They can continue these processes until the community is sufficiently awakened for coöperative regulation of places inaccessible to the young people. Within recent years Cleveland has shown what can be accomplished where there is zealous and enlightened leadership. Along with the activities referred to, pupils can coöperatively undertake the destruction of the flies themselves through the placing of traps, fly-paper, etc. They can carry their surveys still further and show upon another map the distribution of fly-infested food-supplies and fly-protected food-supplies; upon a third, disease-breeding places to which fly carriers have access and from which they may carry diseases. Most of the facts will relate to things over which pupils have no power of direct correction. They will simply be gathering inspectorial facts for the community.

But this is as practical a task as the actual obliteration of the harmful conditions. It is really more important for their civic education, since the things which they can themselves do with their own hands are comparatively few; but the number of things which they are to do coöperatively on the basis of a general community understanding are numerous. The inspectorial labors provide both intellectual and social training for these coöperative labors.

To be fruitful for community life or for education, there must be joint responsibility of adults and children with adults supplying leadership and delegating responsibility to the children. A child campaign alone is a social abnormality, good neither for practical results nor for education.

Other types of incompletely specialized activities in which the students can participate are anti-mosquito campaigns, city clean-up campaigns, current thoughtfulness and care for the cleanliness of streets, back yards, etc., coöperative participation in the ventilation of public places, destruction of vermin and pests of other sorts than those enumerated, etc. These and others of similar type can be carried through on plans analogous to those described in the case of the anti-fly activities. Pupils also have an opportunity to coöperate practically with the labors of specialists of many kinds as these touch the various homes; for example, in the garbage disposal, the smoke nuisance, sewage disposal, the drainage of city lots, quarantine, protection of the water-supply, and elimination of nuisances. After all is said, however, coöperative health activities will largely be taken care of by specialized civic departments: the board of health, city food inspectors, market inspectors, milk inspectors, the city water department, the garbage and waste disposal department, the sewage disposal department, the playground department, the city smoke inspectors, building inspectors, the factory inspection service, etc. The intelligent city, village, or rural region of the future will see that part-time work is provided mature pupils for training purposes in connection with these several coöperative activities. The quantity of responsibility placed upon them probably need not be large. That they be in contact with the realities is the principal thing.

While such part-time participation is needed for substantiality, the major portion of their practical labors in connection with all of these things will necessarily be the gathering of facts, the making of surveys, the preparation of publicity charts, diagrams, statistical tables, reports that are to be used in the inspectorial labors of the total community. This has been sufficiently discussed in a previous chapter. The methods employed will be the same for the social aspects of health care as for any other coöperative group task.

PART V
EDUCATION FOR LEISURE OCCUPATIONS

CHAPTER XVII

THE FUNCTION OF PLAY IN HUMAN LIFE

ALL of our discussion, whether of play or work, assumes that education is preparation for the affairs of the mature world. This is not to lose sight of the fact that the education of the nine-year-old child is to prepare for the life of the ten-year-old; and this in turn for that of the eleven-year-old. But at the same time and in the same way, education during the formative stages of childhood and youth is to prepare for the long stage of maturity.

Attention is called to this, since we are not here primarily concerned with the plays of children for their own sake, but with play-experience as preparation for the leisure occupations of adult men and women. We are discussing training for adult life as fully as in the chapters on vocational or civic education. It is true that play is a large factor in the lives of youth, since it is man's fundamental education; but it is no less one of the largest factors in normal adult life. Dr. Woods Hutchinson has a lecture entitled "Which is the life of man — his work or his play?" His answer is, "It is his play." Play is both end and process.

"Man is a whole man only when he plays," goes the old proverb. As worded by Schiller: "Man plays only when he is a human being in the fullest sense of the word, and he has reached full humanity only when he plays. This proposition will acquire great and deep significance when we shall learn to refer to it the doubly serious ideas of duty and destiny. It will then sustain the entire superstructure of æsthetic art and of the yet more difficult art of life."

Leisure occupations are physical, intellectual, social, and

æsthetic: conversation, observation of men and things, construction and operation of things, hobbies, sports, games, athletics, reading, travel, music, painting; scientific experimentation prompted by interest in science; the reading of history, economics, philosophy, science, foreign languages, mathematics, and technology, when prompted by love of the subject and delight in the intellectual experience; religious meditations and philosophic contemplation. The field is wide.

Men and women have considerable leisure time. A week consists of one hundred and sixty-eight hours. After allowing twelve hours a day for sleep and meals, there remain eighty-four hours per week. With an eight-hour day and Saturday half-holiday, the work-week is forty-four hours and the leisure-week, forty hours. With a labor-week that meets general approval, a man has almost as much time for his leisure as for his work.

There is more opportunity than the figures show. Recreational activities are mingled with work-activities. One's eyes, one's attention, one's thoughts are, while he works, continually roving over the things of his environment for no serious purpose. Very much of this watchfulness and thought as to things going on about him is not an essential portion of his immediate task. It is a leisure occupation as completely as his observations out of a car window. Then there is conversation with his associates concerning things unrelated to his work. Where conversation is not possible, there is meditation, reminiscence, day-dreaming, planning of social activities, and the consideration of one's current problems. The mechanization of industry often provides favorable conditions for this quiet intellectual leisure occupation. The man performs his work with no more mind upon it than if he were a machine. His hands perform the labors, but he himself is out in the wide fields of imaginative experience. Although working eight or ten hours a day at a mechanical trade, many of these may really be hours in which his consciousness is mainly devoted to leisure occupation. Such a man's play-life even during the hours of his work may be larger than his work-life.

And even beyond this, there is opportunity. It consists in transfusing the work-activities with the play-spirit. For example, Mr. Edison is reported to have said, "I think I have never done a day's work in my life." Although devoting ten to twenty hours a day to laboratories and shops, the labors have been so fully vivified by the quickening spirit of play that sense of drudgery and bondage to conditions have been eliminated. When a man thus attains his freedom, when he feels himself master over his work rather than the servant of his work, he has made it one of his large fields of recreational experience. Since work of this transfigured type is really so much more accurate, proficient, and productive of material results, one of the ends of vocational education must be this transfiguration.

Education must take note of the disparities of human character. Even within the same race, men often seem so different as scarcely to belong to the same species. Compare, for example, a group of bankers, bishops, or judges with the hard-handed laborers upon our streets or in our mines and factories. The professional men stand poised, erect, full-statured, physically flexible, buoyant with energy. Intellectually, they are rich in stores of the world's wisdom and their mental horizon and outlook are as wide as the world itself. Their social presence is stimulating, exhilarating, contagiously uplifting. They seem to be a revelation of the nature of complete manhood. On the other hand, the members of the hard-handed army of unskilled labor, especially if they have reached middle life, in large portion present a different picture. Physically they all too often appear worn, hard, and misshapen. Heavy, impassive features reveal an all too frequent sluggishness and vacancy of mental life. Too often they have little information beyond that picked up at random in the course of a meager and sordid experience. Their mental life too often has but a narrow horizon, and but little sky. Their pleasures too often are upon a sensuous level. With exteriors so hard and impassive, with conversation so crude and materialistic, with minds so circumscribed or vacant, their social presence is often wanting in many desirable factors. One feels instinctively that these do not represent the norms of personality. Both high and low turn instinctively to the other type as the norms of what men might and should be.

The differences are largely due, not to heredity, but to differing developmental conditions. The large place of play in the process is well stated by Professor James in one of his striking paragraphs: —

Compare the accomplished gentleman with the poor artisan or tradesman of a city: during the adolescence of the former, objects appropriate to his growing interests, bodily and mental, were offered as fast as the interests awoke, and, as a consequence, he is armed and equipped at every angle to meet the world. Sport came to the rescue and completed his education where real things were lacking. He has tasted of the essence of every side of human life, being sailor, hunter, athlete, scholar, fighter, talker, dandy, man of affairs, etc., all in one. Over the city poor boy's youth no such golden opportunities were hung, and in his manhood no desire for most of them exist. Fortunate it is for him if gaps are the only anomalies his instinctive life presents; perversions are too often the fruit of his unnatural bringing up.

"Sport came to the rescue." Play is Nature's method of building out those aspects of personality that are left fallow by an otherwise incomplete and barren experience. Play is Nature's normalizer.

Defects of personality may be due, not merely to lack of

developmental opportunity, but also to failure to maintain
gains that have previously been made. The classical illustration is presented in Darwin's autobiography: —

Up to the age of thirty or beyond it, poetry of many kinds gave
me great pleasure; and even as a schoolboy I took intense delight
in Shakespeare, especially in the historical plays. I have also said
that pictures formerly gave me considerable, and music very great,
delight. But now for many years I cannot endure to read a line of
poetry. I have tried lately to read Shakespeare and found it so
intolerably dull that it nauseated me. I have also almost lost my
taste for pictures or music. . . . My mind seems to have become a
kind of machine for grinding general laws out of large collections
of facts; but why this should have caused the atrophy of that part
of the brain alone on which the higher tastes depend, I cannot conceive. . . . If I had to live my life again, I would have made a rule
to read some poetry and listen to some music at least once every
week; for perhaps the parts of my brain now atrophied would thus
have been kept alive through use. The loss of these tastes is a loss
of happiness and may possibly be injurious to the intellect, and
more probably to the moral character, by enfeebling the emotional
parts of our nature.

If this dying away of certain of the higher portions of the
personality should be so marked in the case of a studious,
scholarly man like Darwin, who had traveled widely, read
widely, and who was in constant association with the leaders
of science, it is reasonable to suppose that in the case of that
great majority of men and women of lesser opportunity
in whom the original developments were less complete, the
atrophy of the higher powers might well be much more
marked. Thus the large gains during school-days are lost,
soon or late, if there is not continuing exercise for maintenance. Things must be earned before one can possess them;
but they must be re-earned continually in order that possession may continue. One's work-activities are usually too
narrow and specialized to provide for the necessary protection against the decays of disuse; and the conditions grow

worse as specialization increases. Interest-driven leisure occupations alone can provide the necessary counteracting influences. In the face of the maleficent influence of specialization upon personality, play is again Nature's normalizer. It maintains the personality against decay.

Play is as normal for adulthood as for childhood. During childhood it is to unfold the potential powers and make them actual; and at each level to maintain the gains of earlier levels. During adulthood it is to maintain for a lifetime all of the awakened and expanded aspects of personality so as to prevent withering and disappearance.

It is probable that in the newer schools of the oncoming humanistic age, education for leisure occupations will be recognized as one of the most serious educational tasks — if not the largest and most vital of all. Vocational education is receiving enthusiastic and liberal support because it promises increased production of corn and cotton, of machinery and clothing, and the other material means of life. Leisure occupations relate to the production not of the means of life, but of life itself; of fully rounded character; and the continuing maintenance of that character. If we are to educate for efficiency in producing the means of life, we should also educate efficiently for the production of life itself.

In order to develop sufficiently the educational implications, we must introduce a little of the physiology and psychology of play. The first thing to be noted is the relation of *exercise* to the development and maintenance of structures and functions. Everybody knows that muscles require exercise for normal development of both structure and function; and for maintenance. It is not so well known, but just as true, that exercise is necessary for mental functioning, social functioning, æsthetic activities, religious and philosophic contemplation, appreciations of science and literature and art, sympathies and emotions in general; and for maintenance of the power to function.

A second thing to be noted is the *instability of growth-results*. Structures and functions disappear when unused: and relative to man's needs, the atrophy is rapid. It would be a fine thing indeed and make enormously for economy if structures and powers once developed remained permanent and constant. Our educational problem would then be to bring the muscles to their proper level of development and then simply leave them there with a constant strength and power, whether used or unused, for an entire lifetime. The task would further be to develop one's mental powers in desirable measure and then to leave them with unchanged strength during the rest of one's days, whether used much or little, regularly or irregularly. It would be a beautiful arrangement; and it sometimes appears that educational practices presuppose that such conditions exist. But unfortunately man is not so constituted. The moment he relaxes his normal exercise of muscles, heat-producing apparatus, and nerve-structures, or his mental, social, æsthetic, and other activities, whether he be child or adult, that moment the structures begin to atrophy and the powers to decline; and the loss is more rapid than generally realized.

Relative to the abruptness of frequent need, *the upbuilding or re-upbuilding is slow*. This is well illustrated in the present training of our national army. It was predicted that should ever national danger arise, an efficient army would spring into existence overnight. The need came with suddenness; but the men in general were found to be insufficiently developed in muscular strength, endurance, and resistance to climatic conditions. In part they represent incomplete physical development; in part atrophy due to sedentary life. They may assemble under the colors in a few days, but they cannot so quickly call into existence the necessary powers.

A further principle is that *heredity provides the possibility of a much fuller development than demanded by the conditions of civilization; and play must make up the deficit.* Rightly to appreciate this we must look first to the place of play in pre-civilized life.

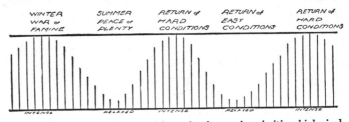

FIG. 8. The varying degrees of intensity in man's primitive biological struggle. Represented by the height of the vertical lines.

Figure 8 is designed to represent crudely the varying intensity in the demands of the primitive biological struggle over a period of time. In those early ages the winter was often a period of scarcity, of famine, of struggle with climatic elements and with competing hostile tribes. Conditions often demanded the expansion and exercise of one's full potential powers. The demand for effort is represented by the distance between the horizontal lines. With the coming of summer, the increase in the food-supply, the decrease in the competition with hostile tribes, and the temporary disappearance of the climate struggle, the demands for strenuous exertion were relaxed. This was so complete that there was no need of the men's doing anything for months at a time. But the seasons brought recurrence of the struggle. The figure indicates that conditions may precipitate the struggle very suddenly; and thus after months of inactivity call for instant functioning of the individual's full powers.

Let us for a moment suppose that there were under such conditions no instinctive tendencies to play. Then in proportion as the demands of the struggle relaxed, the individual would grow correspondingly quiescent in muscular effort, in observation, in thought, in invention, in conversation and development of ideas in conversation, and in other social activities. As exercise thus relaxed, the powers would atrophy in proportion to the degree of disuse. Figure 8, therefore, shows what the rise and fall of the actual powers of the individual under such conditions would be, — provided the atrophy of unused powers was as rapid as the diminution in the demands of the struggle, and the recovery of those same powers could be as rapid as the onset of the struggle where it is relatively sudden.

Unfortunately the latter supposition is not true. Recovery of atrophied powers is relatively slow; yet the need of rapid recovery under primitive conditions was frequent. War came unexpectedly; famine also. Men had always, therefore, to be in a state of preparedness to meet the sudden onsets. Nature could not permit man's exercise, therefore, to diminish in proportion as the struggle grew relaxed. The loss of powers would make the individual the prey of any sudden and unexpected attack. If caught unprepared he would find himself in the condition of an army that has not kept up its drill and which when called to sudden and unexpected war finds itself weak, flabby, and lacking in endurance. Such a condition would not only invite, but under the circumstances would result, in destruction. The man, therefore, during those days had to be kept drilled during the period of relaxation in the biological struggle in order that he should be ready for the times of stress. He must not be caught unprepared.

The level of needed preparedness is roughly represented by Figure 9. The segments of the vertical lines below the

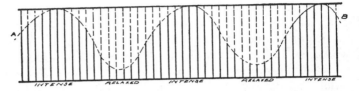

Fig. 9. The relatively constant degree of preparedness needed for the inconstant conditions of primitive life. Needed preparedness represented by the total vertical lines. The portion above the curved line AB to be provided through play-activities.

curved line AB represent the portion of his preparedness provided for by his serious activities. The segments above the line AB represent the portions of his preparedness that could not be taken care of by his serious activities and which therefore had to be otherwise provided for. So far as the struggle of the moment was concerned, this surplus of powers was mere luxury. Primitive man was not intelligent enough to know that during periods of biological relaxation he must keep his body and mind in a continual state of preparedness and that continuing functioning was necessary for the purpose. He was notoriously lacking in foresight; and what is more, his knowledge of educational processes was not sufficient to enable him wisely to choose the best means. When enlightened twentieth-century individuals are so lacking in these things, obviously it could not be expected that primitive man would be continually looking forward to the renewal of the struggle and consciously keeping up his gymnastic exercises of mind and body in order that he be always prepared. And yet the great variety of exercises had to continue. For this reason Nature provided man with his wealth of play tendencies. He was impelled to play at fighting when real fighting was no longer necessary; to hunt and fish for pleasure when not required for the food-supply; to travel about over the region; to move among his fellows;

to converse concerning the tribal experiences; to observe the actions of men and animals and the elements; and all for the mere pleasure of the activities. Although not demanded by the struggle, he ran and jumped, swam and climbed, shouted and danced, in obedience to the promptings of Nature that he exercise and thus keep himself ever ready for serious action when it came. The pleasure was not the end; but it seemed to him to be the end. It was the lure. The man who did not so exercise in play by way of maintaining the necessary surplus of powers was cut down in the next onset of the struggle; and his heredity was cut down with him. Only those endowed with strong play-tendencies were preserved; and to their sons were transmitted the same play-tendencies. In those days as well, play was Nature's normalizer, disciplining individuals whose intelligence — likewise hereditary — was too frail to direct the process.

In those early ages children were differently situated. In periods of greatest hardship, the burden fell first and most heavily upon them. More than with the adults, they had ever to be as completely prepared as possible. With them, therefore, the play-tendencies were urgent and incessant. Not only was there for them this purpose of vigilant maintenance of all of the gains, but there was also the original unfoldment of their abilities. For both purposes the instincts needed to be certain in their action and strongly impelling. Seen biologically, children's play was — and is — the most serious function of childhood. It was then — and to-day should be — the largest factor in the child's education. We refer here, of course, to play in its wider sense, as it includes social, intellectual, and æsthetic activities as well as the physical.

This discussion of the primitive situation is for the purpose of bringing home to us a realization of the present situation and the nature of our educational problems. The potentialities of man developed during those early ages have been handed down to our own generation in heredity. The possible degree of unfoldment of our powers was largely determined for men of the present within those early days. We are but the living portion of the same series of generations. The types of activities which they needed to perform for their full unfoldment, we yet need to perform, — though with modifications to meet artificial conditions. The impelling tendencies which actuated them are also the only ones given to us to-day.

Although man's original nature has not greatly changed, his external environment and the conditions of the struggle have been greatly transformed. Figure 10 roughly indicates

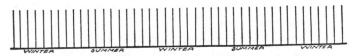

Fig. 10. The relaxed and relatively unchanging intensity in man's present-day biological struggle.

certain changes in the struggle. The distance between the two horizontal lines is intended to represent schematically the magnitude of man's hereditary potential powers; the vertical lines, the quantity of energy to be expended in the twentieth-century type of biological struggle. In large measure, the struggle has been evened over the year. The labors of factories and mines, commerce and transportation, etc., are now much the same from year's end to year's end. In our abundant provision of clothing, fuel, and shelter, we have mostly banished winter and evened the climatic struggle. In developing a world agricultural community, systems of transportation and storage, we have banished famine. In spite of the present atavistic European outbreak, we think that we have done most of the things necessary for banishing war. In the invention of labor-saving machinery, in the specialization of industry, and in organization under trained direction, we seem to have banished the necessity for thought, judgment, observation, accurate and detailed information, and comprehensiveness of understanding of things about us, for the great majority of men. Primitive man had to be watchful, alert, and thoughtful as to the significance of a host of things within his environment. He had to keep informed as to what other people around him were thinking and doing. He had to be kept alive in his social sympathies so as instantly to rally to the support of his fellow tribesmen in sudden emergency. Civilization has diminished the need for these things. A man can now be *little* — in body, in mind, in social responsiveness, in moral responsibility — and yet survive in the relaxed conditions of the modern struggle. Specialization can hold us in such narrow grooves and provide us with such meager opportunities for experiences that we can pass through life in a state of littleness. It is to live but half a life — or less.

Such a state of half-life means, not merely half-realization alone, but also subnormality or abnormality of even that which is realized. It is not good physically to have powers only half-developed. It means flabbiness, incoördination, inaccuracy, lowered physiological inhibitions, susceptibility to disease, lowered reserves of vitality, and a consequent imperfect foundation for one's mental, social, æsthetic, and moral life.

Intellectual half-life or quarter-life is not good for one mentally, even though under another's direction he perform the tasks that fall to his lot. It means intellectual flabbiness, a leaning upon others, uncertainty, inaccuracy, lack of confidence, depleted stores of information, an unobserving mind, lack of initiative and inventiveness, inadaptibility, inertia, and most other intellectual weaknesses. Such an individual lives within a petty environment and fails even to see the things within that environment. He lacks outlook upon the wide world, upon the past, and imagination as to the possibilities of the future. Such a man is not of the type demanded by twentieth-century conditions.

In the same way the half-exercise and half-realization of one's social powers results equally in social ill-health: social disintegration, enfeebled social sympathies, incoördination of individuals within the group except as enforced by external authority, social unresponsiveness, lack of consideration for others, lack of tact, social irresponsibility, and other social ills.

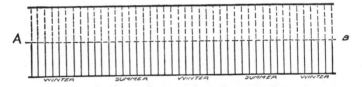

FIG. 11. To represent the portion of man's potential development that in our present civilized state is dependent upon continuing play-activities.

Figure 11 is designed to represent schematically the possible and desirable additional expansion of one's powers. The unbroken segments of the vertical lines below *AB* represent the fraction of one's possible powers that is sustained by one's serious activities; the broken segments above *AB*, the fractional portion that is to be added and sustained through play — or not at all. Herein lies man's opportunity to live above and beyond the ineluctable dictates of stern natural necessity.

The vocational, civic, and hygienic education already discussed seek to lower the level AB, and thus still further to reduce the call for serious activity; and to increase both the opportunity and the necessity for leisure occupations.

Just as in early days, this further expansion is to be effected through activities of the play type. Now as then it is to be at the prompting of normal play-instincts — though the artificial conditions of modern life will make a large amount of conscious guidance necessary. No less than then, the pleasure-motive — under guidance — must be the impelling force in childhood and adulthood; even though this pleasure be now, as then, but a lure and not the end. It is unhealthy to be too conscious of the nature of the ends. The play should long be unsophisticated. It should be largely so throughout life.

Rightly to appreciate the place of play in adult life, one has to examine the activities of men among those social classes where from childhood into adulthood the play-impulses have had full opportunity to function; where they have not been stifled by adverse conditions and barren opportunity. It is best revealed by men and women of the leisure classes and of independent means. They have all they need, and there is therefore no call for them to act. The general social machinery protects them in their idleness. They might sit at home in year-long undisturbed quietude without thought or care. But they do not; and they cannot. They are most miserable if they are not doing something most of the time, and filling life to the brim. They must travel, or attend the opera, play bridge, speculate on the stock exchange, attend dinners, dances, and other social functions, deck themselves in gorgeous plumage, read the latest novels, go cruising in their private yachts, motoring from coast to coast and beyond the seas, hunting in the Adirondacks, fishing in the wilds of Canada, lion-hunting in

Africa, climbing the Alps, placing their money at Monte Carlo, or traveling in the war-zone to get the thrills. In their restlessness is revealed the driving power of the play-tendency in adult life. The results are beneficent. This is particularly true if they have been wise enough to select a balanced assortment of experiences; and if there has been intermingled enough of serious effort to give them ballast. They are instantly recognized to be larger men and women than those who have been held within the narrow grooves of serious vocational, civic, and family duty. They are felt most nearly to approximate the full desirable stature of manhood and womanhood. They may be social parasites, consuming in their play what others have earned in sweat and blood. Nature's rewards on the side of personality are not in proportion to one's economic usefulness and produc-tiveness; but rather to the volume and variety of one's experiences. It is not the conscientious individual who tries to do nothing except what is demonstrably useful who most fully realizes himself.

Professor Groos's volume on *The Play of Man* shows that man is a many-sided creature with plays of great number and diversity, involving all levels of his being. There is, in fact, a hierarchy of plays ranging from the gratification of physical appetites and the pleasures of simple sensation at one end of the scale up to the highest forms of intellectual play as found in science and philosophy. At the lower end of the scale, one finds such activities as eating, drinking, smoking, sex-activities, and crude sensations of brightness, warmth, etc. Somewhat higher are physical sports like wrestling, boxing, athletics, tennis, football, and other games of physical contest. Somewhere about this level pos-sibly we should classify social dancing. Somewhat farther along the scale are the folk-dance, marches, processions, pag-eantry, and the like. A thing that has to be variously classi-

fied as to level is conversation, since it is high or low according to theme and character. Rather high on the scale are
purely intellectual games, such as chess, whist, etc. Still
higher are the fine arts, music, literature, drama, opera, etc.
Naturally the level of these is determined by theme and
artistic character. They may deal with the lowest activities
of man and be near the bottom of the scale, or with man's
most transcendent activities and be near the top. At the
highest end of the scale, most removed from the sensuous,
are the rarefied austere leisure occupations of intellectual
character: history, science, mathematics, philosophy, and
the contemplations of a developed religion.

The levels of this hierarchy are very differently supported
by instincts. The physical activities at the bottom are
prompted by the most powerful and permanent instincts.
These are so compelling that if full opportunities for satisfaction are given, and strong inhibitions do not exist, the
lower activities are almost certain to be carried to excess.
In a state of nature the physical and herd instincts had to
be strong in order that the race might survive. Civilized
men have inherited them in their original strength and often
they seem stronger than needful. Even if not so, they seem
to be disproportionate. Civilized man needs more powerful
and permanent instinctive propulsions for the higher activities. But the instincts prompting to high intellectual en-
deavor, to large-group consciousness, and to humanizing
art are relatively feeble, flickering, and transitory. Man's
original nature, shaped by primitive conditions, is fitted
for simple materialistic small-group conditions; and is not
rightly balanced for the new conditions of civilization.
This makes the task of education for civilization enormously
difficult.

Activities on all of the levels have a rightful place; but
owing to the inequalities of inner propulsion, the amounts

of educational effort required for the different levels are vastly different. Given right living conditions as the environment of youth, the activities on the lower levels are so fully prompted and guided by instincts that the Great School of experience will largely take care of them without much attention from educationists. Those of the higher levels, however, will demand not only a right stimulating community environment but also the greatest possible expert stimulation, encouragement, and leadership from teachers. For the lower levels the curriculum problems on the positive side are small; for the higher, they are the most subtle, complex, and difficult presented to the profession. They involve the development of a twentieth-century democratic type of humanism; one that in an age of efficiency can be made efficiently to humanize all normal individuals. The curriculum-maker has an inspiring task that in large part is new.

Let us now note the relation of this humanistic training to certain problems. There is, for example, the question raised by the arrest of development caused by specialized industry: How are workers, men or women, to keep young and plastic in a specialized age which everywhere demands youth and plasticity and which tends to throw specialized individuals above forty upon the scrap-heap? It is not really a matter of years, but of mentality. Some are old at thirty; others are plastic and adaptable at seventy. We have factories at present where each workman is automatically discharged when he reaches the age of forty. By that age it is felt that the withering results of specialization have so cut down a man's effectiveness that he must yield to those not yet so crippled. In the beginning, the hot blood of youth, its spontaneity and its enthusiasms, lead to such initial expansion of character, outlook, and vigor of action as to give one the efficiency demanded. But continuing life within the grooves and the dwindling of those aspects of personality not exercised by this mechanized existence result inevitably in dwarfing the individual in body and mind and social responsiveness. It means the loss of the vitality required for spontaneity and plasticity; and of ideas, outlook, and enthusiasms. If the individual has not during the blossoming season of youth developed wide ranges of awakened interests, quickened appreciations, habits of participation in an extensive series of leisure occupations upon all levels, including the intellectual, old age is reasonably certain to set in early and bring about an incapacity that is real; and which is recognized by the practical leaders of industry. It is a frequent and tragic misfortune that is unnecessary and due simply to a narrow, incomplete type of education that has not sufficiently established its objectives.

There is a related problem. We have referred to the necessity within a democracy of mutual respect on the part of the members of the various social classes. This doctrine we have long tried to preach into men; but without noticeable success. Here as everywhere it is reality and not sentimentality, however well-intentioned, that in the long run determines. We respect a man according to the character of his personality. We withhold respect in the proportion in which the man falls short of what we consider the desirable stature of full manhood and womanhood. In the long run, therefore, the esteem in which different social classes are held will depend upon the characters of the men and women who make up those classes. The use or uselessness of their labors will have relatively little to do directly with the amount of respect accorded. A man is respected for what he is, not for his economic productiveness.

The deficient esteem accorded labor is not, as often thought, because their clothes and hands are soiled and their faces covered with the dust of industry. The professional man at his golf, his hobbies in home-shop or garden, or on hunting or fishing expeditions, may be no better dressed and carry as great a quantity of dust and grime. In their case, as in all cases, " The man's the man for a' that." The lack of respect accorded heavy-handed labor has enormously deeper roots than mere external appearance. It is the disfigurement of the man's personality mainly due to the lack of humanistic opportunity. It is not the fault of the man, but of the conditions under which his nature was unfolded; of his education. Industrial education designed to increase productive efficiency will not alone solve the problem. It requires the twentieth-century type of humanism, glimpses of which we have tried to present in this volume.

CHAPTER XVIII

READING AS A LEISURE OCCUPATION

PRIMITIVE man had a considerable variety of leisure occupations. But it appears that the one to which he gave the greatest amount of time and attention was observation of the men and things that made up the restricted world in which he lived and moved. As he went about through the little community he kept watch upon his associates, their actions, dress, property, living conditions, habits, manners and customs: also upon animals, plants, climatic conditions, natural phenomena, the heavenly bodies, etc. As he acted upon and reacted to many of them, his knowledge was further increased through various sense-channels.

What he could not observe directly, he observed through the medium of language. Listening to another's report is one kind of seeing. When the constitutents of situations are familiar, it makes relatively little difference in understanding, whether one observes directly through the eyes of sense or indirectly through the eyes of language.

Primitive man was motivated to this direct and indirect observation in part by his serious purposes; but in large part simply by his interest in things in general. In the latter there was no conscious purpose of putting his knowledge to practical use. In fact, he could not judge the value of the information until he had apprehended it. It was mainly a leisure activity; and leaving aside the purely physical, it was probably by far his most important leisure occupation.

Nature's purpose in providing so adequately for this leisure occupation is clear. The man had to move and act within this circle of things and forces and influences, and to shape his conduct to them all. In the unexpected mutations of human affairs he never could know with which of the many things he was to be concerned. He had to be watchful of the whole pageant of community affairs in order to be prepared for the specific adjustments that conditions should demand. Interrelations and interdependencies were innumerable. Rightly to know any part required that one know the whole, and through this all its parts. The most useful thing was an adequate vision of the total pageant of community life and of the conditioning setting or background.

Our interest is in twentieth-century civilized life. We began with primitive life because of the obviousness of the relations. For modern life also this observation of human affairs is certainly the most important non-physical leisure occupation; but for our time it has an enormously larger function to perform. Instead of our being the denizens of a community covering only a few square miles, we are citizens of a world-community. To move with understanding to-day and to see adequately all of the things with which one has vital relation and responsibility, one needs adequate and continuous vision of the whole world-pageant.

Were man's youth sufficiently long and the facilities of travel sufficiently cheap and abundant, he might travel through the world and familiarize himself with it as did primitive youth in his smaller community. For effectiveness of education he needs to come into contact with essential realities the world over. And the most vital contact is the direct. Were it possible, he should visit all parts of the world and observe men and women in all of their affairs. He should participate in all types of activities: in the vocations, the recreations, the social and civic affairs, etc. And he should talk with all social classes concerning their affairs.

More than anything else, this experience would give him much-needed world-understanding and sympathies.

But the physical limitations are insuperable. Only a small fragment of such experience is possible even for individuals most favored: whether for the original observations of youth or for the continuing observations of adulthood. Even could they travel as widely they could see only the present; not the past. And they need nowadays to see both, rightly to see the present; for we are a part of the whole interlinked series of generations. They must therefore do most of their seeing of things past and distant through language, mainly reading.

Our discussion thus far is designed to indicate what man should read. Obviously it is that which will present to him a full and adequate revelation of the vast human drama in which he plays his part; and of the stage upon which it is enacted and by which conditioned. It is to enable him to "see life steadily and see it whole."

The general program is the same for childhood, youth, and adulthood, differing only in so far as demanded by the differing stages of maturity. Just as within the primitive community the child of ten viewed, so far as his maturity would permit, the totality of community affairs, so within the life of to-day the child of ten will, in his readings, so far as his maturity permits, view the affairs of his immeasurably wider community. As the fifteen-year-old or twenty-one-year-old youth of that day continued to look upon the same community affairs acquiring greater depth of understanding, greater knowledge of details, increased insight into relationships and values, so through reading will the fifteen- and twenty-one-year-old youth of our day simply continue his observations of the world-situation for greater depth and generality of understanding. Adulthood will push on farther, continuing the same theme.

In that early day, learning was experiential. Men were not consciously learning or memorizing facts. They *lived;* and the mind was filled with memories, the normal residua of experience. And generalized understanding like the trunk and branches of a tree simply *grew* up imperceptibly and unconsciously so as to constitute the relatively unchanging fundamentals of their mental life, while the deciduous foliage of their transient experiences came and went.

In our day, original human nature is relatively unchanged. We have no reason to think that there is possible any new form of education that can be an improvement upon the experiential education of the past. New conditions demand adaptations, adjustment of proportions, the use of new and improved instruments, etc.; but at bottom as indicated by all of our progressive recent movements in education, it is still felt that experiential education constitutes the best training for the individual. If the principle holds, then the purpose of the reading is *the reconstruction of experience.* It is to be a *mode of living.* It is not to be a didactic verbal presentation of unrooted facts and generalizations to be memorized, recited upon, examined upon, and then in due process forgotten; leaving little more than the unwholesome residua of disagreeable learning experience.

If the purposes are to be accomplished as fully for civilized man in the midst of civilized conditions as they were for primitive man among primitive conditions, then the readings from the beginning to the end of the course, to the end of life itself, need to be as wide and varied as earthly life and to give an adequate revelation of all major types of human experience, in all portions of the world, and with such historical perspective as is needed for each of the various regions. And what is more, it must look not merely to the tangible and easily apprehended things of sense, but also to the intangible forces, influences, and relations without a vision of which the more tangible things are often meaningless. The intangibles are also portions of reality.

We can now particularize the reading program. First it will present a revelation of man in his present dispersion over a diversified planet. Such readings we classify as travels, geography, ethnology, descriptive sociology, anthropology, etc. A second series of readings will reconstruct the historical background. These will include biography, travels (during past ages), history, memoirs, evolutionary sociology, etc. Coming under both of the classes mentioned there will be such sub-classes as industrial readings, commercial readings, civic and sanitary readings, etc. A third type of readings will reveal the essential natures and relations of things: science readings, mathematical, physical, biological, sociological, technological, etc. All of the fundamental sciences need to be read, — naturally in connection with direct contacts, — as modes of viewing the nature of the world in which we are called upon to act. A fourth type of reading is literature, in the narrower sense. It aims to present anything that happens to be chosen as its theme. This may be a single historical incident, a whole historical movement, a single human relation, an interconnected series of relations, the biography of an animal, an aspect of the inorganic world, the nature of immortality, or anything else, tangible or intangible, near or remote, real or mythical, that may enter into human experience. Clearly literature is not coördinate with the others. It cannot be separated from them. Good literature in its narrower sense appears simply to be the *adequate* presentation of any of them.

Let us note some of the more detailed implications, beginning with the geography. In the primary and intermediate grades in addition to the widest practicable direct observations, there will be stories about things that make up the world in general. Much must be oral; but beyond the first grades most of the stories will be read. The book-trade is rapidly providing suitable books. Here are a few titles taken at random: *Little Folks of Many Lands, Eskimo Stories, Around the World, The Wide World, Big and Little People in Other Lands, The Dutch Twins, The Japanese Twins, Little Journeys to China and Japan, Travels in Scotland, Gerda in Sweden,* etc. The more literary the stories can be, in the sense of presenting a true and clear and interesting reconstruction of life and its background in the various regions, the better for the educational experience. The readings offered at present have largely been developed in an educational age of didacticism and fact-memorization, and are often so freighted with information that they do not reconstruct life so that it can be visualized, and relived in imagination. Many books, however, particularly the more recent, have avoided the pitfalls and fallacies of didacticism. They simply present interesting stories that comply with literary canons. They give no appearance of an attempt to be "informing." They are presented upon the sane theory that if children are permitted to enter vividly into the life of a country and view conditions as they are, they will have intelligence enough to see the things that are there, and to carry away a sufficient residuum of memories.

These readings upon the earlier levels should reveal the fundamental aspects of life over the earth. A reconstruction of Eskimo life, for example, should permit the children to see the nature of the houses, the furniture, the mode of heating and lighting, the nature of the clothing, the food-supply, the occupations of the people, the recreations, the religion, the nature of their villages, their transportation, the thrilling adventures at times met with, the climate, land and water forms, lengths of day and night, the aurora borealis, plant and animal life, the nature of family life, the education of the children, etc. The reading should not call attention to these things specifically and consciously. As a drama upon the stage, it should simply present the reconstructed life and let the children do their own seeing and understanding. This will be superficial for some of the things; and this is normal for little children. As they look at corresponding things in their own community, they see them with the same superficiality and incompleteness of understanding. One of the most mischievous superstitions of education has been that when a thing is presented it must be completely understood. Really normality of experience upon all levels results in a full-knowledge of some things, a half-knowledge of other things, a quarter-knowledge of still other things, and the merest fragmentary impressions of still other things. Experiential training expects these normal differences; is suspicious of the normality of the experience if they are absent.

For the grammar grades, it is the same world-pageant that is to be observed by way of further deepening and extending their understanding and sympathies. They too will read accounts that permit them adequately to visualize life in its totality in the various lands. These are to be selected for their more mature understanding, however, and should reveal a wealth of details and relationships not possible on the earlier levels. The stories require for effectiveness in the reconstructions the same types of literary merit; and absence of didacticism. If children do not acquire this habit of world-wide observation of human affairs during school days when the instincts are most fully awake as a healthy and satisfying leisure occupation, they are not likely to continue it during the years of adulthood. It is this continuance at which education should principally aim. This is immeasurably more important at this period than the memorization of deciduous information. But it will take care of the information, — and on the sound presumption that most of it normally is deciduous. Let them develop their appreciations and their habit of world-observation as a satisfying leisure occupation, and the amount of genuine information they will have on tap will be enormously increased. And when they need other information they know how to acquire it expeditiously. But let them during grammar grades simply be dosed with didactic facts, then when adulthood is reached, they will neither have the facts remembered, — except where the learning was accidentally experiential, — nor those habits of observation of world-wide affairs which should constitute the most important non-physical leisure occupation of adulthood.

Unfortunately the major portion of the books supplied for grammar-grade levels are heavily didactic and imperfectly fitted for experiential education. But there is now a clear movement away from the verbal-fact-learning method. Whereas a few years ago in progressive school systems, the textbook was the basis of the training with the so-called supplementary books merely inessential collateral readings, at the present time the geographical readers are coming to be the basis of the training with the standard textbook relegated to the position of reference-book or atlas. The more recent geographical readers make a more adequate attempt to reconstruct living experiences within the various lands and less to presenting merely strings of facts. More and more there is revealed a tendency to read vivid narratives of travel such as the *Cruise of the Cachalot, Two Years before the Mast,* Darwin's *Voyage of the Beagle, Lost in the Jungle, The Land of the Long Night, The Peeps at Many Lands Series, Adventures of Two Youths in Ceylon and India, Boy Travellers in Australia, Around the World in the*

Sloop Spray, How I Found Livingstone, Through the Dark Continent, etc. A still further step is the increasing use of readings that are ostensibly literary with no didactic purpose, but which at the same time present illuminating reconstructions of some region or important life-situation; such as *Heidi, Lizbeth Longfrock, The Young Ice-Whalers,* etc.

The best basis for that geographical problem-solving which we are coming to think should constitute a very large portion of the training experience of the children in this field, is effective contact with essential realities. The more vital the contacts, the better the foundation laid for the problem-solving. It may appear at first glance that in urging reading experiences of the type herein described and in introducing interest and vividness of concrete impressions, we are falling into the error against which we are so often cautioned of making educational experience too soft and easy. As a matter of fact we are urging the kind of experience required by the demands of those hard-headed practical men who insist that education shall result from the most vital contact possible with essential realities. They are very clear as to what these contacts must be within one's local environment: direct observation, practical participation, and the like. We are here only saying that that portion of the world which lies beyond the horizon is also to be given the greatest possible degree of reality in the minds of the children. Abstract didacticism does not give them this sense of reality. A half-page exposition of the cod-fishing industry, for example, off the banks of Newfoundland gives the children no essential realization of the nature of that industry. Let them, however, read Kipling's *Captains Courageous,* and thus indirectly participate in the various activities and experiences of the fishing fleet off Newfoundland, and they will have come into contact with that type of human experience almost as efficaciously as if they had been actually upon the waters. Let them in the same vivid way travel in spirit across the wide plains of Russia, up the rivers of China, through the jungles of Africa or Brazil, across the Polar ice-fields, with the ore-fleets of the United States Steel Corporation, live upon the cotton plantations of the South, the great wheat farms of the Northwest, in the timber regions of Georgia and Oregon, etc., — let them thus know realities from vital contacts with them and only then are they prepared for the geographical problem-solving which should develop an understanding of the more general influences, forces, and relationships. Experiential education aims at the greatest possible educational efficiency, substantiality, and practicality of result. It employs interest for the sake of vividness and massiveness of experience; not for the sake of pleasantness. It *uses* pleasantness as a means; not as an end.

The story does not end with the grammar grades. The geographical program of the past has aimed so little at this adult leisure occupation, that it has tended to stop at the end of the seventh grade. But looked at from the point of view of purposes, it seems clear that this type of experience should continue throughout one's entire training. It is not possible to develop habits and appreciations needed for adulthood in the first seven grades, and then leave them in storage unused for years until taken by up the adult. They will not be there. The only practicable way is for high school and college to continue this indirect observational experience through readings appropriate to their higher levels of mental maturity. There will be increased attention to forces, the subtler relations, and general principles. But mere verbal didacticism apart from essential contacts with reality is no more appropriate for these levels than

for the lower; and will no more lead to the adult habits
desired. A habit is to be acquired in the way it is later to
be exercised. If life-long observation of the practical realities of the world is to be the habit, then during adolescent
years it is a continuing observation of concrete realities
that will develop the habit. The thing that is to be continuous throughout life should obviously be continuous
throughout education.

The limitations of space forbid discussion here of the
reading programs of history and of science. But for both,
there is the same major purpose, and controlling principles.
The present ferment in both fields presages far-reaching
changes. The studies have not been organized as conscious
means of training for this intellectual leisure occupation.
The purpose itself is yet scarcely recognized as legitimate.

Let us now turn to literature, in the narrower sense.
Since we are here dealing with the leisure occupation of
world-observation through reading, good literature for the
purpose is obviously that which presents adequate and
effective vicarious opportunity. To be complete it is to
provide not only for effective visualization but also for
emotional reactions in the reader like those of the original
observer and writer. The canons of literary discourse aim
simply at effectiveness in the indirect or language-obser-
vation method of viewing and experiencing reality.

Now for developing the leisure occupation here discussed, the literature to be selected is that which will give
the widest and fullest and most effective possible revelation of the world as a whole in its multifarious divisions
and aspects. Any selection will be chosen not upon the
basis of literary form or structure; or nationality of the
writer; or language in which he originally wrote; or of the
age in which he lived; or recency of the selection; or fame
of the author. It is simply a question of whether it presents

a clear window through which one can look out upon existence. If it does not, then it matters not how famous the author, or how difficult the selection, or what the wealth of footnotes, it cannot be good for the purpose here defined.

This has profound significance for the curriculum. In the past we have tended to be provincial in our selections. The usual course of study in grammar grades and high school tends to include only the literature of English and American writers and to reveal little more than England, Scotland, and America; and little that is recent. The traditional courses have not, and have not consciously attempted, to present any adequate revelation of Russia, Switzerland, Norway, Japan, Brazil, and most of the other regions of the earth. The purpose has been not so much to reveal human life the world over as it has been to reveal types and technical characteristics of literature. When special teachers of the subject are asked, What is the fundamental purpose in the teaching of literature? the most frequent reply is, The *appreciation of literature*. Almost never do they say that it is an understanding and appreciation of human-kind and human affairs and the general setting of the great human drama.

Acceptance of this latter purpose must work profound transformation in both spirit and content of the literature curriculum. Selections will be chosen for their content-value. They will aim at the greatest possible width of vision, historical perspective, and depth of insight. The curriculum will draw upon the literatures of all lands. For the purpose here stated, good translations are on par with English and American selections. The books of Homer, Virgil, the Old Testament, Dante, Balzac, Maeterlinck, Björnsen, Freytag, Fabre, Sienkiewicz, and Tolstoy must be considered portions of the total revelation that are just as vital and essential as those of Shakespeare, Scott, Dickens, Tennyson, Stevenson, or Joseph Conrad.

The purpose demands catholicity of theme. The literature should reveal war, personal adventure, love, brigandage, philanthropy, religion, travels, poverty, family life, commerce, agriculture, industry, transportation, government, the struggle with nature and with disease, conflicting social classes, the labors of science and technology; and the other major ingredients of human existence. As literature rings the changes upon these things for different historical periods and in different portions of the world, its field is interminable and presents material for a rich and satisfying lifelong leisure occupation. It is the business of early education to start youth upon this inspiring program; to bring him to love it as he loves the simpler visual drama upon the stage or screen; to develop habits in this field that are satisfying and permanent for the intellectual illumination of a life-time.

For the purposes mentioned, men need *to use* literature of different types and structures; but this does not require understanding of the technique of literary types and structures. A man can use a watch for the human purposes of telling time without knowing the technique of the mechanism. In the same way, he can use literature for securing the revelation to which we have referred without knowing how it is made.

The reading should be like witnessing a play at the theater. The play presents an illusion of human life. All that the spectator wants is this illusion. The more complete the illusion, the more successful the play. The man need know nothing about the various devices that were employed by the playwright in producing the effects. As a matter of fact, the more he knows about the technique of securing effects and the more he sees the stage machinery, the less is the play a real illusion of life. It becomes but a tissue of technical devices. The knowledge of the technique not only does not further the fundamental purpose of the play, it actually interferes and prevents. In the same way, an undue consciousness on the part of the reader as to technical literary machinery not only does not further the fundamental purposes of the reading, but may actually hinder.

Should the literary selections used for educational purposes be difficult? No, else clearness and vividness and immediacy of impression were not literary virtues. The more the literature facilitates the vision itself and the less it calls attention to itself the more suitable it is for the purposes. It is simply to say that a window of such clear glass that the glass itself is not seen is better for the purposes of vision than one which calls attention to itself. Or to resume our other illustration, the play upon the stage should be so written and presented as to involve no difficulty, no confusion, few or no allusions to things not generally known by the audience. The witnesses must be able to take in the action as rapidly as it is presented. The play that fails is one that is obscure, confused, makes allusions to things that are not understood, or presents other types of difficulty. It is obvious that the literature which is used for inducing experience in the reader should be of the same clear character.

As a matter of fact, reading should be easy, rapid, interesting, so that much ground will be covered within the available time and also so that it can be done chiefly because of inner motive. We cannot expect adults, even trained adults, to read things as leisure occupations which require constant or even frequent references to dictionaries, handbooks, or notes at the end of the volume. Children's natures are even less adapted to any such machine-method of grinding through a piece of literature. In proportion as the thing is difficult and the reading slow, the pupil gets less of the vision of things he ought to see. It fails to accomplish its purpose. And what is more, it fails to develop within him the much more permanent and fundamental things of appreciations, and right attitudes of mind toward his reading, and right habits of using reading as a richly fructifying life-long leisure occupation.

The way to make reading easy and rapid and pleasant is to have *much* reading from the first grade onward; an ever increasing quantity from grade to grade. Any selection that is so difficult as greatly to impede progress thereby proves that it belongs on a later level, and is to be prepared for by readings that grade upward to its degree of difficulty. There is evidence of insufficient preparatory reading if pupils have to refer frequently to dictionaries, handbooks, or literary notes. As a matter of fact, if the readings are properly chosen, and if they are sufficiently abundant, such *growth* of vocabulary should result that pupils should rarely have to refer to dictionaries in their reading. If they have difficulty with mythological and historical allusions, it means that they have not had that wealth of mythological and historical reading experiences which should precede and be considered a prerequisite to the readings that involve allusions to those things. A mythological handbook does not and cannot give one the true flavor of mythology and therefore the true spirit and significance of a mythological allusion; nor can a historical reference book do any better by the historical allusions. These things rightly to be known must be met with in their proper settings and relationships.

In concluding this section let us summarize. For the generality of men, literature is primarily a thing to be *experienced*, not a thing to be *studied;* to be *used*, not to be *analyzed;* to be pleasurable experience motivated from within, and not tasks arbitrarily imposed from without. The literature need not be old; neither need it be new. It

need not be by authors who are dead; neither is there reason
for holding mainly to authors who are living. It is not primarily to reveal literary types; nor the characteristics of
literary epochs. It need not be only by authors who have
already become famous. It should be easy, rapidly read,
and voluminous in amount. It should provide for lifting
the reader to the higher levels of intellectual and æsthetic
experience. It should begin with fullness in the primary
grades and continue with increasing fullness during grammar grades, high school, and college; and so provide for
proper fullness during the continuing education of maturity. It should present world-literature, not merely that
of the English tongue. It should be all-inclusive in its
revelation, so far as human finitude and fragmentariness
will permit, rather than a revelation of scant and partial
aspects. It should present the full human drama and the
stage upon which it is enacted.

Along with the provision of a rich and appropriate reading opportunity, there is the equally vital problem of providing a teacher who can rightly lead and guide this
reading experience. The qualified teacher is one who loves
reading, and who daily uses it in the renewal of his own vision; who has world-outlook, world-sympathies, a quickened
interest in the varied affairs of mankind; who values *experience as a trainer of youth* over and above memorization
of facts; who is a condition-setter and an influence rather
than a memorization-task-master; who knows the tastes
and interests and loves of the child's unfolding spirit at
each level of maturation so well that he can divine the
reading experiences most effective for awakening and exercising and shaping the child; who can withhold his hand
in patience until the time is ripe, and then can subtly and
unsuspectedly crowd the experiences needed for the child's
unfoldment as the flood-tide of awakening interest reaches

its crest and before the ebb has set in; who feels that his responsibility is to the children, — and to the unfolding men and women within the children, — rather than to syllabi and programs and textbooks and time-schedules; who knows how to use system and organization for effectiveness and economy, and yet keep the elements of spontaneity and freedom of choice as to kinds and places and amounts of experience; who knows a better way of managing child-experience than those who say arbitrarily to the children that at 9.00 o'clock to-morrow you shall experience thus and so, at 9.30 to-morrow you shall experience such and such a second thing, at 10.00 to-morrow your experience shall be of this third type, and who thus mechanically grinds out child-experiences through days and weeks and months of dreary drudgery.

So long has our profession taught that we think the only way to educate is *to teach*. We have not sufficiently known that *to live* will also educate. We have been busy providing the conditions for teaching. Only recently are we coming to know how to provide the conditions for living. Both have a place; and the main thing is living.

PART VI

EDUCATION FOR SOCIAL
INTERCOMMUNICATION

CHAPTER XIX

THE MOTHER-TONGUE

LEAVING aside the physical, man's activities are primarily social; and the mother-tongue is man's primary instrument of social intercourse and intercommunication. It is also the principal vehicle of his thought. It may be said that he needs to use it just well enough to get on with his fellows. If he can understand and make himself understood, and if he can do his thinking well enough in whatever quality of language he may have developed, then nothing else greatly matters. It would appear, however, that an instrument which is used almost continuously throughout one's waking hours for thought and communication, and throughout one's entire lifetime, should be a *good* instrument for the purpose, not a crude cheap one; and that it should be well understood and appreciated in order that it be carefully and intelligently used. The motor-car that one uses for recreation one prefers to be of good design, clean, properly finished, quiet, smooth-running. One is not satisfied with just anything that will run. One's clothing we feel should be of good design and color, clean and not displeasing to others; not just anything, regardless of others, that will keep one warm. In the same way, one's language which is more intimately related to one's life than either of these things and which is a permanent possession, not one that is changed frequently, should also be of good design, correct, polished, accurate and socially pleasing; not just anything that will crudely express crude thought.

It is generally recognized that the major training in the mother-tongue is obtained in one's general social and language experience. In listening, talking, thinking, reading and writing, one uses the mother-tongue of the social class in which one moves; and thereby masters it. In the main he will rise without teaching to the standard of correctness that is set by the language of his social group. Here and there he may need a little help in the grammar and composition, and somewhat more help in his start in the artificial language forms involved in reading, writing and spelling. But if he is to be educated only for the language-life of the group in which he moves, this additional curriculum of conscious training usually need not be large.

We feel however that the language-life of most social groups is on a lower plane than it should be; that the language abilities are inadequate for the language activities demanded by the thought and action of a thoroughly humanized democracy. It is felt that the intelligence demanded requires a type of language fitted to higher, more subtle and more complicated types of thought; and that the social agreeableness and mutual understanding of all classes within a democracy demands a more or less uniform level of language excellence on the part of all people. This does not mean uniformity of type; but uniform elimination of crudeness, or what we may term language-inefficiency.

Since the language-efficiency of all is to be raised to a level above that of most, education is clearly here to be an agency of social progress. It is not only to eliminate the language weaknesses found in children as these are measured in terms of their adult group, but as measured by a standard above that of their group.

Scientific curriculum-making has probably been more fully developed in this field than in any other; though as yet only in its beginnings. Grammar investigators in many cities have been discovering the actual grammatical shortcomings; and on the basis of these, drawing up studies and other experiences for the purpose of eliminating the grammatical deficiencies. Throughout the country, investigators are drawing up lists of words commonly misspelled or mispronounced; the types of composition weakness; kinds of errors commonly made in handwriting, oral and silent reading, etc. These are diagnoses of conditions by way of discovering the particular objectives of conscious training.

Beyond this point of locating the objectives, scientific investigations have not yet gone far. The series of pupil-experiences that are prescribed for attaining the objectives are usually based upon nothing better than the current educational hypotheses that have grown up out of practice.

It is probable that actual procedure often looks too exclusively to the particular errors to be prevented or corrected, and insufficiently to the deeper roots of those errors. In correcting or preventing grammatical errors, it is more important that one ardently *desire* to use correct English than that he memorize all the necessary technical information or have all of his errors pointed out to him. Unless education can first develop this desire, all other more direct efforts must remain futile. Education here must therefore aim primarily at fundamental valuations, appreciations of good language, a critical attitude toward and watchfulness over one's language, a social ambition to use language that is both effective and agreeable, a general social sensitiveness to linguistic errors and weaknesses of types that are to be eliminated, etc. These are particularized objectives just as fully as a list of commonly misspelled words; and far more fundamental. But for attaining these deeper objectives, both educational thought and technique are yet very uncertain. In the discussion that follows, unfortunately brief and general because of lack of space, we can present probabilities more frequently than certainties.

1. The first educational task is to provide each child and

youth with a rich and full language-life of the type desired. Let him hear as fully as possible the language of the kind he is to use, and the undesirable kinds as little as possible. Let him live abundantly in the rich fields of reading experience with language of desired types flowing through his consciousness and unconsciously moulding vocabulary, sentence-forms, and language thought-structures. Let him have diversified experience with realities through direct contacts, participation in action, observation, reading, etc., and at the same time the experience of verbalizing his experiences in conversation, discussion, oral and written report, both informal and formal. Give variety, reality, responsibility and substantiality to the non-linguistic experiences that make up his life; and provide the opportunities for the normal language accompaniment. Make clear and adequate thought as to realities the central feature of his intellectual life; and language an adequate vehicle of this thought. The education that can provide these experiences will take care of practically all needed training in English.

Children and youths mainly need opportunities to *live* their language under rightly impelling conditions and circumstances. There has been too much English *teaching;* not enough English *living.* Even the overworked English teachers themselves admit that after having obtained the lion's share of the curriculum for the English, their teaching is far from successful. And their remedy: We must have still more time. Give it to them, and they will soon be asking for yet more. They have command over the machinery of teaching; but over most of the conditions of a full language-life, they have no more command than other departments. Language-teaching is a matter of adjusting the whole range of educational experiences, and paralleling them with the verbal element. The ordinary English teaching relates to only partial aspects of this total experience.

2. The major training that comes from living a language-life that parallels and verbalizes one's other experiences will fall short at many points when not supplemented by conscious training. Let an individual have the richest language-experience, he will be found making certain kinds of grammatical errors, misspelling and mispronouncing certain words, and making other types of linguistic error. The curriculum of conscious training for each individual will have as its end the elimination of these errors. This means that for one pupil the curriculum will be long; for another, short; all depending on the length of the list of his errors. It means that the conscious curriculum in English will not be the same for any two pupils in the same class; that a uniform English curriculum is unthinkable. There is no more sanity in it than in a uniform treatment of all cases that enter a hospital.

A variety of agencies may be enlisted in discovering the curriculum objectives for each pupil. Fairly early in the course the pupil himself can be set at the task of drawing up his own error-lists for spelling, pronunciation, concord, verb-forms, handwriting, sentence-structure, composition-structure, etc. His labors here need to be brought to the work-level as speedily and completely as possible. This requires that he be conscious of the ends to be reached. His own effort in defining those ends is a necessary portion of the process of developing this understanding and sense of responsibility.

Pupil-committees for each subject will serve in relays in keeping tab upon all English errors of every type made by each individual of the class; and make contributions to the individual error-lists of each pupil. Watchfulness over the speech of others is a more objective process than the subjective watchfulness over one's own speech; it is therefore a good preparation for self-watchfulness. It is easier to develop a critical attitude toward errors when they are seen in others than when seen in one's self; this can then be generalized and made to apply to one's own errors. Such pupil-committee work can be wholly unobtrusive, and yet effective for a variety of purposes. It is a necessary ingredient of training the pupils who do it; not merely a means of relieving the teacher of diagnostic labors.

Where pupil-errors go undiscovered by both the pupil himself and the committees, the teacher will extend the lists by adding any others that he may have noted.

3. After the pupil has his list of errors, and his knowledge of the right forms to be substituted, the next thing is that he *want* to make the substitutions. The pupil is the only individual that can do this. His will must therefore be awakened. This is not a thing that can be normally accomplished through preaching, persuasion, threats, coercion, or setting of lessons and drill exercises. Language is a social process; the awakening is to be secured through those social stimulations that normally incite one to watchfulness over his language, and which produce chagrin or mortification when his language goes astray. It is a sensitive linguistic conscience, one type of social conscience, that will hold him in the paths of rectitude and prick him to effort at return to grace when he finds himself fallen into transgression.

To assert that such linguistic conscience is beyond children is but to confess that one does not know children. The boy who is chagrined when his teacher makes him use "big words" and bookish English, is simply reacting to the linguistic conscience which at the moment happens to rule within the boy-group of which he is a member. He hates to be laughed at — that is to say, condemned — by his fellows for using a form of English not sanctioned by the conscience of his group.

The problem of making a boy *want* to use good English is, therefore, a problem of making his fellows *expect* him to use good English, and condemn him if he does not. The problem of training the boy is one of training those to whom he reacts. It is to reach him indirectly. The task is to make the society of which he is a part genuinely critical of his language. This is not to say that they must be vocal, and rudely point out to him his errors. This will but awaken contrary reactions in him. It is his consciousness of their unspoken condemnation of his failings that is most effective, and which should be the usual thing, — his own consciousness voicing the social conscience and the social condemnation. This does not excite contrary reactions in him, but rather fires him to purge his language of its faults.

The problem, therefore, is how to bring the whole class sincerely to condemn improper English in any of its forms of impropriety. The task appears to have both positive and negative aspects. Noting the latter first, pupils are to be made critical of improper English in others. The pupil-committee tasks of drawing up lists of pupil-errors in current oral and written expression is an effective method of doing this. One who has had extended experience in proof-reading, or in reading student-papers, can appreciate the critical linguistic conscience thereby developed.

On the positive side, there is the problem of developing clarity, accuracy, and orderliness of thinking; and the consequent parallel qualities of language. One so trained tends to condemn slovenliness and obscurity of thought and expression. This positive program is a matter to be taken care of by all teachers who have to do with thought as an aspect of the training; and this means practically all departments.

Thus far we have discussed mainly the expression side of the English. This leaves the problem of the receptive side of language — listening and reading. Listening is so completely instinctive that it does not have to be taught. The way to learn to listen is simply to listen. Reading is the visual analogue of listening. In the purely visual part of it, it is not impelled by instinct, and requires careful setting of conditions and stimulations by teachers. But at bottom the method is the same as for listening. One learns to read by reading. Children will listen and easily learn to listen when the things appeal to them; equally, after once getting a little start, they will read and thereby learn to read, when presented with things that appeal to them. The problem of curriculum-making for the single purpose of mastering the mechanics of reading is mainly the provision of an abundance of interesting reading matter for each grade, adapted to the maturity of the pupils, and graded upward by such easy stages that the pupil can do abundant and rapid reading, usually silent, without being slowed down by difficulty of language or thought. Every pupil of the first grade should have easy and continuous access to not fewer than two or three dozen appealing books; and each grade beyond, an ever-increasing number. Teachers will then find ways of awakening interests, stimulating enthusiasms, getting the pupils started into books; and then leave the children to enter normally, and to lose themselves normally, in the living experiences of reading.

CHAPTER XX
TRAINING IN FOREIGN LANGUAGES

WHAT are the specific mistakes or shortcomings or forms of arrested development that result in our country from a lack of knowledge of foreign languages?

If there are no important deficiencies that result from failure to master one or more foreign languages, then there is no need for including them at public expense in the curriculum. If, on the other hand, there are serious resulting defects, then the nature of the deficiencies will point to the foreign language training that will prevent such undesirable results.

In order to avoid the pitfalls into which both the protagonists and the antagonists of foreign languages are prone to fall, we must particularize the problems. What are the deficiencies in one's performance of the labors of his calling that result from lack of knowledge of foreign languages? This question has to be separately put for each occupational class and for each grade of labor from the simplest routine levels up to the most complicated professional levels. Then the questions continue through other fields. What are the defects in civic performance that are due to an inadequate understanding of foreign languages? What are the deficiencies of personal hygiene and community sanitation that result from a lack of knowledge of foreign languages? What are the aspects of family life that are generally or frequently suffering because of the inadequacy of training in foreign languages? What are the shortcomings in the moral and religious life that are due to an insufficient knowledge of foreign languages? What desirable leisure occupations are faulty or seriously insufficient because of a lack of knowledge of foreign languages? What are the specific defects in our use of our mother-tongue which result chiefly or largely from ignorance of foreign languages and which can be corrected most effectively and economically through the mastery of such languages?

The problems need to be particularized in another direction. Are men to be trained for a speaking or only a reading knowledge of the language? The curriculum for the latter purpose alone will be fundamentally different from the one demanded by the first. While reading will be a large element in the first case, the principal element must be speaking. Classes must be small, meetings frequent, and much time and labor given to grammar and composition. In the second case there need be only a little speaking in the beginning for giving pronunciation and certain language-imagery. The chief need will be an abundant supply of fascinating reading materials, so graded in degree of difficulty that after a start has been made, the gradient of vocabulary, word-forms, sentence-forms, etc., is so imperceptible that through fullness of reading without much help from teachers or dictionaries or grammars the individual can attain reading proficiency. In this latter case classes may well be large and class meetings infrequent.

Languages needed for occupational efficiency

The problems suggested are so numerous and complex that we can here touch upon only a few of the more fundamental. Let us look first to the occupational values of the foreign languages. The occupational argument is the one most urged by our colleges in the case of modern languages; and the college influences the lower schools. The argument takes several forms. One is that all college men and women must read the technical literature of their specialties in the foreign languages in sufficient degree to justify the expenditure of some years of preparatory language-training for the purpose. Since the high schools do not know which of their students are going on to college, they proceed to require the foreign languages of everybody; and so far as this vocational argument is dominant, they encourage the modern languages. The second occupational argument is commercial and clerical. Business houses need clerks, correspondents and agents for foreign fields who are thoroughly conversant with the foreign languages involved. In other cases it is urged that foreign languages should be taught for the promotion of the business interests of immigrant communities.

For the occupational argument, let us make the matter concrete by taking the case of the teaching profession. There are upwards of six hundred thousand elementary and secondary teachers. As completely as any other profession, theirs requires fullness of knowledge, width of outlook, and ability to handle complex problems. Now what are the shortcomings in teaching ability that are due mainly to a lack of knowledge of foreign languages? When one goes for answer directly to the teacher's work or to the testimony of specialists, one finds enumerated many kinds of teaching deficiency; but not one of them appears to be strictly and inevitably due to a lack of knowledge of modern languages. As one reads the judgments of superintendents, principals, normal-school presidents and training-school directors as to the causes of teaching deficiency, one does not find them mentioning ignorance of modern languages as one of the causes. If it were a major source of weakness, or even moderately important, it would be discovered by some of them.

In a former chapter we discussed the need of the workers in any field keeping abreast of progressive technical discoveries and developments anywhere throughout the world. Education is a field of the widest kind of experimentation in all progressive countries. The teacher therefore should obtain ideas concerning any important advance in educational thought or technique wherever it is being made, whether in the United States, in Canada, in Great Britain, France, Germany, Denmark, Norway, Sweden, Switzerland, Italy, Russia, Japan, Argentina, Chile, Brazil, Australia or New Zealand— to mention countries where progress is being made. Also the teacher needs the professional stimulation and width of outlook that comes from feeling himself a member of the world-wide professional group. This can result only from vital contacts, mainly through socializing reading, with the profession throughout the world.

Another equally valid statement is that they should employ economical methods in securing this technical and socializing information. Time and money at present are needed for so many things that they must not be wasted where more economical methods can be found. And what is more, the technical and social needs require that the things be carried through effectively and not in a perfunctory and slip-shod manner. With these generally admitted presumptions in mind, let us look at the situation.

There are two conceivable ways of accomplishing this aspect of teacher-training. One method is to teach the languages of all of the countries enumerated — about ten languages in all — then to expect the teachers in training, in colleges and normal schools, to get their technical and socializing information from the reading of the original literature in the various languages; and further to expect them in some yet undiscovered way to secure the current literature of these various lands in the towns where they teach and look through it in order to find the portions that can be helpful for the purposes enumerated. The other possible plan is that which for some years has been developing in the United States Bureau of Education, namely, the issuance of specially prepared bulletins which present in English the selected aspects of educational developments in the various countries of the world. A few of the titles are illustrative: —

1. Some suggestive features of the Swiss School System.
2. Educational system of rural Denmark.
3. The folk high schools of Denmark.
4. The Montessori system of education.
5. German Industrial Education and its lessons for the United States.
6. Educational system of China as recently reconstructed.
7. Latin-American universities and special schools.
8. The training of teachers in England, Scotland and Germany.
9. The auxiliary schools of Germany.
10. Secondary Schools of Central America, South America, and the West Indies.
11. Some foreign educational surveys.
12. Demand for vocational education in the countries at war.

While this work of the Bureau is not yet sufficiently developed, it already goes much beyond the demands of the profession in general for the technical and socializing information. Let there be a widespread and clearly-voiced demand for a still more adequate bulletin literature, and the Bureau can soon supply all professional needs. It will be necessary to employ a few specialists each of whom has a thorough knowledge of the needs of teachers in our own country and an equally thorough knowledge of the educational conditions in the foreign land upon which he is to report. The knowledge of the foreign language, the foreign education, and its professional literature, needs largely to be acquired by these specialists upon the grounds. It is by living within a foreign land at least half the time and as a life-long vocation that such workers will be enabled to give effective examination to all of the work that is to be reported upon;

and to make effective choice of just the things that American teachers need. Only through vital contacts with both sides can investigators make rational selection of technical facts; or prepare effective socializing readings.

The foreign language method is highly expensive in time and money. And for the two professional purposes mentioned, except in the case of a few specialists, it is wholly ineffective. To teachers in general the foreign literature is inaccessible; it is not written from the point of view of their needs; it is voluminous, discursive, fragmentary, confused. Teachers have not time to read a tenth of our own over-discursive professional literature, much less that of foreign lands. They scarcely have time to read the latter when it is carefully selected and organized for them by specialists familiar with their needs, and put into English.

This is not to deny the necessity of the foreign languages for a few hundred professional research workers. Quite obviously those engaged in searching through the literature of foreign countries for the sake of finding the technical or other information needed for immediate application or for dissemination through our own country must have the languages of the countries from which the facts are drawn. This justifies the foreign languages for strictly professional purposes for perhaps one in a thousand. It is too expensive a method to require the same of the other 999 in order that the one be accommodated.

In discussing the situation of teachers at such length it has been our intention to reveal the nature of the modern language situation as regards all of the professions. Let one examine medicine, engineering, finance, law, divinity, architecture, music, art, journalism, politics, and the professional levels of commerce, banking, transportation, agriculture, mining, etc. He will find that the members of these professions also need technical and socializing information from all progressive countries of the world. But they too need to use *effective* and *economical* methods. Each needs a few highly specialized research workers who know the foreign languages and who can bring to them in English the valuable things from all lands.

Let one calculate the relative costs in either money or time of the two plans, and the one suggested will be found the more economical in a ratio of probably not less than a hundred to one. In degree of effectiveness *for the profession as a whole* its relative advantages must be even greater.

When one looks to the rank and file of farmers, mechanics, miners, housewives, milliners, and all others below the professional level, one can discover reasons for vital contacts with their occupational confreres throughout the world. We are coming to be, and we think we ought to be, cosmopolitan-minded on all social levels. Men and women therefore of all ranks and classes should read; but it is obvious that for effectiveness and economy the reading should be in the mother-tongue. It will be a hard enough task to get it done even through that easy medium. Unless specially situated, therefore, there seems to be no occupational reason for foreign languages for the millions of workers below the professional levels.

It will be argued that commerce has international relationships which involve other occupational needs than those mentioned. The large business houses having contact with foreign lands need correspondents, agents, and clerical workers who have a thorough familiarity with the language of the country with which the house is dealing. When they deal with Brazil their specialized employees must know Portuguese; when with Japan and China, it is Japanese and Chinese; with Russia, Russian, etc.

In large measure the foreign agents, clerks, and correspondents will be native to the country itself. So far as

native — and the degree is an increasing one — there is no
training problem for our schools. It is necessary, however,
we are told, to have a certain percentage of native Americans
for this work, especially as leaders. They need to be thoroughly trained for the purpose. They need a high degree
of proficiency in understanding, speaking, and writing the
foreign tongue. To be effective they must know the turns
of phrase, the subtleties of expression, the idioms and everything that is effective in making appeal to intellect and emo-
tion within the country. They must both think and speak
in the language, not translate, hesitate, and talk like a book
— or worse. Such proficiency is to be attained only by living in the land where the language is native.

Quite clearly this is but a minute field of specialized vocational training. In proportion as a field calls for but few
workers, especially if the training must be intensive and
thorough, vocational guidance should see that but few are
trained. It is possible to urge that since one in each thousand high-school students will go into positions requiring
Spanish, and since we do not usually know which is to be
that one, we should therefore permit or encourage all to
take the Spanish. To train the hundreds who do not need
it merely to meet the needs of the one that does is a highly
uneconomical method of meeting the needs of the one. And
it loses sight of the needs of the hundreds. After public
education has provided adequate vocational training for the
millions who do not go into this narrowly specialized vocational field, then it will be time to undertake the specialized
training of the few hundreds who do.

Language needed for civic activities

What are the defects in civic performance in our country
that are demonstrably due to a lack of knowledge of foreign
languages on the part of the citizens? Social leaders, polit-

ical parties, and newspapers are busy, each from its own point of view, in pointing out numerous social deficiencies and their causes. They do not, however, point to ignorance of foreign languages as one of the important sources of generally admitted civic inefficiency. When so many thousands of eyes are scanning the field, and when they are so often rendered acute by self-interest, it is not probable that any really fundamental cause of civic shortcoming can escape all eyes.

In other chapters we have referred to readings necessary for developing national and municipal large-group consciousness. It is certain that the mother-tongue is most effective for giving understanding; for arousing emotional responses; and for developing sympathetic attitudes of mind. But when we look to the international situation, the problem is different. Man needs also to read for world-democratic sympathies and understandings. Is the English the only language that we need for the purpose?

There are two conceivable ways of entering into world-experience. The foreign language advocates present one of these. We do not, they say, rightly enter into the experiences of other peoples unless we think their experience in the same language-terms in which they think that experience. Rarely or never do they carry out their argument to its logical conclusion. It contains the implication that we should learn the languages of the nations throughout the earth. Naturally the deprovincialization would be most effectively brought about through learning those of the largest nations in case only a portion could be covered. The most important languages, therefore, for the purpose would be Russian, Spanish, Chinese, Portuguese, Hindustani, German, and French. These with English would perhaps sufficiently cover the earth. It must be observed that the thing wanted is a planetary consciousness, not a mere

French one from learning French, or German one from learning German, or Roman one from learning Latin. If foreign languages are the necessary means for this purpose, clearly the ends cannot be reached through the study of just one foreign language, or even two.

The alternative method is reading the history of nations in the English tongue and the literature of nations in good English translations. As a matter of fact, human experience in its fundamentals is much the same the world over, differing only in details and proportions. It can be expressed about equally well by any of the world's developed languages. The basic thing is not the language but the experience in the mind of the writer upon the one hand, and the reconstructed experience in the mind of the reader upon the other. It matters little what system of symbols is employed in the transmission of this experience from the one to the other; or whether it starts in one language and through translation arrives in another. The only thing that counts is adequacy of reconstruction of the experience. Emerson once said: "I should as soon think of swimming across the Charles River when I wish to go to Boston as of reading all my books in the original when I have them rendered for me in my mother-tongue."

Foreign languages needed for family life

It is obvious that under normal conditions the mother-tongue is all that is needed for family life.

We have a serious problem, however, in the case of immigrant populations, the adults of which bring a foreign tongue to our country, while the children grow up within an English language atmosphere. The immigrants, in most instances, are laborers. They often use a corrupt variety of their native tongue. They are not greatly familiar with the literature of their own land. Their social status often causes

them to be looked down upon by the native population; and
their language also. Children growing up within an American atmosphere unconsciously adopt the American attitude
toward their ignorant parents. They lose respect for their
parents and for the parental tongue. They drift prematurely
away from the parental influences. This family disintegration is often highly disastrous to the children; and destructive of cherished parental hopes.

The disintegration is due to many factors. But language
being our major social bond, one of them certainly is the
lack of a common language. Children decline to use a
despised language; and the parents are not sufficiently
plastic to take on that of their children. A partial allevia-
tion could be produced by bringing the children to respect
the parental tongue. This could best be accomplished by
having the children read the stimulating literature of that
tongue. While the basic language of all American schools
should be English, in an Italian community the children
might well be brought also to read the interesting literature
of Italy; in a Polish community, that of Poland; in a Hun-
garian community, the literature of Hungary. The children
will come to respect the language which the school respects
and which the literature reveals to them as a high and honorable tongue.

If education here will look accurately to the social results
to be aimed at and include nothing not demanded by such
results, the task ought not to be a difficult one, nor to con-
sume any large amount of time. A reading knowledge is
all that the school need concern itself with. The children
will get their speaking practice in their homes. The latter
may not be grammatically accurate. But *training must
always be related to purposes.* In this case the children are
to be brought to respect the language of their parents. If,
therefore, the parents speak a rather ignorant type of the

language, the less the attention of the children is called to this, the better for all concerned. This will eliminate the necessity of teaching the grammar, composition, and the other things that require time.

The schools will only take care of the reading. They need an abundance of the most fascinating stories obtainable in the language; and so well graded that the gradient is imperceptible. As children master the mechanics of reading English, it will be easy to master the mechanics of reading their parental tongue. There need not be much classwork — only enough to introduce the social motives and stimulations. Their textbooks and supplementary reading books in history, geography, literature, etc., might occasionally be in part in their parental language.

All of the other purposes of the training of these children are to be kept in mind at the same time so that this one shall not be exaggerated and receive an undue proportion of time or energy. Harmonious family life is but one end of many for which these children are to be trained. The reason disappears in the second generation. Educational inertia can then be no justification for retention of the language.

Foreign languages and leisure occupations

All admit that the reading of good literature is a healthy and desirable leisure occupation. This literature exists in a few ancient and in several modern languages. It is generally accepted that except for those forms of poetry where the effects are so largely dependent upon rhythm and other sensuous elements, a translation properly done is practically as good as the original. It may be better. But among the essences of leisure occupations are variety, novelty, and freshness of experience. Stale experiences do not satisfy. In music, for example, one likes to hear selections produced through different media: orchestra, band, piano, organ, voice, chorus, opera, etc. This employment of different media greatly widens and diversifies the musical experiences and increases the sum total of enjoyment. In literature likewise, one enjoys different media. Literature in the foreign tongue often brings a tingling of new and eager interests that is less evident when the same literature is received through the routine grooves of vernacular habit.

This appears to be a higher or less sensuous form of spiritual recreation than music. It cannot then represent a less justifiable type of leisure occupation. It is not improbable that for some, who can really use it as a satisfying leisure occupation, it is even more justifiable and more fruitful. The chief question that arises is, Is it not too high and rarefied a type of recreation for people in general? Clearly it can be justifiable only in the case of those in whom it will actually function as a leisure occupation. This end cannot in any degree justify forcing the language upon the unwilling. The literature probably can have humanizing effectiveness, can expand and enrich the personality, only when it is read with fully aroused emotional reverberations. If it is read as a prescribed task, laboriously and without zest, little of value can come of it. It is not good as a training experience; it will not lead to the desired recreational habits.

A thing that is to function as a leisure occupation must be got as a leisure occupation. When this is the dominant purpose of learning a foreign language it seems certain that the learning should be of the play or interest-driven type. The teacher's business will be to provide favorable conditions, to lead, to stimulate, to encourage, to supply the contagions of enthusiasm. On the side of actual teaching, the teacher must give the pupils a start in vocabulary, pronunciation, fundamental grammatical forms, etc.; but the novelty of beginning a new language, if the teacher is competent in finding the springs of pupil-interest, fills this initial learning with the play-spirit. The start having been made, then the less teaching the better — just as upon the play-field, the less play-supervision the better. Since the end is reading and not speech or writing, the pupils' experience will be mainly reading — at the dictates of interest. The teacher will see that the necessary abundance of attractive readings are at hand, and so well graded that pupils can mainly be emancipated from grammars and dictionaries, and *learn to read by reading.*

When the training is mainly through an abundance of easy and interesting reading, the pedagogy relates mainly to leadership and control of motives. There is no longer justification for that perverse practice on the part of language teachers of pouncing upon the hard spots, the unfamiliar words, the difficult and irregular grammatical forms and relationships; and thus demanding explanations of just the things which the pupil has not got; ought not to have got at his stage of learning; and ought not to be required to explain.

We find here another example of the fallacy that a thing must be fully known in order to be known at all. As a matter of fact, little children listen to the speech of their parents and understand the general drift of thought without fully understanding the meaning of every word; and without being able to explain any of the grammar. As they grow older and have fuller experience both with things and language, the difficulties disappear without thought or effort. In the same way, one can read the easy literature of a foreign language, and move in the full current of the story without knowing the meaning of all words met with, and with little knowledge of the grammar. Let this experience continue, week after week, month after month, and year after year, and the meaning of the unfamiliar words will gradually unfold without effort.

The present technique of education is largely an elaborate technique of prematurity. It is attempt to teach prematurely what later would develop naturally through the normal processes of living.

This reading plan of recreational training does not require society to invest so much money and time in the teaching of foreign languages as at present. Only those who like the languages will take them. When a pupil's interest so slackens that he will not under normal stimulation continue his reading, clearly he should drop the study. This will leave only those who are moving under their own power. A great amount of teacher-effort will not then be required. Classes may be large and need not meet frequently; or if small may have pupil-leaders. And there is the saving of most of the energy now given to grammar and composition and vexation of spirit.

Let these conditions be brought about, and it is the prediction of the writer that there will be a considerable proportion of our population who will take advantage of this recreational opportunity, and effectively go through with it; and who will reap the good harvest that must come from such non-sensuous type of recreational experience.

The arguments for this type of leisure occupation are not strong until we become a reading people, and read our own rich English literature. This is the largest of the world's literatures. It is the most diversified of all, owing to the Anglo-Saxon dispersion. It is the most cosmopolitan. It alone will de-provincialize one. It contains most of the best of all literatures ancient and modern in good translation. Within itself, it employs many media of expression. It is a thing of infinite moods. Compare the military-band style of Kipling with the symphony orchestra style of Shakespeare, the "big bow-wow style" of Scott, as he himself termed it, with the "fine cameo style" of Jane Austen. Let one note the acid of Dean Swift, the geniality of Chaucer or Charles Lamb, the thunders of Carlyle, the varied music of Tennyson and Byron and Milton, the virile grace of Stevenson and Joseph Conrad, and the varying moods of Uncle Remus and Mark Twain and O. Henry. Let one note the diversified wealth of lyric, epic, idyl, drama, novel, essay, humor, oration, and religious or philosophical meditation. Let one then look into the diversified media and moods provided in translations: the English Bible, Homer, Virgil, Plato, Cervantes, Dante, Dumas, Balzac, Tolstoy, Omar Khayyám, Björnsen, Ibsen, Freitag, Maeterlinck, and Tagore.

There are moods and media enough in the literature of the English tongue to satisfy the present recreational literary cravings of most of our population — most even of those who go through the high schools. In large measure it is now unutilized opportunity. We believe that men and women should be trained for foreign-language recreational reading if they will actually take sufficient advantage of their opportunities; but it is absurd beyond expression to train them for any such opportunities when they do not even take advantage of the infinitely rich and diversified literature of their own tongue. Beyond the conventional two or three books of each, few people, even those who have gone through high school and college, have read Scott, Stevenson, or Conrad; or in translation, Björnsen, Tolstoy, Balzac, or Ibsen. Much less do those same high-school and college individuals who have had to take foreign languages for some undefined purpose, use them for recreational reading.

Suppose a foreign language is to be offered in high schools

for leisure reading, which is to be chosen? Quite evidently it is the one which contains the largest and best literature. In order to ascertain this the writer took the more than seven hundred volumes of "Everyman's Library" which aims to bring together the best of all of the world's literatures in English translation. Since it is a commercial enterprise, producing books at low price which will appeal to the reading tastes of the population in general, its selections ought to reveal the literatures which have the largest number of books of general appeal. Omitting those of English-speaking peoples, the number of volumes from each of the world's most important literatures are shown in the accompanying table: —

French	52
Greek	23
Russian and Polish	14
Latin	11
German	11
Scandinavian	10
Italian	8
Oriental nations	5
Spanish	3

Other book-lists afford confirmation of these figures. Among modern literatures, there can be no doubt that the literature of France stands head and shoulders over every other literature except the English. If only one language is to be studied for the purpose here discussed, it should doubtless be French.

If one wants a second language for this purpose it looks as though it might as well be Greek, Russian, Scandinavian, German or Italian. It is unfortunate that this purpose does not point more clearly to Spanish. This justification is really needed to support other valid reasons for studying Spanish, which in themselves, without this one, are scarcely sufficient, except in special instances.

Foreign languages needed for proficiency in English

Few urge modern languages as aids to training in English. There is, however, a common presumption among teachers that the large place accorded Latin is justified on this basis. But the scientific curriculum-discoverer cannot proceed upon ill-defined presumptions. He must know with definiteness and particularity just what the serious deficiencies in our use of English are that are demonstrably due to inability to read, translate, and explain the grammar of Latin; and which have no other sufficient remedy.

Let us locate these if they exist, by a method of elimination. In the first place in the English training the most fundamental things to be developed are: genuine desire to use good English, right valuations or appreciations of good English, and habits of watchfulness against errors of all kinds. These attitudes obviously result mainly from social stimulations and contagions. They are developed mainly by living within a language atmosphere in which good English is spoken and read and valued. Language valuations are almost wholly social matters, obtained from one's associates chiefly through unconscious imitation. Latin has little or nothing to do with the matter.

English training further aims at the development of the habits, skills, and technical knowledge involved in pronunciation, choice of words, construction of sentences, use of English inflections and concord, construction of the larger forms of discourse, oral and written presentation of thought, reading, spelling, and handwriting. If one has right valuations, and can do all of these things well, he will have a pretty secure control over his English. In each of the things, deficiencies are common. But examine them one by one, and in most cases there is not even a remote probability that the deficiencies are due to inability to read and explain Latin.

Latin has a slight value for spelling; though on the whole it is the Saxon words that give most trouble; and if one cannot remember the English spelling, how can he with greater assurance remember the Latin?

It is urged for sentence-construction and concord, through aiding in one's knowledge of English grammar. Doubtless it will help; but it is a tremendously expensive way to get the little grammar really needed for correcting some twenty-five kinds of English errors. Those whose English is so seriously defective that they need Latin for the purpose generally do not get it; and those who get it generally grow up in such a cultivated language-atmosphere that they do not greatly need it for the purpose mentioned.

The argument simmers down to vocabulary-development. One needs Latin, French, and Anglo-Saxon for the etymology of the five thousand words that one uses; and for the fifteen thousand that one reads. The presumptions are two: (1) the etymology gives understanding of meanings; (2) one should learn the languages from which English comes to understand the etymology. There is some truth in both; and more error.

One must note the psychology of vocabulary-building. The simplest and usual condition of vocabulary-learning is where one meets with some new thing, action, quality, or relation; and at the same time gets the word that expresses it. In the presence of any new aspect of reality one is not easy in mind till one has the necessary word in terms of which to think it. The presence of the reality calls for the word. When brought together they associate so closely as to fuse into a single conception. The basic condition of vocabulary-building is *contact with the realities*. If one is to have a wide and varied vocabulary then the first condition is that he come into vital contact with numerous and varied aspects of reality; verbalizing his experience. If, for example, one would require the vocabulary of the motor-car — limousine, chassis, carburetor, commutator, differential, magneto, muffler, transmission, etc. — let him operate the car, repair it, make adjustments, consult handbooks for the necessary information, talk over matters with others, etc.; and the full vocabulary will grow up so easily and naturally that one does not notice how or when he acquired it. *Make experience central and the vocabulary will take care of itself.* If one would acquire the vocabulary of a farm, a steel-mill, a hospital, the game of golf, a science, a religion, or anything else, material or immaterial, the principle holds. Let one study Latin till he is gray, he will find that for vocabulary-building it is a poor and pale substitute for reality.

The older plan was to use simple well-known English words for explaining the meaning of the Latin vocabulary; and then to use that Latin vocabulary to explain the meaning of other English words. It was a matter of pouring meanings from English into Latin, and then back again. It was to use a small body of meanings got from a little contact with reality to produce a large body of substantial meanings without any further contacts with realities. It reminds one of the street-fakir who from an ounce of soap produces three barrels of foam. There is increased iridescence; and one is impressed; but no increase of substance. The schools of the past were places of words not realities. It is not therefore surprising that this primitive faith in verbal methods should linger.

And yet etymology has legitimate functions to perform. Let us illustrate some of them. We have in English some **twenty** or thirty commonly-used prefixes borrowed from the Latin, such as *bi-*, *circum-*, *contra-*, *semi-*, *post-*, *trans-*, *uni-*, etc. We have another twenty or thirty more or less common prefixes imported from the Greek: *anti-*, *mon-*, *mono-*, *pan-*, *penta-*, *poly-*, *tri-*, *hemi-*, *iso-*, etc. We have also some sixty or eighty suffixes variously derived from Latin, Greek, Old French, and Anglo-Saxon: *-fy*, *-ed*, *-hood*, *-tion*, *-cion*, *-ise*, *-ize*, *-less*, *-ish*, *-ie*, *-kin*, *-ling*, *-ness*, *-able*, *-ly*, etc.

Now, it does not really matter from what languages these have been imported. They are essential portions of the English tongue. They have become completely naturalized and they are as much a portion of the living English as its Saxon element. It is no more necessary to study the Latin in order to get the significance of a hundred and fifty English affixes than it is to study the ancient Aryan, which preceded the Latin in order to understand the terms which the Latin borrowed from it.

Given favorable conditions their mastery involves practically no problem. Bring the children into contact with the actual realities in relation to which the prefixes and suffixes have significance, call attention to this significance, in so far as pupils need to be made conscious of it, and the work is done without effort. For example, in the mathematics let the children know that *bi-* means *two*, as they come into contact with *bi-nominals*, *bi-sections*, etc.; that *tri-* means *three*, as they come into contact with *triangles*, *tri-sections*, *tri-nominals*, etc. Let children meet with *semi-weekly*, *semi-annual*, *semi-circle*, etc., as verbalized realities, and it does not require a great deal of effort on the part of teachers to make them conscious of the significance of *semi-*. Let them come into contact with both realities and diminutives like *doggie*, *lambkin*, *duckling*, *hillock*, *eaglet*, etc., and the understanding is acquired without thought or effort. This is but to apply the central principle of reality-teaching rather than verbal-teaching to the vocabulary-building.

The roots or stems of many English words have also been imported and naturalized; as, for example, *dico* or *dicto* in *diction, dictionary, dictate, dictum, abdicate, contradict, predict, edict, interdict, verdict, dictator*, etc. Of these root-terms there are several score in common use that probably should be generally known; and even a few hundred that may be known with profit by those who would acquire a finished knowledge and appreciation of English. Most of the root-terms have been naturalized and are now as much parts of the English as they ever were of the Anglo-Saxon, Latin, or Greek. They are the common possessions of any language that cares to adopt them. The meanings are mainly read into the root-terms by associating them with the realities to which they refer. These terms can be broken out of their English matrix, the generalized meaning revealed, and then used in the study of families of English derivatives that employ the root-terms. One can thus study the etymology of English without studying Latin, French, or Anglo-Saxon. Most of us who have not studied Greek appreciate the etymology of such words as *psychology, theology, pantheon, biography, biology, bibliography, philosophy, phonograph*, etc., about as completely as we appreciate the words from the Latin which we have studied. And we can use the roots borrowed from the Greek just as efficiently in analyzing derivatives.

In general, it is not through etymological associations that one acquires the meanings of words. Take, for example, the derivatives *serve, serf, servant, servitor, service, servitude, serviceable, servile, subservient*, etc. All come from a single root. A dictionary knowledge of the meaning of this root will not give one any inkling of the finer nuances of meanings. The root-term, for example, does not reveal the subtle differences of meaning in *servant, serf,* and *servitor;* or between *service* and *servitude.* One gets these delicate but vital differences through contacts with the realities themselves, either immediate or imaginative. One who reads and observes widely and accurately but who has never noted the etymology of these words will acquire the finer shades of meaning as completely as one who is familiar with the etymology. And if he can get the subtler flavors of words in this way, surely he can thus also get the crass meanings of the root-terms.

A further question relates to the technical terminology of specialists: biologists, physiologists, physicians, etc. The basic thing needed for making them specialists is full, varied and intimate contacts with the realities of their specialized fields. At bottom they need to know *things,* not words. But adequate knowledge of things involves the use of words — the improved vehicles of human thought. But the reality-method of getting at the things makes the language aspect easy. The presence of the thing calls for the language necessary for thinking it. Let the young physician once learn, for example, that *hœma* means blood; and then let his daily experiences involve such terms as *hœmachrome, hœmabarometer, hœmacytometer, hœmaphobus, hœmatozoa, hemorrhage, hemoglobin, hemoperitoneum, hemophobia, hemoscope, hemotropic,* etc., — he will very easily learn the value and significance of *hœma-* as a root word for his technical field. Let him read Greek literature for twenty years, and he can never thereby acquire any better understanding of this word. And he can learn his other technical terms in the same way. Rare terms he will have to look up in a dictionary — like ordinary people. There is always a fringe of little-used words that require the use of the dictionary.

It must be kept in mind that we are here discussing but

a single phase of the problem. To assert that a mastery of Latin grammar and literature is not *necessary* for a thorough understanding and appreciation of English is not equivalent to saying that Latin should not be studied for this purpose by those who are willing to employ this method. Many of those who appreciate linguistic study as recreational experience will be justified in taking Latin for immediate and subsequent recreational uses. As it then gives them a goodly portion of their etymological background, it will have accomplished a double purpose. It cannot serve as a substitute for the reality-method; but it can substantially reinforce it. Latin will then be taken only by those of linguistic appreciation, with the students mainly moving under their own power. The Latinists should then supply them with the wealth of interesting readings needed for the imperceptible gradient of experience that will permit them to learn to read the language by reading it. Under such circumstances those who want the Latin can get all that they want without requiring too much effort and expense on the part of teachers and school systems. Under present teaching conditions, the cost, especially in time and loss of other more important things, is usually disproportionate to the returns.

Foreign languages needed for humanistic experience

It is generally supposed that there is an intimate, even indissoluble, relation between the classical languages and humanism. Before one can rightly note the relation, however, one must first define humanistic experiences in terms of twentieth-century life; and in their particularized forms. This we have tried to do in some measure in previous chapters. To look with wide and sympathetic vision over all human affairs, near and remote, recent and ancient; to enter freely and sympathetically into all worthy kinds of

human experience, directly through participation and observation, and indirectly through conversation and lecture
and wide reading; to range with quickened mind through
the rich and inspiring fields of science and art and philosophy and religion; to feel a oneness with one's race, and
to be fired with its highest aspirations; to act with one's
fellows vigorously, joyously and whole-heartedly in the
coöperative provision of a full and rich life-opportunity
for every human being, — such as these are humanistic
experiences. Those experiences in which man realizes his
full humanity constitute the *substance* of humanism.

This is not to give a new definition to humanism. It is
but to rescue its original one; and to state it in terms of
twentieth-century thought and life. It is to see that humanism is not a thing of language alone; but rather of the
full texture of life. Any language in which one can live and
think can be the language of humanism.

In the day of the Renaissance, the classics provided
the languages and much of the thought of the wider humanistic experience. But vernacular literatures have since
arisen which can not only provide the same experiences, but
the far wider ones of modern life; and which also can
serve the humanistic needs of all, a democratic requirement, and not merely those of a small leisure class.

The classicists of to-day are much concerned because of
an alleged attack upon humanism. As a matter of fact,
there is little discernible attack upon actual humanism.
The attack is only upon the conception that only the ancient languages can serve in a democratic age as the vehicles of humanistic experience. One has but to look about
him to see that, in spite of the apparent contradictions of
war, the world grows more humanistic in its conceptions,
aspirations and practices. More and more we would bring
to all social classes the varied and essential humanistic

experiences that have hitherto fallen only to the lot of the intellectual and social aristocratic few. To all we would give fullness of vital contacts with men, with nature, with literature and history and art and high religion. To all so far as possible we would give the far vision outward and backward and upward. There are aristocrats and Philistines who are indifferent to this wide diffusion of humanistic experience, or who are skeptical of its possibility. But in general they are making no active attack upon it.

It is under the circumstances unfortunate that classicists should have the erroneous idea that humanistic experiences require the ancient vehicles of thought; that the world is a decadent affair in which modern languages are so wretchedly weak and shabby as not to be able to carry the ancient experiences; and even that modern human experience is inferior to that of the peoples of old. There is attack and justifiable attack upon such pessimism and puerility. The attack however is not because of hostility to humanistic experience. It is brought by the optimistic, forward-looking friends of twentieth-century humanism. To them humaneness and richness and nobility of spirit seem so good for the world that they would have these things for all men and women; and therefore they would employ for the purpose the language of our democracy rather than the ancient outworn languages of the intellectual aristocracy.

The classicists have not defined humanism in terms of the essential realities. They have defined it only in terms of the symbols of thought: of the verbal associates of the older humanistic experience of centuries ago.

As a matter of fact, reading the ancient literatures in the originals is not an essential factor in developing humaneness, or gentleness, or richness and elevation and nobility of thought and feeling, or high appreciation of æsthetic art, or of any of the other essentials of high character. The cynical disbelief on the part of the classicists of the possibility or desirability of democratic diffusion of humanistic experience to all makes them unsafe defenders of actual humanism in our democratic age. Their major effort is not to find means of the greatest possible amount of such diffusion; but rather to retain an impossible vehicle of diffusion.

It is the social-minded men and women of to-day who are the real leaders of modern humanism. A few are linguists; most are not. Some are in the educational profession; most are in other fields of labor. But it is those whose primary interest is in their fellow-men rather than in languages, and whose fundamental faith is in mankind rather than in symbols, who are to-day leading and guiding humanity toward fullness of self-realization.

CHAPTER XXI

SOME CONCLUDING CONSIDERATIONS

In this volume we have tried to look at the curriculum problems from the point of view of social needs; and thereby to develop, in some measure at least, the social point of view as regards education. In a single volume, one can present but glimpses of a limited number of the detailed tasks. Others of similar type stretch out apparently endlessly before us. Our profession is confronted with the huge practical task of defining innumerable specific objectives; and then of determining the countless pupil-experiences that must be induced by way of bringing the children to attain the objectives. We have lacked space for discussion here of the administrative problems. But let us refer briefly to a few of them.

The first necessary thing is for our whole educational profession to acquire a social, rather than a merely academic, point of view. The writer fully appreciates the difficulties in the way, as may be illustrated by a personal reference. Soon after the American occupation of the Philippine Islands, the writer was a member of a committee of seven appointed to draw up an elementary-school curriculum for the islands. The members had all taught or supervised within the islands for two or three years and were reasonably familiar with their peculiar conditions. It was a virgin field in which we were free to recommend almost anything by way of meeting the needs of the population. We had an opportunity to do a magnificent and original constructive piece of work.

And what did we do? We assembled upon a table in the committee-room copies of the American textbooks in reading, arithmetic, geography, United States history, and the other subjects with which we had been familiar in American schools. We also assembled such American courses of study as we could find; and without being conscious of it, we mobilized our American prejudices and preconceptions as to what an elementary-school course ought to be. On the basis of these things we made out a course of study for the traditional eight elementary-school grades. We provided the traditional amount of each subject for each grade, distributed them as in American schools, and recommended American textbooks for the work.

The thing was not adapted to the conditions within the islands. As a matter of fact, we did not try to adapt it to those conditions — though we honestly thought that we were doing the thing needed. The difficulty was that our minds ran so completely in the grooves of traditional thought that we did not realize the possibility of anything else. We greatly needed something to shatter our self-complacency and bring us to see education in terms of the society that was to be educated. We needed *principles of curriculum-making*. We did not know that we should first determine objectives from a study of social needs. We supposed that education consisted only of teaching the familiar subjects. We had not come to see that it is essentially a process of unfolding the potential abilities of a population, and in particularized relation to the social conditions. We had not learned that studies are means, not ends. We did not realize that any instrument or experience which is effective in such unfoldment is the right instrument and right experience; and that anything which is not effective is wrong, however time-honored and widely used it may be. Fortunately for the people, the Director of Education was better able to look at essential realities; he cut the course down to six grades, unceremoniously threw out irrelevant materials, and without regard for the time-hallowed sanctities brought bodily into the course a number of things then far more than now regarded as superficial and plebeian, such as shop-work, cooking, sewing, weaving, rug-making, etc. We were properly horrified.

We needed something that would shake us out of the grooves and which at the same time was violent enough to obliterate them, and set thought free. Attention is called to this personal experience because of a belief that it is an example of a wide-spread obstructive influence in American education to-day. A large portion of our profession appears to need something that will lift them out of the grooves of routine traditional thinking — or rather out of an imita-tion that is not thought— and which will so obliterate the grooves that their minds will be free to think out new prob-lems. For in the field of the curriculum, the whole world to-day is presented with a magnificent opportunity for origi-nal constructive work. The present social *débâcle* demon-strates the inadequacy of types of education upon which we have relied in the past.

Some of the things necessary for the liberation of thought have been attempted in these chapters. They are written with the assumption that we must establish fundamental principles and employ scientific methods in formulating systems of training. All of the advance in the curriculum field at present — and there is much in all progressive school systems — is pioneer, experimental, suggestive. In these chapters we have tried to formulate some of the curriculum-thought that is in a state of ferment throughout the field. There is nothing recommended here but what is actually being done somewhere and in some measure by practical and progressive school men and women.

At the present stage of developing courses of training it is more important that our profession agree upon a *method*

of curriculum-discovery than that we agree upon the details of curriculum-content. The writer has been chiefly
interested in this volume in suggesting a method, and fundamental points of view. The reader may or may not agree
with the conclusions. That is of little consequence. The
main thing at present is that each find scientific principles
and methods of curriculum-formulation which he can himself accept; and which will make thought the basis of curriculum-making rather than imitation. Without such principles at the present moment, one is like a ship in the wide
seas without chart, compass, or stars.

Our professional vision must be greatly in advance of our
practice. We shall move forward only step by step with feet
on solid earth; but we must be able to see far beyond our
immediate next steps in order that they be taken in the
right direction. The work of our profession, more than that
of any other, requires foresight and far sight. For this reason, in our discussion of ends and means, we have not looked
merely to what is practicable next year, or even five years
hence. Often we have discussed matters that are to be developed only through a slow-moving program covering a
long series of years.

A superintendent who recently listened to the suggestions
made in this volume presented this question: "What should
a superintendent actually *do* by way of improving the curriculum in his schools?"

To begin with, he should accept the situation in his city
as it is. He should look upon it as the normal, and therefore
proper, result of the institutional growth-influences that
have been operative in that city. He should therefore accept the conditions as right and good in the sense that they
represent a growth-stage, conditions being what they are,
through which the city must pass before it can arrive at its
next normal stage of healthy growth. He should expect the

curriculum to change and grow from year to year, rapidly or slowly. Naturally he would like to have rapid growth; but he would have to accept conditions as they are. The only normal thing is for the growth to continue with a rapidity that is determined by the conditions within the city. This would mean in one city rapid growth; in another, slow — at least until this could be normally accelerated.

Even if given a free hand, he should attempt no abrupt reorganization of the work, nor any sudden reformulation of the studies. In other words, he should not attempt to accelerate the growth beyond that which can be normal and healthy; and permanent after it is once accomplished. The details of the work have to be carried out by teachers who have been trained both in their academic courses and in their professional experience to certain types of work. He could expect teachers to assimilate only those suggestions for improvement which do not mean radical departure from what they have been accustomed to. But after having taken these first steps, he could expect them then to be prepared to go a little farther; and then later, to take other steps in advance. The readjustments in the teacher's thought and practice must be gradual. This is true also of school board and community. They are not prepared for any type of re-organization that greatly differs from that with which they are familiar. Like the teachers they can shift only gradually. All must be a growth-process. And what is more, the super-intendent would find that his own ideas were insufficiently worked out in detail for directing reformulative procedure which broke in any sudden manner from the old. He would have to think out innumerable details and try them out in practice. While this was being done, he would want the best that has been accumulated in the years past to continue until he was reasonably certain as to the exact details of the next steps that are to be taken. If he is to make mistakes, it is better for him to continue the old mistakes than to invent a new series.

The superintendent will remember that inertia is as much a factor in the general human economy as dynamic forces; that the conservation of gains is as important as making further gains. He will be content with neither without the other.

Along with principals and teachers on the one hand and school board and community upon the other — for he should insist not only upon democracy of opportunity, but also of responsibility — he should look over the work in every subject within the system, elementary school and high school, in the attempt to find those places where further growth is demanded by community needs; especially those where teachers, school board, and community are prepared to take the natural next steps of progress; and where they are in a mood to accept leadership in that direction.

For example, he will find manual activities going on as a portion of the course. He will try to find the dozen or so relatively small ways in which the work can be improved; and he will try to get those relatively small things done. In locating them, he will consider the educational principles relative to making work real, making it pleasurable, intellectualizing it through mathematics, science, and design; socializing the activities by introducing the history, geography, and economics of the field; the introduction of observational activities, practical participation, reading for vision and social appreciations. Making no changes except where there is a clear guiding principle, moving by short steps, trying out everything before going far, it is possible to make progress that is relatively sure in direction and relatively certain to be permanent. This small amount of progress accomplished, the stage is set for taking another short step. This step can lead to a third; and so the process may continue indefinitely.

He will then turn to another subject, history, let us say. He will find many good results being secured. But he can find, on the basis of curriculum principles, a dozen ways or more in which it may in some measure be improved without confusing the thought or practice of teachers or community. He doubtless can take some reasonably long steps in advance provided he can secure the necessary reading materials.

In the same way through making a multitude of little changes in each subject he can with assurance arrive by the stages of normal growth and with reasonable speed at a curriculum that is better adapted to social needs. By enlisting the active coöperation of all concerned, all can move forward together.

To keep from getting lost among the innumerable details of many subjects, distributed over many grades, superintendent and staff should coöperatively draw up a concise summary of the curriculum principles to be kept in mind in connection with each subject. In some of the subjects there should probably be different lists for different grade levels. These should be printed so that they could be continually used in checking and rechecking the situation as regards each subject. They, too, should be subjected to continual revision.

The superintendent will not try to advance more rapidly than teachers, school board, and community are prepared for. He will consider his position to be not educator *for* the community; but rather only a specialized *leader* of the community in its labors of educating its children. In other words, he will conceive the responsibility of education to be not his primarily, but rather one that rests squarely upon the total community. He is but a specialized helper and leader in the work. If he goes faster than they can or will go and leaves them behind, by so doing he abdicates the responsibility that they have delegated to him. As a leader he must take the community with him; or he is no longer its leader. If they are backward and slow, his pace must be determined by their pace; except as he can normally accelerate it. If they are awake and progressive and eager and able to proceed rapidly, he must lead in progress of that character. It is not inconceivable that his task of seeing that work is substantial and permanent may sometimes require restraint upon an over-eager community.

He will assume that not all progress is to be made in this generation; that something is to be left for those that come after us. And yet, he will attempt all of the progress for which conditions are ripe, and for which he can without forcing make them ripe.

INDEX

INDEX

Aims of education, in general, 3–7, 41–52; vocational, 56–57, 63–70, 71, 87–88, 94–95; civic, 117, 130, 131, 160; moral, 163–64, 166; health, 173–79, 185, 189–90; recreational, 209, 212, 224–26, 229; language, 255–56; double-aim of work-activities, 20; vague aims of the past, 41; need of specific aims, 43.

Antecedent aspects of work-experience, in general, 26–33; relation to extra-mural activities, 39; administrative aspect, 40.

Apprenticeship training, 24.

Capital and labor, education for mutual understanding, 76–86.

Citizenship training, general, 117–62; major objective, 117–30; training for large-group consciousness, 131–62; on play-level, 13; on work-level, 22, 37; relation of physical education to, 176; foreign languages needed for, 262–64.

Civics. See Citizenship training, Social studies.

Classics, the, 5, 272–81.

Concrete experience. See Shopwork, Observation, Reading, Practical activities.

Cooking, introduction of responsibility, 34–35; as general training, 102.

Coöperative part-time work, 21–24, 39–40, 83, 144, 155, 190, 202–04.

Culture advocates vs. utilitarians, 3–7.

Curiosity, as educational motive, 9–11.

Deficiency as symptom of training need, 44–46, 50–52, 56–57; in occupational matters, 63–70; English,

248–49; foreign languages, 255–56, 272–73.

Double aim of work-activities in schools, 20.

English language training, general discussion, 247–54; motivation of responsibility, 22–23; assistance of foreign languages, 272–78. See Reading, Grammar, Composition, Literature.

Exercise in relation to function, 212–13.

Extra-mural activities necessary for finding responsibility, 20–22; general theory, 34–40; occupational, 21–24, 105–08; civic, 149–57; sanitational, 185–88, 202–04.

Foreign languages, general discussion, 255–81; utility vs. culture, 5–6; method of discovering purposes, 255–56; needed for occupational efficiency, 256–62; needed for citizenship, 262–64; for family life, 264–66; for leisure occupations, 266–71; for proficiency in English, 272–78; for humanism, 278–81.

French, 271.

Gardening, 34, 35, 102.

Generalist, education of the, 78–82.

Geography, reading, 12, 231–37; occupational, 112; for civic purposes, 146–48, 160.

Grammar, errors as indices of training needs, 45–46, 248–49; motivation of training, 249; general discussion, 247–54.

Health training, in general, 171–204; major purpose, 171–79; physical

AMERICAN EDUCATION:
ITS MEN, IDEAS, AND INSTITUTIONS
An Arno Press/New York Times Collection

Series I

Culver, Raymond B. **Horace Mann and Religion in the Massachusetts Public Schools.** 1929.

Curoe, Philip R. V. **Educational Attitudes and Policies of Organized Labor in the United States.** 1926.

Dabney, Charles William. **Universal Education in the South.** 1936.

Dearborn, Ned Harland. **The Oswego Movement in American Education.** 1925.

De Lima, Agnes. **Our Enemy the Child.** 1926.

Dewey, John. **The Educational Situation.** 1902.

Dexter, Franklin B., editor. **Documentary History of Yale University.** 1916.

Eliot, Charles William. **Educational Reform: Essays and Addresses.** 1898.

Ensign, Forest Chester. **Compulsory School Attendance and Child Labor.** 1921.

Fitzpatrick, Edward Augustus. **The Educational Views and Influence of De Witt Clinton.** 1911.

Fleming, Sanford. **Children & Puritanism.** 1933.

Flexner, Abraham. **The American College: A Criticism.** 1908.

Foerster, Norman. **The Future of the Liberal College.** 1938.

Gilman, Daniel Coit. **University Problems in the United States.** 1898.

Hall, Samuel R. **Lectures on School-Keeping.** 1829.

Hall, Stanley G. **Adolescence: Its Psychology and Its Relations to Physiology, Anthropology, Sociology, Sex, Crime, Religion, and Education.** 1905. 2 vols.

Hansen, Allen Oscar. **Early Educational Leadership in the Ohio Valley.** 1923.

Harris, William T. **Psychologic Foundations of Education.** 1899.

Harris, William T. **Report of the Committee of Fifteen on the Elementary School.** 1895.

Harveson, Mae Elizabeth. **Catharine Esther Beecher: Pioneer Educator.** 1932.

Jackson, George Leroy. **The Development of School Support in Colonial Massachusetts.** 1909.

Kandel, I. L., editor. **Twenty-five Years of American Education.** 1924.

Kemp, William Webb. **The Support of Schools in Colonial New York by the Society for the Propagation of the Gospel in Foreign Parts.** 1913.

Kilpatrick, William Heard. **The Dutch Schools of New Netherland and Colonial New York.** 1912.

Kilpatrick, William Heard. **The Educational Frontier.** 1933.

Knight, Edgar Wallace. **The Influence of Reconstruction on Education in the South.** 1913.

Le Duc, Thomas. **Piety and Intellect at Amherst College, 1865-1912.** 1946.

Maclean, John. **History of the College of New Jersey from Its Origin in 1746 to the Commencement of 1854.** 1877.

Maddox, William Arthur. **The Free School Idea in Virginia before the Civil War.** 1918.

Mann, Horace. **Lectures on Education.** 1855.

McCadden, Joseph J. **Education in Pennsylvania, 1801-1835, and Its Debt to Roberts Vaux.** 1855.

McCallum, James Dow. **Eleazar Wheelock.** 1939.

McCuskey, Dorothy. **Bronson Alcott, Teacher.** 1940.

Meiklejohn, Alexander. **The Liberal College.** 1920.

Miller, Edward Alanson. **The History of Educational Legislation in Ohio from 1803 to 1850.** 1918.

Miller, George Frederick. **The Academy System of the State of New York.** 1922.

Monroe, Will S. **History of the Pestalozzian Movement in the United States.** 1907.

Mosely Education Commission. **Reports of the Mosely Education Commission to the United States of America October-December, 1903.** 1904.

Mowry, William A. **Recollections of a New England Educator.** 1908.

Mulhern, James. **A History of Secondary Education in Pennsylvania.** 1933.

National Herbart Society. **National Herbart Society Yearbooks 1-5, 1895-1899.** 1895-1899.

Nearing, Scott. **The New Education: A Review of Progressive Educational Movements of the Day.** 1915.

Neef, Joseph. **Sketches of a Plan and Method of Education.** 1808.

Nock, Albert Jay. **The Theory of Education in the United States.** 1932.

Norton, A. O., editor. **The First State Normal School in America: The Journals of Cyrus Pierce and Mary Swift.** 1926.

Oviatt, Edwin. **The Beginnings of Yale, 1701-1726.** 1916.

Packard, Frederic Adolphus. **The Daily Public School in the United States.** 1866.

Page, David P. **Theory and Practice of Teaching.** 1848.

Parker, Francis W. **Talks on Pedagogics: An Outline of the Theory of Concentration.** 1894.

Peabody, Elizabeth Palmer. **Record of a School.** 1835.

Porter, Noah. **The American Colleges and the American Public.** 1870.

Reigart, John Franklin. **The Lancasterian System of Instruction in the Schools of New York City.** 1916.

Reilly, Daniel F. **The School Controversy (1891-1893).** 1943.

Rice, Dr. J. M. **The Public-School System of the United States.** 1893.

Rice, Dr. J. M. **Scientific Management in Education.** 1912.

Ross, Early D. **Democracy's College: The Land-Grant Movement in the Formative Stage.** 1942.

Rugg, Harold, et al. **Curriculum-Making: Past and Present.** 1926.

Rugg, Harold, et al. **The Foundations of Curriculum-Making.** 1926.

Rugg, Harold and Shumaker, Ann. **The Child-Centered School.** 1928.

Seybolt, Robert Francis. **Apprenticeship and Apprenticeship Education in Colonial New England and New York.** 1917.

Seybolt, Robert Francis. **The Private Schools of Colonial Boston.** 1935.

Seybolt, Robert Francis. **The Public Schools of Colonial Boston.** 1935.

Sheldon, Henry D. **Student Life and Customs.** 1901.

Sherrill, Lewis Joseph. **Presbyterian Parochial Schools, 1846-1870.** 1932 .

Siljestrom, P. A. **Educational Institutions of the United States.** 1853.

Small, Walter Herbert. **Early New England Schools.** 1914.

Soltes, Mordecai. **The Yiddish Press: An Americanizing Agency.** 1925.

Stewart, George, Jr. **A History of Religious Education in Connecticut to the Middle of the Nineteenth Century.** 1924.

Storr, Richard J. **The Beginnings of Graduate Education in America.** 1953.

Stout, John Elbert. **The Development of High-School Curricula in the North Central States from 1860 to 1918.** 1921.

Suzzallo, Henry. **The Rise of Local School Supervision in Massachusetts.** 1906.

Swett, John. **Public Education in California.** 1911.

Tappan, Henry P. **University Education.** 1851.

Taylor, Howard Cromwell. **The Educational Significance of the Early Federal Land Ordinances.** 1921.

Taylor, J. Orville. **The District School.** 1834.

Tewksbury, Donald G. **The Founding of American Colleges and Universities before the Civil War.** 1932.

Thorndike, Edward L. **Educational Psychology.** 1913-1914.

True, Alfred Charles. **A History of Agricultural Education in the United States, 1785-1925.** 1929.

True, Alfred Charles. **A History of Agricultural Extension Work in the United States, 1785-1923.** 1928.

Updegraff, Harlan. **The Origin of the Moving School in Massachusetts.** 1908.

Wayland, Francis. **Thoughts on the Present Collegiate System in the United States.** 1842.

Weber, Samuel Edwin. **The Charity School Movement in Colonial Pennsylvania.** 1905.

Wells, Guy Fred. **Parish Education in Colonial Virginia.** 1923.

Wickersham, J. P. **The History of Education in Pennsylvania.** 1885.

Woodward, Calvin M. **The Manual Training School.** 1887.

Woody, Thomas. **Early Quaker Education in Pennsylvania.** 1920.

Woody, Thomas. **Quaker Education in the Colony and State of New Jersey.** 1923.

Wroth, Lawrence C. **An American Bookshelf, 1755.** 1934.

Series II

Adams, Evelyn C. **American Indian Education.** 1946.

Bailey, Joseph Cannon. **Seaman A. Knapp: Schoolmaster of American Agriculture.** 1945.

Beecher, Catharine and Harriet Beecher Stowe. **The American Woman's Home.** 1869.

Benezet, Louis T. **General Education in the Progressive College.** 1943.

Boas, Louise Schutz. **Woman's Education Begins.** 1935.

Bobbitt, Franklin. **The Curriculum.** 1918.

Bode, Boyd H. **Progressive Education at the Crossroads.** 1938.

Bourne, William Oland. **History of the Public School Society of the City of New York.** 1870.

Bronson, Walter C. **The History of Brown University, 1764-1914.** 1914.

Burstall, Sara A. **The Education of Girls in the United States.** 1894.

Butts, R. Freeman. **The College Charts Its Course.** 1939.

Caldwell, Otis W. and Stuart A. Courtis. **Then & Now in Education, 1845-1923.** 1923.

Calverton, V. F. & Samuel D. Schmalhausen, editors. **The New Generation: The Intimate Problems of Modern Parents and Children.** 1930.

Charters, W. W. **Curriculum Construction.** 1923.

Childs, John L. **Education and Morals.** 1950.

Childs, John L. **Education and the Philosophy of Experimentalism.** 1931.

Clapp, Elsie Ripley. **Community Schools in Action.** 1939.

Counts, George S. **The American Road to Culture: A Social Interpretation of Education in the United States.** 1930.

Counts, George S. **School and Society in Chicago.** 1928.

Finegan, Thomas E. **Free Schools.** 1921.

Fletcher, Robert Samuel. **A History of Oberlin College.** 1943.

Grattan, C. Hartley. **In Quest of Knowledge: A Historical Perspective on Adult Education.** 1955.

Hartman, Gertrude & Ann Shumaker, editors. **Creative Expression.** 1932.

Kandel, I. L. **The Cult of Uncertainty.** 1943.

Kandel, I. L. **Examinations and Their Substitutes in the United States.** 1936.

Kilpatrick, William Heard. **Education for a Changing Civilization.** 1926.

Kilpatrick, William Heard. **Foundations of Method.** 1925.

Kilpatrick, William Heard. **The Montessori System Examined.** 1914.

Lang, Ossian H., editor. **Educational Creeds of the Nineteenth Century.** 1898.

Learned, William S. **The Quality of the Educational Process in the United States and in Europe.** 1927.

Meiklejohn, Alexander. **The Experimental College.** 1932.

Middlekauff, Robert. **Ancients and Axioms: Secondary Education in Eighteenth-Century New England.** 1963.

Norwood, William Frederick. **Medical Education in the United States Before the Civil War.** 1944.

Parsons, Elsie W. Clews. **Educational Legislation and Administration of the Colonial Governments.** 1899.

Perry, Charles M. **Henry Philip Tappan: Philosopher and University President.** 1933.

Pierce, Bessie Louise. **Civic Attitudes in American School Textbooks.** 1930.

Rice, Edwin Wilbur. **The Sunday-School Movement (1780-1917) and the American Sunday-School Union (1817-1917).** 1917.

Robinson, James Harvey. **The Humanizing of Knowledge.** 1924.

Ryan, W. Carson. **Studies in Early Graduate Education.** 1939.

Seybolt, Robert Francis. **The Evening School in Colonial America.** 1925.

Seybolt, Robert Francis. **Source Studies in American Colonial Education.** 1925.

Todd, Lewis Paul. **Wartime Relations of the Federal Government and the Public Schools, 1917-1918.** 1945.

Vandewalker, Nina C. **The Kindergarten in American Education.** 1908.

Ward, Florence Elizabeth. **The Montessori Method and the American School.** 1913.

West, Andrew Fleming. **Short Papers on American Liberal Education.** 1907.

Wright, Marion M. Thompson. **The Education of Negroes in New Jersey.** 1941.

Supplement

The Social Frontier (Frontiers of Democracy). Vols. 1-10, 1934-1943.